GOING

TWO YEARS SAILING ARC

Charlotte – with best wishes

[signature]

ex libris
F & B Fitzgibbon

Journey's End
Myrtleville, Co. Cork

GOING WEST

TWO YEARS SAILING AROUND THE WORLD

BARBARA FITZGIBBON

MERCIER PRESS

MERCIER PRESS
5 French Church Street, Cork
16 Hume Street, Dublin 2

Trade enquiries to COLUMBA MERCIER DISTRIBUTION,
55a Spruce Avenue, Stillorgan Industrial Park, Blackrock, Dublin

ISBN: 1 85635 357 5

10 9 8 7 6 5 4 3 2 1

REMEMBERING
SUE, DERRY & KATHLEEN

Printed in Ireland by Colour Books Ltd.

CONTENTS

MAPS AND DIAGRAMS

ACKNOWLEDGMENTS

Heartfelt thanks go to my skipper, friend and husband, Frank, who took the major responsibility for the trip, and encouraged me to continue writing when it seemed fruitless. Thanks to Liam Fitzgibbon without whom the voyage would never have taken place. Thanks to all those who crewed with us, particularly our forbearing family, in order of time spent aboard: Rachel, Cathy, Sarah, Gary, Andy and Dave. Ruth and her dad served their time, as did my godfather Andy, John and Monika, and Shailesh. My brother John and family made us feel at home down under. Mag was undisputedly the best correspondent, and Brid, Joe and Anne, John and Marion, Séamus and Ide were there when we needed them. Thanks to Mary Feehan for all her practical help with getting the book together, and to Niall and Hugh for editorial comments. Thanks to all the sponsors who helped us out in the early stages of the project: RTE, Esat, Sony, Collins McNicholas, Guinness, Dubarry Shoes, Tambrands, Erin Foods, Kelken, Texaco and Ballygowan. To Tom MacSweeney a big thank you for keeping us alive on radio, and to the RCYC for help and support. Allan Briscoe helped us delve into the mysteries on *Atlantic Islander*. John Murray, Tim McCoy and Declan O'Connell helped with video knowhow. Hugh Coveney, whom we all miss, was such a source of inspiration to us and to the valiant crew of *Golden Apple* who voyaged with hope and did so much good. *Go raibh míle maith agaibh go léir* to all those family and friends who held us in their hearts and kept us in their prayers. And a big thanks to Mark O'Sullivan, Liam Devane and Ben Aliaga-Kelly from Glenstal who set up a marvellous website on our return.

To all the gallant sailors we met throughout our wanderings: Paul, Des and Adrian, John and Carol, Brendan and Frances, Gearóid and Orla, Edvind and Jørgen, David and Roger, Graham and Mary, Geoff and June, John and Fred, Richard and Jacqui, Connie, our lifesaver in Sudan, Trish and Kasper, John and Roz, Iain and Berit, Joan and Peter, Eric and Walter, the *Blue Biscays*, *Sprays*, *Enarkays*, *Little Blues*, *Storm Vogels*, *t'Early Birds*, *Iron Maid* and all those who befriended us en route: fair winds to them all.

And finally, tribute to my dear sister Sue, who did so much ashore for us. *Ar dheis Dé go raibh a h-anam dhílis.*

PROLOGUE

Las Palmas de Gran Canaria. Sunday, 21 November 1995

The hands of the theatre clock pointed to noon. I lay on the operating table with a green sheet pulled up to my chin, my right arm outstretched as the resident surgeon and her intern prodded and jabbed at my injured fingers. A drip fed into my left hand, and a nurse stood by my head monitoring its flow. Outside, in the bay off Puerto de la Luz, scores of yachts were making their final preparations for the start of the tenth Atlantic Rally for Cruisers. Frank and I were to have been among them, but I knew now that *Atlantic Islander* would *not* be starting with the 180 other boats. Perhaps in a few days time we could try to catch up with them and make our first transatlantic crossing as part of the fleet? This would be the first major step in our two year circumnavigation, which had begun three months before, and was a vital leg, our longest passage by far; a distance of 2,670 miles which we wanted to undertake with the backing and experience of an organised group.

It was Sunday, not the best day of the week to be on an operating table. I hoped that the on-call doctors would not be in a hurry to patch me up, but would refer me to a specialist next day. I was not disappointed.

'You have done quite a bit of damage to your index finger, and we will simply clean and dress it until our plastic surgeon can see you first thing tomorrow. The second finger we will stitch now, and send you back to A&E for monitoring.'

The young intern had spent a summer in Cork and spoke excellent English: up until now I had been labouring in my rusty Spanish to the amusement of the nurses.

'I suppose I will need surgery? How much time will I have to spend in hospital?'

I began to have visions of being stuck in port for up to a week or two, thereby messing up the Rally for our French crew-member who had arrived from Paris just two days before. Christophe and I were to share the cooking duties on board as he is an excellent chef. He had a much tighter schedule than we did, and would have to be back in his office in a month's time. The Atlantic crossing had been a dream of his – as of ours – for many years.

'Naturally the plastics consultant will be able to tell you more precisely, but if I were you I would consider going home for treatment. You are likely to be in hospital for up to five days, but will probably need about a month to five week's outpatient treatment before being able to rejoin your yacht.'

I was devastated! All our preparations and plans lay in ruins – and all through my own fault. If I hadn't tried to reposition the mooring lines a few hours before, when the boat was pitching in the heavy swell at the Las Palmas marina ... But three strong ropes had already snapped through during the night, and their replacements were very near breaking point ... Frank and Christophe had gone to the Immigration Office to clear us all out of the country, and I was alone on board. But why had I not left the blessed warps alone? Why had I not ignored them, and carried on with the simpler task of washing down the portholes and deck with fresh water, thereby keeping pre-start nerves at bay? Why, why, why?

The tears that I had valiantly fought since the accident were close to falling now. But I shook myself internally and remembered that I had a lot to be thankful for. I had been very fortunate not to lose the top of my finger, as the bone had remained intact though much of the tissue of the inner tip had been crushed, caught between the ropes and fairlead. I had received the best possible help from the two people who come to my aid as I shouted for help from the bow of our boat: a neighbouring French sailor who had suffered a similar injury some years before, followed swiftly by a local doctor whose yacht was berthed further along the pontoon. With such excellent attention I had been expertly bandaged before the ambulance arrived to take me to the hospital.

The doctors finished their work. An analgesic kept most of the pain at bay, and I was relieved that the more delicate plastic surgery would be left to the experts – and to a general anaesthetic! As I was wheeled back to the Accident and Emergency Department, where Frank waited anxiously for news, I looked more calmly at the possibilities which lay open to us.

It seemed clear that I should follow the intern's advice and make arrangements to receive treatment at home in Cork. But there was no reason why Frank should come with me, or that Christophe's hard-earned vacation be cut short: they should look for an additional crew and join the rally as soon as possible. It all began to fit into place, and when Frank mentioned that he had met two young Danes whom we knew to be looking for berths, both recommended by a famous Norwegian round-the-world yachtsman, our fate was sealed.

By the time I was discharged Christophe had had an initial meeting with Jurgen and Christien, and felt that they were competent *and* compatible. Over a special dinner that Christophe had carefully prepared we looked at the reality of the boat carrying on without me. He would have to take my place as chief cook and second-in-command, and was somewhat overwhelmed by this unexpected turn in events as it was many years since he had sailed seriously.

Frank too was in a state of shock. Barely recovered from surgery in Madeira three weeks before, he was now faced with a totally untried crew for the longest ocean passage he had ever attempted: yet to abandon the project at this stage seemed unthinkable. None of us had expected something like this, and each had their own fears and worries that night. I found it impossible to sleep: the wind was still extremely strong, and with every creak of the mooring lines I relived my experience, and had to force myself to read in order not to succumb to the horror of that memory. At about four a troubled sleep came.

By 9.00 next morning we had met the local plastic surgeon who passed me fit to travel. Arrangements were made with a consultant in Cork, who would operate the following day. The final interview with the Danes had gone well and Frank was pleased enough that all four would cope well with the passage. I was flattered that it took *two* 25-year-olds to replace my 50 years!

With the help of my doctor rescuer I was on the next flight to Madrid: everything was slotting into place, though we were all three still in shock. Our farewells were of necessity more hurried than emotional, which was probably just as well. How would the crossing go? How would my surgery work out? How would Christophe and the Danish boys settle down together? How would Frank work with such a hastily-gathered team? It was not the ideal beginning to a world cruise – but surely things could only get better!

Two days later I was out of hospital. There was no way of contacting Frank, though the Rally office in London was able to give me one position fix after about ten days: it looked like *Atlantic Islander* was making very good time. My skin graft had taken well and the doctors were very pleased at my progress. On 15 December the longed for phone call came through: all safe and well in St Lucia. When was I coming out?

Two days before Christmas I *finally* got the all clear from the doctors: I could rejoin the boat! Hurried arrangements were made for flights, and though I felt guilty at leaving my family yet again, at this special time of year, they and I knew my place was with Frank. On Christmas Eve I flew high above the Atlantic's waves and currents, longing to see him!

During the five weeks at home there had been plenty time to ponder. Why were we attempting to circle the world in a relatively small sailing boat – at this stage against several odds? What drove us on despite the set-backs that we both had encountered? As I sat in the comfort of the big 737, gliding over the ocean thousands of feet below, my mind went back to the very beginning ....

1

Origins of the Dream

It was early January 1994. A howling gale tore at our 100-year-old house, which faced north over the sleeping village of Crosshaven, inside the mouth of Cork Harbour in the south of Ireland. Rain lashed at the tall windows, and wind found its way through their time-worn frames. The shutters were tightly closed and yet the long curtains shivered in the stealthy breeze. A huge log fire roared up the chimney, and we were tucked into our armchairs, drawn up close to its warmth. The big house was deserted except for us two: four of its five bedrooms empty. Our family of six had flown the nest and were scattered to universities in Cork and Dublin and Edinburgh, in the mainstream of life, and we, like the old windows, were rattling round the once-bustling home, alone.

Frank stirred in his seat and passed me a slender brochure which had arrived in that morning's mail.

'Read this, and tell me what you think', he murmured as he resumed his favourite evening occupation – reading the current *Yachting Monthly* which he devours from cover to cover and which pastime renders him almost totally incommunicado for several evenings on end!

I set aside my knitting and examined the slim booklet. Its cover showed a ketch at anchor in an aquamarine bay, dipping palm fronds etching arcs on the white beach in the foreground. *Trade Winds Cruising Rally* invited the title, and I read, entranced, of an eighteen-month world cruise to be organised by members of the RAF Yacht Club, taking in exotic destinations I had often dreamed of – Caribbean, Galapagos and South Sea Islands, Fiji, Australia, Bali, Singapore, Thailand, Sri Lanka, Suez and the Mediterranean: a total of three oceans and nine seas, and countless lands and islands! Much of the difficult preparations and worldwide arrangements would be taken care of by the organisers in advance, and expert advice would be given by specialists and members of the RAF Yacht Club in the form of seminars and lectures ashore prior to the rally's commencement in October 1995. While at sea full safety and communications back-up would be assured during the passage. Here, on a plate, was every aspiring circumnavigator's dream come true: the luxury and adventure of being their own master on a challenging voyage, with most of the anxiety and pre-trip hassle reduced considerably. I became more and more entranced.

Ever since I was a child in Limerick, listening to my father's tales of far-away places, I wanted to travel, and ever since Frank and I had moved to Crosshaven nineteen years before, I had been involved in boats in some capacity or another – never, I must confess, with the same enthusiasm as he – but for the past sixteen years I had accompanied him in racing and cruising adventures. He had often spoken of making an extended cruise, and while I was never too keen on being at sea for days on end, the prospect of getting somewhere new and different was reward enough for the broken nights and rough-and-ready meals (we Taureans like our comforts!) Here, however, was the opportunity of being hand-held while making a far greater voyage than we had ever dreamed of: I would visit more countries than I had ever hoped for, and Frank would have enough sailing to satisfy him for some time to come. It seemed heaven-sent, and as soon as I had finished re-reading the list of magical places the cruise would visit, I was ready with my answer.

'Are you *really* serious about this? It sounds absolutely fantastic!'

Frank was usually the one who needed to be coaxed into the annual foreign holiday – but never needed pushing to take the boat away, whereas I usually preferred getting on a plane and reaching somewhere different as quickly as possible. Within the normal two-week time frame this for me was a necessity: cruising always took so *long* to get anywhere, but here was an opportunity to go everywhere I ever wanted within a year and a half, *and* in the luxury of one's own home – like a water-borne snail! It sounded too good to be true!

'But first of all, we had better get the family's reaction. They might think it was a crazy scheme, and be worried about us.'

My motherly conscience began to itch. While all the family were very independent and happily out of the nest, those still at university would be left to fend for themselves in our absence, and it seemed only fair to put the proposition to them first. With that, we picked up the phone and spoke to all six young adults. Each one in turn was excited and delighted, and not at all as sur-

14

prised as we had expected, but hopeful of being part of the Great Adventure during their holidays. They were all keen travellers and good sailors.

And so, in a matter of half-an-hour, the decision of a lifetime was made: we would lease out our consultancy business (career change and development, recruitment and training), rent out our house, and take a well-earned sabbatical. The seven-year-itch which had prompted regular career moves and had taken Frank up the Human Resources ladder from banking in Dublin to pharmaceuticals in Cork, and thence into the electronics industry before setting up his own consultancy, now had got a grip again, and his thirty-six years of working long beyond nine-to-five surely now deserved an eighteen-month break. I too had had a variety of jobs, and while I had really enjoyed the last eight years working with Frank as general *factotum*, by now the novelty was wearing a little thin and our lives were lacking adventure. My parents and Frank's mother had died in their early sixties, and fearful that a similar fate might befall us, we felt strongly that such a project should be attempted now, in our fifties, rather than waiting for 'retirement' age.

The first and most important part of this undertaking would be to find a suitable boat ... Our present Moody, at 31 feet long, was too small to complete such a journey in comfort, though it had served us well in pleasant trips to the south of England and along our south-western shores as well as putting in regular credible appearances in weekly racing leagues. Prior to that we had owned a Cobra 850, bought 'sight unseen' from a charter fleet in Sardinia – in the ensuing delivery trip organised by the broker some difficulty was encountered with the main halyard during a storm: the incompetent crew abandoned the boat to her fate midway between Sardinia and Corsica, and took a ride on a cargo ship. *Étude* was subsequently found by the Coastguard and safely brought ashore for a professional delivery from there to St Malo. The story of how we rescued the poor, woe-begotten, holed vessel whose engine was totally seized would take far too long to recount here – but her restoration and subsequent voyage to Cork was more than memorable and provided a sharp learning curve to the six family members who were involved. The following year we survived a never-to-be forgotten return from Plymouth with four of the children (then aged between six and twelve) when we met a 48-hour gale on the nose and were close to calling for assistance, exhausted and anxious without the security of an extra adult on board. Four French trawlermen met their deaths off Castletownbere in the next storm a few hours after we reached home.

Before settling in Crosshaven we had had no sailing experience whatsoever. Frank picked up the rudiments through crewing on a well-run National 18 with skilled and patient friends who had grown up with boats. In love with this new sport, he subsequently restored a battered 4.3-metre wooden dinghy in which we did our early family practice. Our first serious yacht was a 6.4-metre Puppeteer, which we bought new in basic *sail-away* mode, and christened *Barbara* in time-honoured tradition. She was a superb racing boat in which he and I and our eldest son slowly built up experience and managed to carry away many prizes in the several monthly leagues right up to the frostbites! Our sailing career had been varied but limited, yet we felt that we were now ready for a challenge.

We waited a week or two for the idea to really settle in our minds, and consulted a few close friends for positive reactions, before committing ourselves to a £500 Rally deposit (ten percent of the total fee). It was very difficult to carry on a normal daily life while waiting for the response!

Within a fortnight a letter arrived from the Trade Winds organisers in the Isle of Wight: the Rally was already oversubscribed by several boats, and they were returning our deposit while holding us on a list for a second venture to commence in 1997, if we were still interested. We were devastated, and the building excitement was instantly deflated – but not for long: we had already discussed the possibility of not getting a place, for one reason or another, and had also weighed up the pros and cons of travelling such a distance in a large, homogeneous group, with organised activities, regulations and possible restrictions. Having committed ourselves mentally it now seemed impossible to postpone our departure for another three years, when we would both be that much older, and we had made up our minds that if necessary we would go it alone, at roughly the same time as the Rally – the optimum time from a wind and weather point of view. So in a sense we were relieved to have the freedom to make our own decisions, to go where and when we pleased, though we were quite apprehensive at our ability to manage alone. In compensation, the

£5,000 saved would certainly help in our budgeting for a replacement boat.

We navigated our own way through the masses of literature and specialist advice available to dreamers of the circumnavigation dream. We avidly read every practical book on the subject – and there are plenty. As working weeks shorten and career spans are diminished through 'down-sizing' and increased technology, more leisure-time is available to more people, and the number of couples involved in opting for several years afloat grows annually. Many of these adventurers write well on the practical aspects of this lifestyle, and so our book-shelves began to swell with helpful titles like *Sell Up and Sail, Blue Water Countdown, Just Cruising* and many more. We contacted people who had done extensive sailing themselves, and extracted from them as much information as we could: all were generous with their time and advice. Frank consulted hundreds of magazine articles, seeking practical help, while I wrote to the embassies of all the countries we were likely to visit, to get information on visa and other entry requirements. Frank gathered information on radio operators' licence courses and boned up on his navigation and electronics. During the previous 16 years he had completed his Yachtmaster's Offshore Certificate and had sailed or skippered a good 7,000 miles. I had completed an excellent First Aid course with the Red Cross, and was a fair hand at French and Spanish, which would cover most of our language needs: I had recently acquired a TEFLA certificate (Teaching English as a Foreign Language to Adults) which would come in handy if we needed to find work abroad!

The list of things to do was endless, but before we could really get down to pre-trip planning, we needed to sell *In Pursuit* and find a more suitable floating home: a long-distance, comfortable, manageable seaworthy boat as soon as possible! It proved to be a much more difficult and time-consuming task than we could have imagined!

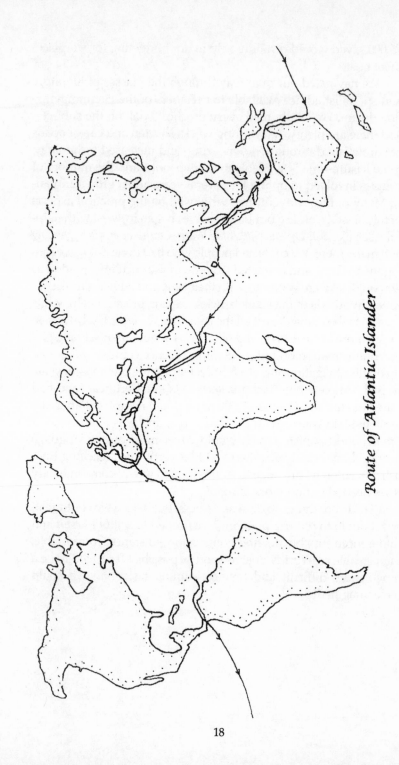

Route of Atlantic Islander

2

BUYING THE BOAT

Many experienced sailors have given their views on the best type of boat for extended warm-weather cruising, and like all newcomers we avidly read everything we could find on the subject. Experts agreed on basic common-sense principles such as seaworthiness, top-class fittings, a good engine with world-wide parts availability, lots of stowage space and airy livability, particularly in the cockpit area – and given either limitless funds or an available and willing ship-wright/electrician/electronics expert in the family with a lot of time on hand, there are many boats that more than adequately meet, or can be adapted to meet, all these criteria. But add a tight budget and limited time-frame, and the task of finding the near-perfect boat becomes a little more complicated, as we were soon to find out!

In the spring of 1994 we became regular visitors to the bigger boatyards in southern England. The UK is a more obvious source of boats than the small and limited Irish market, and with VAT restrictions greatly simplified in the past few years inter-market purchases are so much simpler. We investigated scores of boats – but they were either too dear, or needing too much work, and we eventually concluded that autumn would yield better deals. We continued our search in Ireland throughout the summer months, but found nothing to fit the bill. As the year grew older we became more anxious. We needed to find our boat in time to get to know it thoroughly before the following August. But despite intensive searches, we still hadn't found a suitable craft.

In October, in desperation, we flew to New York and drove a hired car north to Boston and south to Annapolis and back, checking out ten boatyards which had interesting possibilities for sale. The standard of US boats is extremely high, with excellent interior finishing and a sturdy overall construction. We were particularly impressed by the Shannons and Island Packets – but all the boats within our price-range had one big draw-back from our point-of-view: they lacked the aft-cabin arrangement of French and English-designed boats – a layout that we felt would greatly ease communal living when additional crew were on board. So we sadly had to forego many a lovely teak deck and mahogany interior, and leave the United States without a solution – just a memory of glorious fall colours in New England and warm reunions with family and friends. Time was moving on with alarming speed and we seemed no nearer to our goal.

In February our second-eldest daughter, Cathy, having completed a degree in Architecture the previous June, set off for Cambodia to work a year with Goal, an Irish charity. We saw her off with much emotion, though we looked forward to her joining us for much of the circumnavigation as she was the family's second most experienced sailor, and had been the first female bosun on the Irish sail training ship, *Asgard II*.

By March 1995 we had narrowed our quest down to two fine boats in the UK, both second-hand Oysters needing quite a bit of equipment and modification to bring them up to the electronic and safety requirements of such a trip: for this reason either could be had for a very reasonable price but their refits would bring us well over-budget ever before the trip proper began, and would also take quite a bit of precious time. By this stage it seemed we would have to sell our house, which was in any case too big for us. As we were making preparations for the final journey to the south coast of England to choose one of the Oysters, a hand-written fax came through to our office from a broker whose previous offerings had been ideal in everything but price. Here on pages of hastily scribbled inventory seemed to be the answer to all our months of search: a solid, perfectly equipped boat at a reasonable price. We faxed back immediately and arranged to see it at Swansea Marina.

The drive was worth every mile! Lovingly cared for for the past ten years by a careful, highly technical owner quite a bit older than ourselves, *Atlantic Islander* had every piece of equipment we needed, most of it duplicated. The minute we stepped on board we knew she was right, and while we were truly sad that the reason she was for sale was because her owner had died suddenly, (and many of her complex secrets buried with him), we felt that he would have been proud to have her take part in such a noble adventure. We later learnt that he had been preparing her for the long passage to Lisbon that very summer: she would now certainly fulfil that destiny and far exceed it.

The boat, an 11.8 m Atlantic Ketch built in Broadstone in Dorset in 1979, weighs over 14 tons, coming from an era when fibre-glass was thickly applied. She was a logical successor to an earlier line of fifty-four timber-built sister ships designed by Walter Raynor of Poole, which found themselves owners worldwide, among them the soprano, Joan Sutherland. Her lines were graceful despite the sturdy coachroof which would protect us from wind and rain in northern climes, and, more importantly, from the searing sun in the tropics. She had two masts with lightweight steps on each, and all the controls for raising and lowering sails led back into the central cockpit for ease of handling – ideal for a couple to manage. Roller reefing mainsail and genoa would greatly assist a short-handed crew, though many writers warn of the potential trouble in roller-reefing systems. An electric anchor winch was a luxury which delighted us as the physical labour expended on hauling the heavy anchor and chain would quickly take a toll on dodgy backs. Lots of locker space on deck for all those sails and ropes and other paraphernalia – and down below she was just home from home. Loads of well finished but un-fussy teak, five opening portholes giving plenty of air to the saloon: the immediate impression was of space and light combined with total security. The seat covers would need changing into some bright cotton, as would the berths which were fitted out warmly for wet northern summers. The aft cabin opened off the cockpit with a good-sized double berth and a cot berth on the port side beyond the compact heads. Here again was loads of storage space, hanging lockers and drawers as well as a beautifully finished bookshelf running the length of the starboard berth. We love fresh air and would have plenty in this cabin, with the fully opening hatch and porthole. Forward double berths were adequate for our visitors, and had excellent storage space and opening hatch, just forward of the main heads which was one of the most spacious and well fitted we had seen on this size of boat – and more important still, both heads had top-of-the-range loos, a vitally important factor to most sailing women – and usefully were situated on opposite sides of the boat, to cover all angles of keel!!

A small but well-designed galley ran along the starboard side of the saloon, and comprised a good sized sink with electric and manual pumps for fresh water and the essential manual sea water pump: on long passages we could wash the ware in sea water and save precious drinking supplies. A front opening fridge would not be ideal at sea, but this one was so beautifully built in beneath the fully stocked cutlery drawer that I had to admire it! An adequate gimbaled gas stove with two burners, grill and oven would serve us fine, and the neatly partitioned storage areas above and below held all the crockery and equipment we would need. The saloon settees had roomy cool lockers beneath – more than adequate storage for the large supply of tinned and dried foods that we would need to carry.

Aft of the galley was the navigation area with a good sized chart table and a dazzling array of navigation and communication equipment: at least two of everything. (In fact there was so much additional gear stored for the winter in the owner's home that we would have to hire a van to collect it all). Both built-in and portable GPS systems were installed – this is the miraculous global positioning by satellite which lets users know exactly where they are to within a matter of a quarter of a mile anywhere in the world – together with two top quality radio transmitters (short-range VHF for in-harbour or near-ship communication and the essential SSB for long-range reception and transmission at sea). There were also three forms of auto-pilot, which enables the yacht to sail herself, literally, while the electric or wind-driven systems keep the boat on a set course. A pair of outboard engines and dinghies let us chose the stronger ones and barter the others for essential charts and books. Luxury items included an excellent world-wide AM/ FM radio, top-class radar, a Weatherfax and some valuable practical books – all this helped in keeping within budget and yet being more than adequately equipped.

On the negative side she had a deep and very short cockpit, impossible to stretch out in on watch but excellent protection from high waves. The wheel was very small but we were used to tiller, and this would be an easy transition. Add-on roller reefing to the main placed a third question mark over an otherwise perfect boat. There was little to debate as we made our way back to Ireland. Of the three boats *Atlantic Islander* was well in the lead. Even her name seemed ideal, if a little long! We phoned the broker on Monday morning and told him we wanted to buy. Within a few days the purchase was successfully completed, though a second broker did try to gazump the sale and we were blessed with sound advice and assistance from our original contact. Nevertheless, we had a day or two of high anxiety before the deal was finally signed and sealed. We returned to Swansea Marina during the Easter break to take proud possession of our new, round-the-world yacht. It was sad meeting the owner's widow, but she seemed pleased that the boat he loved so much was to embark on such an adventure, and wished us all the best. Allan, the loyal second mate who had sailed her for the past 10 years, kindly travelled quite a distance to help up with queries and questions, though most of the electrics and electronic work had been the preserve of the skipper. (Later Allan would come to Crosshaven and spend some days onboard.) Aided by our daughter Rachel and her boyfriend, regular crew on *In Pursuit* (which we had now sold), we quickly mastered her basic quirks and motor-sailed her on a pleasant 36-hour passage to the RCYC marina in Crosshaven to begin the difficult work of finding out exactly how everything worked and where everything fitted!

Layout of
ATLANTIC ISLANDER

PLAN:

PLAN:
1. Lazerette (ropes,fenders,vegetables)
2. Coffin berth (clothes)
3. En suite (wine & wellies)
4. Under deck (paints & repair equipment; spares.)
5. Wheel & instruments
6. Oven & grill (pots & pans under)
7. Sink & fridge (filing cabinet)
8. Sailing jacket, boots & axe (for emergencies)
9. Dry goods under
10. Butter and beer (in bilges under floor)
11. Anchor locker
12. Spare film & sewing machine under
13. Guest / Crew accomodation
14. Main heads (first aid)
15. Table (drops to make large double bed)
16. Tinned goods
17. 4 no. gas tanks (batteries under)
18. Books, computer, flags & spares
19. Seat (storage under)
20. My wardrobe
21. Double berth (at a pinch)
22. Books

SECTION:
1. 80HP Mercedes diesel engine
2. Lazarette
3. Cockpit
4. Water tank
5. Lead keel
6. Anchor well
7. Under berth storage

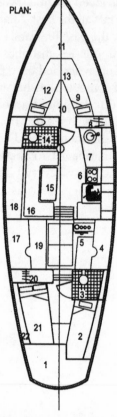

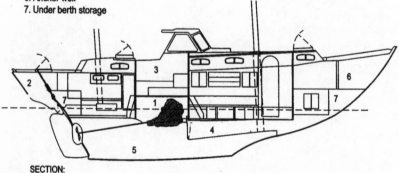

SECTION:

24

3

PREPARATIONS

April came and went in a flurry of excitement with friends coming to admire our new purchase. We wanted to be away at the latest by early September – ideally mid-August, which I felt was impossible. Our time-frame now was getting too tight, and we were both still working nine-to-six at the office. We were blessed in the intervention of Frank's brother Liam who is a veritable mine of electrical and electronic know-how. Having put together a series of motor boats he was currently restoring an old 6.7-metre wooden yacht to her former glory. Liam's engineering job began and ended early each day, and he would then spend most of the long evenings working on *Atlantic Islander*'s electrics. Her past owner had installed a complicated and intriguing series of fail-safe systems as safety was his major concern. Many of the circuits were adequately outlined and documented, but as many more were a source of mystery and had to be traced with a lot of patience. Liam worked his way through each complex layout, and little by little the mysteries began to reveal themselves to him and through him to Frank.

I stayed well clear of these highly technical procedures, and as our house was now on the market I was busy making it respectable while tackling the daunting task of sorting, sifting, storing or clearing out 27 years' accumulated treasure and junk. Eight people can amass quite an enormous amount of both! Several nostalgic weeks were spent sitting in piles of old clothing, photographs, books, school reports – feeling sad and reminiscing on the days when the children were young and all around us! Only once before had we moved house, when Frank took the big leap from the security of a *pensionable* banking job in Dublin, with its privileged financial perks and preferential mortgage, to take up the position of Personnel Manager with a multi-national pharmaceutical company in Cork. I remembered with intense emotion how emptied I had felt on that last morning in our first home – bared of all its furnishings – which had seen all the joys and sadness of our first seven years of married life. But that move had certainly changed our lives for the better, and we had enjoyed a wonderful 20 years in our second home where the children had had a freedom growing up in a small and safe village that they would never have had in the urban sprawl we had left behind. In Crosshaven we had been blessed with excellent schools, good transportation to the city and every possible recreational facility all within walking distance of our lovely home with the magnificent view! The house sold quietly in a mere two weeks, and we had a final brief month ashore before moving on board *Atlantic Islander*. We paid off our mortgage and purchased a small south-facing site nearby overlooking the Atlantic. Little did anyone know then of the Irish property boom just around the corner!

Having sorted and stored the house possessions we now had a more difficult *déménagement* to arrange: finding a good home for our dear Maxi, the black Labrador who had been so much the family friend for the past seven years. Many candidates put themselves forward, for Max was a much-loved and very gentle dog. Finally the ideal solution was found: friends living in a similar sea-side environment had a growing family of three boys all clamouring for a dog. Visits were arranged and all parties seemed agreeable, and so Maxi and his kennel proceeded in state to their new home, where the transition was a total success.

How did our family feel about this dramatic reduction in the home-life they had known? House gone, dog gone, parents soon gone – they were feeling rather deserted and abandoned. Where would they spend Christmas? Where would they do their laundry? Whom would they call when sick? Our eldest daughter Rachel and my only sister Sue, who had worked with us for the past five years and would continue to liaise with clients in our absence, each had houses in Cork and would act *in loco parentis* for the homeless brood, while kind friends and neighbours would offer alternative shelter from time to time. We were almost too busy to realise what a huge step we were taking, and how much worry would be mixed with their pride in our sense of adventure.

It was important to have an official launch and blessing of the boat which would be so vital in our changed lifestyle: this was a tradition in Crosshaven as in many other fishing and shipping centres. My Benedictine uncle and my aunt from the Sacred Heart order were pressed into willing service, and early in June a simple but moving ceremony was held on board, attended by close family, and followed by a cruising lunch. This was a very significant moment in our adventure, as it was the last time before our departure that almost all the family members would be together. The weather was reasonably kind, and a celebration dinner followed which would be the last in the family home – but was enjoyed greatly by all. So many happy gatherings had been round this same table over the past 20 years: this one was probably the most poignant. Soon the three youngest headed off for summer jobs: David to the States, Gary to the UK, and Sarah to return to *Ileán Cléire* (Cape Clear) for the fourth year in a row. It was difficult saying each goodbye – though initially only for a short period: we would return in October to see them settled back into college.

A hastened frenzy of clearing, storing, parting, forsaking and we were finally ready to vacate *Solimar*. We moved from our 9-roomed, 186 sq. m. semi-detached, high-ceilinged house with gardens front and rear, to a 12-metre boat with a headroom of 1.8 metres and a bedroom of 2.4 x 3 x 1.8 – the river Owenabui for its yard and the Royal Cork Yacht Club its annex! We relinquished the 4.5 x 4.5 kitchen with electric oven and gas cooker, dishwasher, microwave, freezer and big island unit for spacious food preparation, and adapted to the 1.8 x .9 compact sail-away *Atlantic Islander* galley. The transition was not without its share of tensions: our morning shower now entailed a brisk walk to the Yacht Club, clutching towels and undies. Living on the marina meant a far more public existence than we were accustomed to, with interested members and visitors hailing us at all hours of the day or night! But it gave us an invaluable opportunity to become more at ease with the boat, and to get over the inevitable bruising and knocking that are part and parcel of changing one's personal relationship with available space! We also became fitter and leaner as more bending and climbing was required than in the wide open spaces of our former home!

Acclimatising slowly, Frank soon stopped sharing the small and awkward double bed and moved across to the cot berth in the aft cabin – a practical but strange solution after 28 years together! Personal space became more and more important, and we took up 'positions' as we would at home – his and her places at table, and in the cockpit! We even had the possibility of a bathroom each, though in practice the main heads off the saloon was more spacious and inviting than the little en suite in our cabin. Our relationship was under quite a strain at this period, but we were so busy on the myriad final preparations for the trip, and in settling our business affairs, that we had little time to think about it. Short words were sometimes spoken – but generally we pulled together as a team: it was essential for survival to do so.

Getting financial arrangements into shape was no easy task: we were blessed with an understanding bank staff who facilitated our needs and minimised the difficulties, and we soon devised a method of covering our expenses while away. With Sarah, David and Gary still at university and partially dependent, we had to ensure that adequate funds be available for them, and cash for ourselves from the farthest corners of the oceans. The sale of our house had eliminated that mortgage, and renting/selling our business together with some investments would almost fund our needs. However, we still needed more capital, and I turned my attention to possible outside sources.

Late the previous year RTE, the Irish national broadcasting company, had advertised their round of Outside Broadcast requirements for the following year and my attention was caught by the video diary category where suitable material was being sought for interesting home-videos. With the kind help of a local film-maker I put a proposal together, and sent it off. They liked it and agreed to supply video equipment and film, with an option on the footage we might eventually produce. Based on this success I now approached the national telephone company with a request for communications equipment – we were particularly interested in having an INMARSAT mobile communications module which links directly to satellite and enables voice and data communication as easily as a telephone call. They were interested in our project but slow to show commitment. ESAT, the then newly set-up and first private Irish telecommunications company, boldly came to our aid with a sponsored global call card – which would be a boon in keeping in contact with home and office. Food and drinks manufacturers showed an interest in our plans and donated valuable products, as did others. All this was invaluable help as our budget ran alarmingly high.

Another high-expense item was a laptop computer, which I had tried unsuccessfully to inveigle from the many electronics manufacturers now based in Ireland. I was beginning to panic and look for older, second-hand portable machines when the Galwaybased recruitment company which took over part of our business, and employed my sister Sue, donated an Apple PowerBook, and good friends provided additional memory and batteries.

As the final weeks drew in the pressures of leaving were greatest. Friends and family treated us to a whirlwind of dinners and farewell parties, and we in turn held a gathering at the Club for business associates, family and friends, at which the Admiral presented us with a beautifully framed Club burgee commemorating the 275th anniversary of the oldest yacht club in the world. Earlier in the summer our President, Mary Robinson, had honoured the Club with a visit to celebrate this significant achievement, and we were now proud of the opportunity of being its ambassadors. Gifts and well wishes came from all around, and we were overwhelmed by the kindness and interest shown by so many. We conducted many brief tours of the boat, and were interviewed on radio and local television, and began to feel like celebrities – but all the while the multifarious task of getting the boat ready to sail was our first priority. Most experienced people say that one can never be really ready, and we soon found that this is true: better to set a definite departure date and leave then, regardless!

All that remained was to complete our provisioning lists and stock the boat with food and vegetables – this would be one of the last things to do, before getting rid of our car. A massive onslaught on the nearby supermarkets filled our remaining storage areas with tinned meats and vegetables, bottled sauces, brown bread mix, flour and cereals, dried soups, herbs and spices, oil and vinegar, coffee and tea, while our drinks locker was stocked with plenty of Irish whiskey, brandy and gin – as well as space-saving tins of soft-drink concentrates. Oranges, potatoes, onions and carrots were found a home in the cool lazarette, while the fridge was stacked with Irish butter and a plentiful supply of *essential* rashers and sausages! Jams, biscuits, eggs and chocolate were stowed away. Frank felt we had enough food for a very long siege! Toiletries too we bought in bulk – no one wants to run out of loo paper in mid-Atlantic – and a doctor friend supplied us with all the first-aid equipment and drugs we would be likely to need, though we seriously hoped we wouldn't use most of the stuff: certainly I felt squeamish at the possibility of having to suture wounds – but emergencies might have to be faced and it was essential to be prepared. Some sailing and medical professionals advocate having appendices removed but we felt that the likelihood of these erupting in our early 50s was slim. We did have thorough dental and medical check-ups, and niggling problems were investigated. In Frank's case one procedure left 'optional' almost became a major crisis within a short three-month period.

The swallows had been twittering about and getting restless. As I made my way along the RCYC marina one glorious August morning, they were gathering on the boom of a nearby boat, making psychological preparation for their forthcoming departure to sunnier climes. I envied the simplicity of their pre-trip procedures: stocking up on insects, waiting until the time was right, and then on the self-appointed day, without map or compass, flying off on a several thousand mile journey to central Africa. Why did our forthcoming departure have to be so complicated in comparison? But now our time too was near, and our pre-trip labours were coming to an end. A final round of visits and farewells, and suddenly it was time to leave: we were conscious of a really hollow feeling deep down inside. Now the dream was becoming reality – would we be able to cope with its considerable demands? Would our limited sailing experience stretch to a range of possibilities we couldn't even contemplate? Would we last the pace?

We awoke on 15 August to a glorious sunny morning. Liam arrived as planned to see us safely out of the harbour, and Frank's oldest brother from Dublin turned up unexpectedly with him! Rachel, the only one of the six still in Ireland, and her boyfriend, had stayed with us the previous night. We had a quiet, tearful send-off as our four well-wishers accompanied us to the mouth of the estuary in the Club launch, filming us as we filmed them! After all the whirlwind activities and intense farewells of the past few weeks we were in fact relieved to be finally under-way, and to have some quiet days ahead, away from stress and tension: time to restore our tired bodies and overtaxed emotions. We waved until all were out of sight, and cast many a last long lingering look at the fading greens of the Irish coast: it would be two years before we would sail past Roche's Point lighthouse again, and who knew what adventures would befall us between times.

4

FRANCE AND SPAIN

The sea was blue and still, and the sky was cloudless. After the emotional departure from Crosshaven, we motored towards the gas rigs, then turned off the engine, and just soaked up the sun, waiting for a breeze. Exhausted physically and mentally it was healing to simply drift, and let our cares evaporate. After an hour or so a light, following breeze stirred, but we needed to augment our sails with engine for a good part of the 290-mile journey, with our third and invaluable crew-member, the auto-pilot, doing most of the steering for us.

It was difficult to get into the nightly watch-keeping routine, particularly on the second night when we were passing through the heavily trafficked waters of St George's Channel approaching Ushant: here the busy VHF kept up a constant stream of French as Traffic Control monitored all passing commercial and pleasure craft. It's a strain peering at the endless procession of red or green lights and trying to figure out whether they are on a collision course or not! We attempted a night-watch pattern that had been recommended by an experienced long-distance couple: two hours on, two hours off, followed by four hours on and four hours off. The two hour stints were easy for the person on duty – but too short to sleep well, and it was very hard to stay alert for four hours at the wheel. Each of us had the horrible experience of nodding off unintentionally, despite the cold, and waking with a jolt just too near a cargo ship for comfort: this was not a good beginning! However, despite these difficulties, the three days and two nights passed relatively quickly, as we got into the rhythm of the sea and experimented with the sails. All the boat systems seemed to be functioning perfectly. Only the humans were out of condition!

Our first port of call was Morgat-Crozon, in Brittany, recommended by friends for its marina and facilities. We arrived in the evening, and began the first of many berthing operations that would become more polished with time! Then we opened a bottle of champagne, a farewell gift from friends, and congratulated ourselves on the first significant step of the grand voyage! Irish lamb and home-grown potatoes provided a welcome dinner, as the

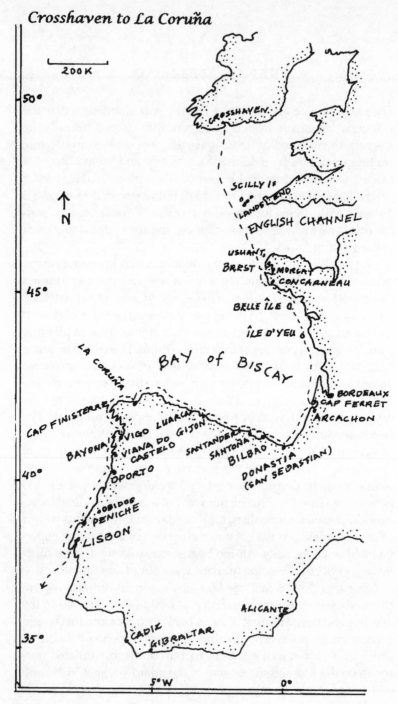

Irish flag fluttered in the breeze near the amenity building: Inter-Celtic games were planned for the weekend!

After two nights' recuperation we were soon away on the morning's tide for a pleasant sail south. This coast is scattered with jagged rocks exposed only at low water and many are unmarked. It's necessary to navigate quite carefully – but it is well worth the effort, and the range and variety of marinas is excellent. The entire Brittany coastline is indented with marvellous bays and coves: one could spend weeks exploring, though the tidal extremes make it difficult for deep keeled boats in some places. In Concarneau we were in time for the annual *Fête des Filets Bleus* when locals wear the traditional dress of the region, the women with delicate lace headgear, and later we witnessed a magnificent fireworks display from the walls of the old mediaeval town: our cockpit provided a grandstand view!

The Bay of Biscay always conjures up dread in sailors hearts, associated as it is with storms and shipwrecks: we decided that our best approach was to stay close to shore and thus be able to run for shelter if bad weather was forecast. We had promised friends in Arcachon that we would visit them *en passant*, and so we headed south, to Belle Île and Île d'Yeu, two totally contrasting islands which are favourites of French sailors and a 'must' on southbound itineraries. A gentle north-easterly wind of about 5 knots helped us most of the way to Belle Île. From about 4.00 in the afternoon we began meeting the fast one-design single-handed boats completing the last leg of the *Figaro* race, a gruelling thousand-mile course from Brest to our neighbouring home-port of Kinsale, and from there to Gijon in Northern Spain, and back to Brest, passing to the east of Belle Île on this final leg. These dedicated men and women are on watch day and night, through warm and cold, wind and calm – and keep their speeds to the absolute maximum. We saluted them from the comfort of our cosy cockpit as they passed at irregular intervals into a glorious sunset while the mauve and peach sky blended and fused into a ruffled sea in the freshening evening wind.

Belle Île's small port was crowded, as visiting yachts moor to several buoys just inside the breakwater – five or more boats to a buoy. Frequent ferries arrive and depart at top speeds, bringing crowds from the mainland. A stroll next morning on one of the many cliff paths showed us why this is such a popular holiday destination with the French – a delightful, unspoilt place with pristine beaches and a wealth of flowers, birds and animal life, combined with its pretty towns, excellent restaurants, and superb organically grown local vegetables, abundant fish and delicious honey.

Early next morning we were away, a nice following breeze of 5–6 knots filling the spinnaker, but sadly our auto-pilot soon refused to steer. Despite Frank's best efforts and lots of patience, we couldn't get the wind-vane working properly either, so it was a long 55 miles at the wheel. By now our fridge was beginning to give up (troubles come in threes!), but we managed to get some cooling from it – enough to keep the butter from going runny: we would have to find someone to look at it before too long. We bought fresh fish in Île d'Yeu and cooked up a nice dinner before retiring early. I still had a lot of thank-you cards to write and post to our many well-wishers.

As we were dependent on high tide for our release from the lock, we couldn't leave until 14.18 next day (Lock opening was as punctual as the French trains!) From Île d'Yeu to the Bay of Arcachon is a passage of 150 miles, and with ever strengthening winds it proved as difficult as we expected. Contrary seas, a broken wind-vane, uneasy stomachs and general malaise did not help the hours of hand steering which lay ahead. We were for the first time face to face with an unfriendly sea and an inhospitable coast with nowhere to run for shelter south of the Gironde. A glance at the map of France shows the inviting bays and coves of Brittany give way to an almost straight line of coast right down to Spain. Here the full Atlantic heaps its strength, and piles the breakers onto mile after mile of windswept beach. In the southern arm of the Bay of Arcachon the sand is swept onto the highest sand-dune in Europe, le Dune du Pyla, 500m, and this in turn encroaches the pine-wooded littoral which is a national park. I felt thoroughly seasick, and wished I was back safe on land, not responsible for bringing a heavy boat through unfriendly waters. For two days and nights we battled against the elements, forced to remain at the wheel for an hour at a time during daylight and two hours at night so we could get *some* sleep. Tempers became frayed, and it was too rough for Frank to effect repairs on the wind-vane. We were extremely glad to finally make out the northern entrance to the Bay of Arcachon!

Cap Ferret where our friends have a summer home, is tucked inside the northern arm of the bay, its back to the wild Atlantic. Rip tides of 6 to 8 knots along the narrow access channels are enough to scare the fainthearted from this delightful enclave. I had been busy translating the French pilot book's dire warnings about only attempting entry two hours after the high tide, and under no circumstances turning back in the channel, so we were extremely anxious on our approach. Suddenly a big passenger ferry, appropriately called *Atlantic Princess*, came steaming out toward us clearly showing the way, and we thanked the Lord and turned in with engine running at full revs. The channel is well marked with port and starboard buoys, but with vast sandbanks on either side combined with extraordinary tides, it is indeed a disconcerting passage, and not until we were actually tied up at Arcachon's huge marina did we relax, collapsing early into a deep, much-needed sleep before contacting Christophe and Éléanore.

As we nosed carefully out of the marina next morning a long, elegant motor boat approached us, filled with shouting and waving people: alarmed, we felt they must be warning us of further dangers ahead. As they came nearer we realised with relief that they were our friends who had come to lead us to a safe anchorage across the bay! The group was augmented with their friends and neighbours – a big reception committee brandishing bottles of chilled wine and aperitifs! We followed them along the twisting sinuous channels of the shallow bay, and dropped 40 feet of heavy chain to keep our anchor firm. Soon the welcoming group came on board and we exchanged greetings and glasses of wine and Irish whiskey! Christophe and Éléanore had been really caught up in the excitement of our decision to go round the world, and had been quite insistent that we should come here *en route* so they could inspect the boat and give the trip their blessing. The news had gone round, and others became involved. So it was a really happy occasion for us to be with such a welcoming and interested group of people. There followed a memorable few days, with dinners and parties in our honour and energetic rows in the dinghy against an incredibly strong tide to get to and from the boat. We were treated to an unexpected group send-off at 7.00 am the day we left. Christophe had decided to do the Atlantic crossing with us, so it was *au revoir* and not goodbye!

Spain called, and our 90-mile passage to San Sebastian (or

Donastia as the Basques prefer to call it) was thankfully uneventful: sunshine, flat seas, and little wind. How easy is this transition from one country to another! The VHF changes language, and *Appel à Tous!* *(all stations)* becomes *Llamada General!* We motored most of the way and entered the incomparable La Concha bay just after sunset, as teams of local oarsmen prepared for a rowing regatta in a few days time. Once again we had free moorings, as the small yacht harbour was completely full and we had to anchor in the bay. The Yacht Club provided a courtesy 24-hour ferry service which we greatly appreciated, as we could leave our dinghy stowed on board. It was 29 August, and the beautifully sited resort was bubbling with Spanish holiday-makers, enjoying the *paseo* and overflowing from the many *tapas* bars in the old town near the YC. I took a bus to the nearby commercial harbour certain of obtaining the Spanish charts we needed: but the government office was closed until mid-September, and we would have to carry on to Bilbao using only the Michelin Guide! The Autohelm was still acting up despite installing a part sent out from home, and the main self-steering was still faulty. On top of this the indispensable Philips GPS – our built-in electronic navigation system – was refusing to compute, and we were relying on a back-up hand-held one. And, just to complete our litany of hitches, the fridge had by now totally packed in! We were using the old reliable student method – a wet cloth draped over the cool-bag for butter and milk! Things mechanical/electrical were not going well. But we counted our blessings: we had successfully navigated the Bay of Biscay and reached Spain under our own steam: we would sort things out.

Frank had excellent reports of the Yacht Club in Bilbao, and also of the repair facilities in such an important industrial port, and despite my childhood memories of a dirty town, we headed there with all speed. The club was comfortable and welcoming beyond our wildest dreams, and we celebrated the first year-and-a-half anniversary of peace in Northern Ireland mentioned in the local paper, while the long-serving head barman told us that he had been held at gun point some years before by ETA: several of the Yacht Club members were on ETA hit lists. Hope of peace there still seems slim.

Next day we bused into the city (about 7 miles up the river Nervión) and I was amazed how it had been cleaned and polished over the years, and now looked quite resplendent. This was before the Guggenheim brought cultural fame to the industrial town. We bought charts for north-western Spain and western Portugal from the Department of the Marine – an armed military policeman carefully supervising our transactions – and arranged our electronics repairs with a certified agent who could hopefully complete the work in a few days.

We decided to head west for a day or two, to cleaner air, but had quite a bit of difficulty disentangling ourselves from the mooring buoy to which we were tied astern, and managed to get its line wrapped around the propeller. So there was nothing for it but for Frank to don the older of our two wetsuits and slip into the oil-rich waters to cut us loose. (This would prove to be one of three such unwelcome harbour swims – all in the filthiest water possible.)

Santoña is a small fishing port which attracts Spanish holiday-makers mainly from Bilbao, but very few foreigners. The main industries are fishing and canning fish, and local housewives earn a few extra pesetas selling home-potted anchovies and tuna. At the turn of the century the place was full of prosperous old houses, most now torn down in the name of progress and replaced with horrendous flats, jerrybuilt and ugly. It was quite an important sailing and ship-building town in centuries past, and Columbus' navigator Juan de la Cosa was born and lived here. Built into the south-facing arm of a steep tree-clad limestone promontory, Santoña looks back over the Cantabrian Mountains across an almost land-locked expanse of shallow mudflats where hundreds of birds breed. A large bullring is sited near the fishing harbour, and the restaurants cook sardines and tuna on outdoor barbecues. It was our twenty-seventh wedding anniversary, and we celebrated with two relaxing days ashore, walking miles and eating well. Frank saw his first bullfight while I made do with spying on the efficient butchering activity at the back of the ring. 6 Bravos Toros 6 would soon reappear as steak on Madrid plates!

Bad news awaited us in Bilbao: our steering equipment would have to be sent back to the makers – so this was a wasted few days and only one of many frustrations to beset us! Luckily Frank had fixed the wind-vane, but we needed more practice to get it right. Time was running short and we would have to move on with speed. Obligingly the wind picked up and we had some excellent sailing all along the magnificent northern coast – where the lofty Picos de Europa and the Cantabrian Mountains run down to the sea, enfolding hidden towns and villages which become smaller and more rural the more further west we went. Sophisticated Santander, former summer home of the Royal family, provided elegant shelter while we were storm-bound for six days. In San Vincente de la Barquera a magnificent fortress-like thirteenth century church houses the statue of Nuestra Señora de los Angeles, miraculously washed up on the shores in an unmanned fishing boat in the fifth century! Gijon, capital of Asturias, was devastated in the civil war but is being lovingly restored. Here we were marina-bound once more, as huge seas lashed over the thirty-foot harbour wall, and other yotties warned of worse to come. Impatient, we made a memorable dash for the nearby secure port of Luarca, a picturesque tumble of ancient slated houses and winding alleys. And finally La Coruña, oversupplied with Yacht Clubs, and last port to the ill-fated Armada which disastrously came to the Irish aid in 1601. Torrential rain caused us to stay, and gave us the opportunity to make a brief pilgrimage of thanks and supplication to ancient Santiago de Compostela where we asked the apostle for protection from misadventure.

We were really worried about 'rounding the Cape'! Cap Finistere's headland marked the end of the known world in Roman times (*Finis terra* in a larger sense than Land's End), when to sail beyond it was to invite disaster. It is still infamous as an area of storms and contrary currents, but thanks to St James we had the most benign of seas and favourable winds as we headed south. Despite tearing the mainsail just as we left La Coruña (Frank managed to fix it temporarily with spinnaker tape) we made the 125-mile journey in good time, passing the fabled cape in glorious sunshine and reaching busy Vigo at dawn – a difficult time with the confusion of shore lights – but with good charts at last we made ourselves secure at the marina before falling into that deep and relieved sleep so necessary after stressful times at sea.

This was our second mail-drop, and I collected a healthy bundle from the marina office, and read avidly through a shore-side lunch. Letters from home give such joy to those away: we had been using our sponsored phone-card most of the time to keep in touch – but the written word can be savoured several times and remain treasured!

Vigo's Real Club Nautico was undergoing renovations and at £10 a night offered really good value for money. Nearby is the old transatlantic liner terminal from which the many emigrants to South America would leave their homelands, most never to return. Since Roman times Vigo has had important maritime traditions, and was one of the principal ports to which galleons returned with treasure from the New World, running the gauntlet of pirateers and enemies. The town itself is on one's doorstep, and is a sophisticated and self-assured metropolis – an excellent place for further repair work which we needed to do. Here Frank had to tackle the mainsail's hauling gear which was giving trouble: this involved a day and a half of difficult work on the top of the mast, scaling the purpose-built steps almost twenty times (and all this on a repair that had been tackled professionally before we left Crosshaven!)

A friendly Norwegian family who had taken a year's sabbatical to cross the Atlantic told us they were completing the ARC, the Atlantic Rally for Cruisers set up some 10 years before by Jimmy Cornell, an ideal introduction to long-distance sailing in company – and encouraged us to take part. *Merrimac* was a Sweden 38 with charming parents, 15-year-old daughter and 12-year-old son aboard: the young people at good ages to take a year out of school. We were to meet them again several times before the start of the rally, and afterwards. They suggested we visit nearby Bayona, which many friends in the RCYC had recommended. We made the short trip westward and stayed there for one night. Situated at the mouth of the fjord-like ria on which Vigo is built, Bayona's friendly marina is perched under an imposing walled castle which has been transformed into a *parador*, offering a delightful circular walk around the headland to the boisterous Atlantic beyond. The town dates back to mediaeval times when it was an important centre for sea-trading and sail-making, and boasts being the first point of call for Columbus' *La Pinta* in 1493 having discovered the New World!

It was hard to believe we had been in Spanish waters for 25 days, had visited ten of its myriad and varied harbours, and had completed 1,100 miles since leaving Crosshaven on 15 August – almost six weeks before. Ahead lay unknown waters, and we wondered what was in store! Northern Spain had been enchanting, and as we sampled a bottle from a newly acquired case of delicious *rioja,* we vowed we would return to Bayona when we had completed the long journey ahead!

5

DISCOVERING PORTUGAL

Portugal was a complete surprise. We had never been here before and were unsure what to expect. We were fortunate that *Atlantic Islander*'s existing library contained some excellent pilots of the area, and we thus felt fairly confident in heading into foreign waters yet again. The fact that neither of us had more than two or three words of Portuguese made me less than sure – but we would find that all the officials, marina personnel and bar and restaurant staff had excellent English and there were never any real language difficulties.

For the third time we experienced the simple, anti-climactic passage from one territorial water into another: no frontier to cross, just the change of radio sounds, and a lessening of habitation along the wooded coastline. We had a welcome northerly wind to speed our short 25 nm journey to Viana do Castelo, though the seas were still big after all the recent storms. This is an important commercial port with its small and friendly marina one mile up the Lima river. We were assured that the long-drawn-out, computerised registration here would eliminate the need for such detail in future places and we felt it was therefore well worth the wait. Rates were quite reasonable at about £12 per night, and ARC competitors had a special discount which made it an obvious gathering place en route to the Canaries. Already *Merrimac* was there, and Dutch friends from Bayona – so we were able to compare notes and get the local information. Once checked in we were anxious to take our first steps on Portuguese soil! We were enthralled by the elegant simplicity and uniformity of the town's architecture – mirrored throughout western Portugal – with buildings clad in white plaster, while cornerstones, window and door surrounds were all of grey granite, as were the paved roads. Footpaths in contrast were a crazy paving of marble chunks, a random mosaic which in the bigger cities would be formalised into waving patterns, remarkably pleasant to walk on. Numerous pastry shops had delicious fare on display: these were too difficult to resist! And so we began to develop the Portuguese habit of buying 'a little something' to have

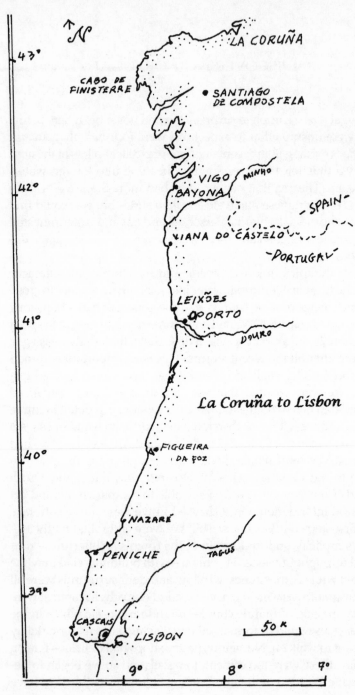

La Coruña to Lisbon

with our morning coffee or after lunch on board! The local super-market had a far greater selection of fruit and vegetables than we had been able to purchase in Spain so we stocked up for several days.

Leixões (*ley-shosh*), a dirty commercial port, lay 25 miles south. Here we spent one night as it was a handy spot for visiting the home of port wine. We had a rendez-vous in Oporto with a crew-member who would sail with us to his temporary home in Lisbon, so we bused to the old city to orientate ourselves. We were over-whelmed by the place! Probably the most seductive element is the luminous quality of the light – colours shine as in Venice, though the pinks are here replaced with yellows, worn and peeling. The heart of the city, its raison d'être, is the fast-flowing Douro river, which for centuries has carried barrels of port wine down from the vineyards in the upland plains, to cool wine lodges in the city, where the liquid matures for several years before being bottled and shipped worldwide. Across the river, imposing buildings tier up the steep north-facing gorge, their names painted in white on their long, tiled roofs: Sandiman, Crofts, Cockburn, Càlem. The two banks are linked by an elegant nineteenth-century cast-iron double bridge. What is unique about this bridge is that both levels carry motorised traffic – rather than the usual locomotive/motorised twinning. Nearby we spotted a handy floating pontoon, and de-cided to berth there the following day.

Next morning we bustled through all our marina-bound jobs, washing the decks, spring-cleaning the interior in preparation for our visitor, and catching up on the laundry – so much easier with piped water – and then left Leixões to make our way the short five miles or so to the infamous, current-torn, Douro bar. It had such a bad reputation that Frank had been loath to attempt it, but I urged him on because of the beauties beyond! As luck would have it one of the fishing fleet which harbour just inside the estuary was mak-ing its approach at the same time: this turned out very much to our advantage. We carefully followed the pilot book's instructions, but hadn't reckoned on the force of the outflowing river, which lit-erally picked up the boat and carried us towards the sand. Frank immediately slammed into 25,000 revs, and made for a mark to the right of the channel. But a shout and frantic signals from the overtaking trawler indicated that we should stay north, and Frank hauled with all his might on the wheel to bring us into line to follow the helpful fishermen. It was probably the most tense moment in our travelling to date, and we thanked the stars that someone was there when we needed them most. Attaching ourselves to the pontoon was another difficult task, and we needed triple warps to guard against the incredibly strong current.

Relieved to have successfully arrived, we sat on deck taking in the beauty of the place, and knew that it had been worth the effort to get in. The Douro, in its Spanish incarnation *Duero*, rises in far off Old Castile near Soria, and marks the northern limits of Moorish rule in Spain. Here in Oporto it is heavy with silt and over the centuries has carved a deep gorge out of the granite rocks. The residential and commercial city occupies the sunny south bank, its terraced six- and seven-storeyed houses tumble down to the river's edge where the old wharves and quays seem lost in time as the shipping which built the wealth of the city has long ceased to come this far, diverted now to Leixões. It is so easy to dream oneself back to the eighteenth century, when sailing ships from England would lie three and four deep to these same quays, unloading Newfoundland dried, salted cod – the original *bacalhau* – and English woollen cloth, filling their emptied holds with barrels of port.

A strong whistle from the shore announced a tall, well-built figure standing at the river's edge, with sports' bag over his shoulder, and a kitbag in the other hand. Frank and I exchanged glances: Hugh would never fit in his assigned quarters in the freshly tidied forecabin – we would have to reorganise the sleeping arrangements! Frank rowed ashore while I put the kettle on: being English he would probably prefer a cup of Earl Grey to a warm beer at this stage of the day. And I was right! We stowed away his gear, promised him the saloon berth, and talked of our mutual offspring! (His daughter Ruth was our Andrew's girlfriend.)

Later we took the lower, pedestrian section of the double-decker bridge, and clambered up into a warren of tenement housing on the northern bank. Dark-eyed children darted to the standpipes, collecting water in tin buckets, while black-clad women dashed the household washing in four-legged concrete tubs outside their tiny front doors. TVs and radios blared, dogs barked and skinny cats skulked at every corner. The steps were steep, a limestone worn smooth by generations of use, and had an ingenious drainage system by means of slanted holes, so rain and household waste was washed to gullies beneath. We were reminded of the Limerick of Frank McCourt's childhood, without the rain, and while in sympathy for the occupants we felt a strange sense of regret that this community may well be rehoused in concrete bunkers far from the city centre.

Next morning we visited the bustling city market, where we found an opulent array of produce and flowers. Never had I seen such displays of fish – much of it still alive, panting on the crushed-ice-covered counters. Beside the fresh fish were great tubs of frozen fish – and most eye-catching of all, giant octopus in metric frozen cubes, one thawing corner dripping a suckered tendril! Each stall was run by one or two women, their flowery wrap-around pinafores reminiscent of those worn when I was a child. They wore short wellington boots over long knee socks, and cardigans over their pinnys, and many had rollers in their hair under chiffon scarves – another reminder of times past! All were joking and laughing, and the air of good humour was infectious. Most had started work before 4.00 am and it was now noon! Men worked equally with women in the poultry stalls. Here the small counters were divided into boxed sections, each one containing piles of chicken parts which we would not see thus displayed at home: mounds of yellow feet, heads red with coxcombs, livers, hearts, breasts, wings, legs and gizzards. Two women sold live fowl from round, lidded baskets – hens, cocks and ducks: movement in a tied hessian sack indicated perhaps a turkey or goose, ready for transportation.

Dense fog prevented us leaving on the next morning's tide, but by lunchtime the city was again bathed in luminous light, and all boded well for our departure. We were nonetheless justifiably nervous as we approached the bar, where the sand bank was clearly visible, and the ebb much fiercer than the flow. Once again the engine was put into full revs to negotiate the bend where the height of tidal pull is felt. We breathed sighs of relief to be belched safely out into the Atlantic.

Our destination was Peniche, a walled town and important fishing centre some 150 miles south – a convenient stop between Oporto and Lisbon, and an excellent launch-pad for a trip inland which Hugh had said would be really worthwhile. Obidos (*oh-be-dosh*) in former centuries was washed on three sides by the sea, but now is about 20 miles inshore, surrounded by rich alluvial farmland. Built on high ground, its protective walls are visible for miles around. A traditional wedding gift of the kings of Portugal to their brides ever since 1282 when it was still an island, virtually nothing inside the walls has changed since then. Hobbles of tiny two-storeyed limewashed houses, their corners painted in bold bands of egg-yolk yellow or delphinium blue, their terracotta roofs sagging precariously yet withstanding the rains and sun of centuries, run at crazy angles from the winding main street, and tiny cobbled alleys lead between minuscule, flower-laden gardens to the many access steps to the ramparts, from where, in normal weather, one has a panoramic view. After the mist the place was redolent with the perfume of oleander and hibiscus, and it seemed like a thousand birds were singing in the aged trees.

Fog greeted us again at 6.30 next morning, Monday 2 October, as we nosed carefully out of the harbour breakwater and into the rolly ocean. By now Hugh's sea-legs were confirmed despite the lay-day ashore, and our journey to Lisbon was a mere 50 miles of down-wind sailing – the land shrouded in fog but a clearance to seaward. Coastal navigation was impossible and we had to carefully watch our position on the GPS to estimate when to make our approach to land. At least there was more success with the fishing line here, and Hugh landed a small mackerel – the very first fish of our voyage! That called for a celebratory drink.

Lisbon has been an important maritime centre since the Visigoths set up a base there in 585 AD. Before them the Phoenicians and Romans were here and later the Moors had a strong presence until 1147, still visible today. On the northern shore of the wide Tagus estuary, sheltered from the prevailing winds, it commands a stunning south-facing position over miles of sheltered quays, and straddles two hills with a deep valley between. Approaching from the north one nudges eastwards round the popular resorts of Esteril and Cascais before entering the city limits at the striking monument to Henry the Navigator. The father of modern navigation, he initially set up an important school of maritime studies at the extreme south-western tip of Portugal in Sagres, where many of Europe's finest cartographers, astronomers and mathematicians gathered and put Portugal to the forefront of sea-going nations for generations. It was a fitting place as the springboard for our voyaging, and our intentions were to rest here, and leave the boat at one of the several city-centre marinas while making a brief visit home to ensure that all the students were safely back at colleges, and to tie up final business details.

As luck would have it, we happened to have hit on peak season for visiting yachts, and were turned away from four marinas – all were full to bursting and couldn't help us, or suggest where we might go. It would be impossible to throw anchor in the busy estuary, with strong tides and a continual stream of ferry traffic to the industrial southern side of the harbour, as well as the east-west flow of shipping of all kinds. We had one last option – failing which we would literally be stranded! We nosed our way into the small Aporvela marina in a particularly nasty swell, alarmed to see a large tug partially blocking the already narrow entrance. We were even more alarmed to see the top section of a mast sticking out of the water just beside the tug: not exactly a welcoming sight in any anchorage! The place seemed full of boats, and as usual there wasn't much room for manœuvring. A kindly Swiss yachtsman gesticulated to a free berth near his boat, and gratefully we made ourselves secure. He told us that there was a lot of roll here – hence the presence of the tug to eliminate some of it. The sunken mast belonged to a German boat which had misjudged the strong currents at the entry, and hit against the quay wall holing the hull. Her distraught elderly owner would spend all day every day diving to salvage his worldly possessions from the muddy bottom. Once safely moored, our priorities now were to make the boat and ourselves as ready as possible, and to leave Lisbon by mid-October.

A quick visit home was a strange mixture of rejoicing and loss: we were happy to see the family, but sad that we would soon again be saying goodbye – possibly for almost two years. It was strange also to be house-less and car-less: visitors in our own village and dependent on Sue's hospitality and any transport we could beg! Our sense of independence which had been heightened over the past two months was now totally dented, but we greatly valued the rock-like support that friends and family extended, and successfully completed the purchase of our site and other unfinished business, leaving our slate clean for the remainder of the voyage.

Back in our floating home we set to work cleaning the dust and grime which had accumulated during our 10-day absence, and tried once again to complete the fridge repair, having brought

47

out the suspected replacement part. Electricians were recommended, and a tense afternoon was spent in anticipation of a successful outcome. Sadly this was not to be: the problem was found to be unsolvable, and we resigned ourselves to using the empty fridge as a store for documents! At any rate we were so used to managing without it now that surely we could manage until the Canaries, where we would make a final attempt to find a competent specialist. We still had the cool-bag and the wet towel! But what would I do with the six new pounds of Irish butter? The weather was still wonderfully hot and the butter was finding the challenge too much! Finally it was decanted into a deep plastic container, and stayed in the cool of the bilges near the water tanks.

Unable to find a nearby laundrette, I enjoyed the unique experience of washing our double sheets and quilt covers in the marina's concrete tub with built-in washboard – a replica of those we had seen used in the poor quarter of Oporto. I had to wait for a few days until the misfortunate shipwrecked German completed his wretched salvage of bedlinen, sails, ropes and clothes, dredged laboriously from the muddy harbour bottom.

Between jobs we took time off to explore some of the wonders of Lisbon. The Aporvela marina is situated in what was the old wheat dock, just under the fascinating Moorish quarter of the city known as the Alfama, an intriguing warren of once stately homes fallen into disrepair and divided into working-class apartments. One day the main *rua*, no wider than four or five feet – enough space for a donkey with panniers to pass through – suddenly became a fish market, as women spread their offerings of fresh sardines and eel-like *espada* on makeshift counters in doorways. We couldn't resist the thought of grilled sardines, and purchased enough for lunch from an amiable, buxom vendor, who, in deference to our obvious visitor status, wiped her fish-wet hands on her aproned bosom before giving our change notes the same treatment!

The Baixa (Lower Quarter) was a total contrast – spacious, European, showy, with big shops and impressive squares and avenidas; but then the unexpected: a city-centre funicular and an art nouveau elevator to transport pedestrians to the western heights of the Bairro Alta – the equivalent of Montmartre – with its famous nightlife, bars and restaurants: we had no time to wander this far. Old-style wooden trams which wind up through both the Bairro Alta and the Alfama are in grave danger of being replaced by modern, efficient, soul-less creatures unless someone protests. Lisbon was like no other capital we knew – so full of life and contrasts, rich and poor, old and older – the out-of-place modern thankfully out of sight apart from the vast humming bridge which soars out over the river at a height of 100 metres, its tiny cars and trucks making the sound of a million bees on the metal struts that carry the roadway to the industrial areas and the south, into the arms of a huge, Rio-like Christ on the opposite bank.

We tended to cling to the city's protective arms. We had to remind ourselves that Lisbon was for many centuries the ultimate centre for exploration and navigation, and would not shelter us indefinitely. On the morning prior to our departure we woke up to see the huge masts of the German Tall Ship *Alexander von Humboldt* berthed on the seaward side of the dock wall, just beside us. In a few months we would be experiencing the cold, north-flowing Pacific current named after the Prussian explorer. There were no further reasons to delay. We had bought all the fresh provisions that we needed – fruit and vegetables and a little milk and some fish. All that was holding us were our fears of the unknown ... just as they too must have unnerved those magnificent explorers in the fifteenth century. And how much better we were equipped than they! We cast our fears to the wind, started our engine, and sped out on the top of the tide. The sunken yacht had been lifted from the muddy bottom, and our spirits lifted to the challenge ahead.

6

First Steps

Henry the Navigator pointed the way as we motored past his imposing marble figure on the afternoon of Friday 21 October, bound for Madeira, 550 nautical miles south-west. It would be chilly and winterish back home, but was still pleasantly warm at this latitude. We were barely out the busy harbour mouth when a thick pea-soup fog again descended, obliterating all signs of the coast and of the frequent shipping departing and arriving. Once more our radar proved invaluable, as it gave us eyes to see the pattern of invisible activities around us. I left Frank on watch, and went below to prepare the evening meal before darkness set in. When I came back on deck it was impossible to see beyond the boat, and Frank was blasting off deafening signals to a very large blob on the radar screen, so close it merged with our own outline. A huge *boooom* would answer him seeming to come first from our left, then from our right – frighteningly close by. We waited for what seemed like an inevitable collision – it was a chilling time and we both prayed fervently. We peered anxiously through the fog – but absolutely nothing could be seen. Just the deafening blare answered by our high-pitched, panicky signal – and then, miraculously, the larger blob disentangled from the central blot on the radar screen, and the sound of their foghorn seemed less strident – we were out of danger. Our appetites had more or less vanished, but quickly returned when I lifted the lid on the pot of bubbling stew, and once more we thanked the Lord for getting us through such a tight spot! There could be no room for complacency on a journey such as ours. Frank soon went to bed, worn out from the strain of the previous hour. I sat on the pilot seat, eyes glued to the deep blue screen, frightened by every flickering dot – though most of them were merely sea-birds and did not recur in the following sweep. I knew that the cruise liner *Canberra* was expected at this time – we wouldn't want to come into contact with her or anything of her size! But was it with her we had so nearly collided?

This is the watch I grew to like least at sea: the unknown night stretches ahead and I alone am responsible for the safe passage of our boat. Will the wind increase, or change direction, and push us where we don't want to go? Will the fog lift or remain? Will approaching boats be monitoring their screens, and see us? Will I have to call Frank? He needs more sleep than I do as he does all the heavy physical work, and I hate to disturb him – but often may need to when worried by decisions that have to be taken on the spot.

Other worries fill my mind on this first night at sea after such a long time ashore. Will I be able to last the course of such an ambitious voyage? Until now I've never been more than four days at sea at any time – usually with more than two on board. Will I cope with seasickness, loneliness, impatience in confined spaces? Will Frank and I get on each other's nerves? All these unanswerable questions crowd into my brain: only time would tell the answers. So far I had managed fairly well, and we were both proud of our progress and growing competence in unknown waters and at strange anchorages.

After another hour, as suddenly as it had come, the fog lifted, and my spirits with it. Beautiful Venus became visible at last, followed by the millions of stars so few of which we know, Orion overhead and the Plough to the north: I looked forward to having Cathy with us – she is the expert stargazer of the family and would have lots of time to teach me during the final months of the voyage. Traffic had thinned out completely, and the coast of Portugal was now well behind us: during most of the days we had sailed near it fog had obliterated it from our view.

The final hour of my first watch passed without incident, and I was able to call Frank, then gratefully curl up in the warm vacated berth and close my eyes for a full three hours of luxurious sleep, before going on watch again at 1.00. Next morning brought glorious sunshine but little wind, so we motored until lunch time and then flew our genneker – a cruising spinnaker rather than a racing sail, but light enough to catch what little breeze there was, and we were able to doze off from time to time to augment the missing night-time sleep!

Our third day out was not to prove so benign: the wind at sea is always unpredictable, and now picked up strength and turned south-westerly – right on our nose. It would be perfect were we heading straight for the Canaries, but we had a rendezvous with Rachel in Madeira, and would have to face the winds to get there. Sailing is an inflexible method of travel, and generally it is diffi-

51

cult to be tied to place and time: but to follow the dictates of favourable winds would deprive us of the comfort of having family and
friends join us from time to time. We had reckoned on the voyage
taking us five to six days, giving plenty of time to be in port before
Rachel arrived. Instead of being almost half-way there, we were
still only 150 miles from the coast of Portugal, with 400 miles to complete in four days. Given good wind from the right direction, we
should average 120 miles a day ... but luck was not with us.

By nightfall the winds were up to Force 8: 30–35 miles per hour
and impossible to steer into even if we were prepared to take turns
on the wheel all night long. Frank decided we needed our rest, and
hove to – putting the very reduced sails in contrary positions and
thereby placing the boat 'in irons' – virtually stopped. This made
it possible for us to get to bed – though with the huge motion of
the seas it was almost impossible to sleep. Waves crashed into the
side of our cabin with horrendous noise, and the running rigging
slapped relentlessly in the heightened wind. Squalls of heavy rain
meant we had to tighten down the hatch and close the windows
in our cabin, reducing essential air and making conditions even
more unpleasant. It was an uneasy, fearful night but we held on
to each other, and felt less afraid.

Tuesday morning saw no improvement in the wind's strength
and direction, and the fact that we had made absolutely no progress over the past 12 hours did not help our morale. Our first longest voyage was turning into a battle, and we began to doubt our
ability to go through with the immense undertaking of circling the
entire globe. If we couldn't get ourselves to Madeira what hope
was there for us over a distance of 30,000 miles? We rationalised
that better weather was surely just over the horizon – and we had
our trusty 80 horsepower engine to speed us along – though it would
be uncomfortable pounding into the ever increasing waves.

On a routine inspection Frank noticed that diesel had been
spilling into the bilges – it was impossible to say for how long but
we might have lost many gallons during the beating of the night
before. Our gauge is a most complicated instrument, particularly
difficult to read in a storm, and we could seldom trust it absolutely: Frank reckoned that we would have to save the remaining fuel
for emergencies and for our tricky entry into Funchal harbour – so
regardless of our rendezvous we would have to sail most of the
way. Just to prove that troubles come in threes, the water supply

was also running low and all wash-up had to be done in salt water: sensible but not to my liking. I was still feeling seasick, and wondered when I would get my sea legs. Thankfully the wind speed had reduced to Force 4 during the day and we were able to make slow but steady progress under increased sail area.

My diary reads: *It's strange, but with all the bad weather we are more anxious about those who are at home expecting to hear from us, than about our own safety. We have tremendous confidence in the boat, and feel that even the most violent storm will not shake the strength and relative stability of this 14 tons. So our worry turns on our own frailty, our decision-making abilities, and our relative lack of practical technical knowledge when small things go wrong. Frank has a great ability to source a problem – but it takes a lot of time and patience, and each new problem brings new needs for inventiveness.*

The weather had been too rough for him to try to establish the source of the diesel leak as to work in the cramped engine compartment under the cockpit floor would be folly in these circumstances. Without the engine the batteries cannot charge – but at least we had a simple solution for this: a small petrol-driven generator which we had added to the boat for just this sort of situation. That at least gave us enough charge to run the navigation and instrument lights at night – but not enough to operate the electric self-steering which had been a real boon since we left Lisbon (with the winds so high the wind-vane was also giving us trouble at this stage, and we had to steer manually for most of the time). We were beginning to lose patience. No engine, no batteries, no self-steering, little progress, and worries about contacting home!! And if all that weren't enough, Frank seemed to have contracted a urinary infection, and was having difficulties passing water.

The storm lasted another two days, but on Friday night the wind changed direction, blowing strongly from the west – enough of an angle to double our speed towards our destination, and certainly arrive by Sunday. We were jubilant, and all the cares and troubles of the past week seemed to vanish as though they had never been. Frank sourced the leak – a minor problem where fuel had been siphoning out from the level gauge – and established that the fuel loss had been relatively small. The sun shone brightly and we were able to rest, for the past two nights had brought little sleep. At 7.00 on Sunday morning Frank could make out the mountains of Madeira. Two hours later we motored into the crowded yacht harbour – eight-and-a-half days after leaving Lisbon. Boats outside the harbour wall were tossing alarmingly in the heavy swell, and it looked as if we might have to join them as there seemed little space inside, with yachts rafted eight deep against the sea-wall. But our valiant captain spied a really tricky opening that all the visitors had spurned, behind the huge bow-sprit of a local boat, and managed to slip *Atlantic Islander* into the impossibly tight spot without contacting the offending projection! We rafted up to a friendly UK boat – with an Irish crewman from Cork – and were just three out from the quay wall, the inside boat being a local catamaran which was in for repairs and would be there for some time. Our UK neighbour *Annie Belle* was another ARC contender, and we were to become good friends with Paul and his crew over the ensuing months.

Eager to make contact with home, we hastened ashore. Phone booths abounded – but none that would accept our call-card. Finally we found a hotel which understood our needs and were able to put a call through to Cork. I was amazed when Rachel herself answered – just on her way to the airport and a bit anxious that she hadn't heard from us – she would arrive that evening on the 20.30 TAP flight. Everything was working out perfectly, and we need not have worried so much!!

Funchal is beautifully situated at the foot of lofty mountains rich in flowering trees and sub-tropical plants, and the town proudly displays samples of the most beautiful of these trees and shrubs in many parks and gardens, and along most streets. Back on board we marvelled at the beauty of the setting and a welcome absence of motion. All around us was frenzied boat activity as cruising yachts gathered for several rallies – some for the ARC, others part of the Trade Winds Cruising Rally, and big numbers involved in French races across the Atlantic. Madeira is the major stepping off point before the Canaries, and being such a green and fertile island is a very popular stop. There was endless friendly hailing – people hadn't seen each other since Gibraltar or Lisbon – and a lot of not-so-friendly exhortations not to tie up alongside, as the rafts became too compacted and inside boats felt the pressure from heavier boats out in the swell. Despite the protection offered us by the off-putting bowsprit, by evening we had accumulated four outer neighbours and so now were in a raft of seven, with the disabled local catamaran taking all the strain.

We tidied the boat that afternoon, making things ready for Rachel's arrival. She would take over the forepeak, which we had been using as a sort of box room, so we re-stored all the junk and aired her bedding in the hot sunshine. Waiting a long time at the airport I finally realised that Madeira was one hour behind Portugal, and my watch was still on mainland time!! This was something that would happen often in the forthcoming months. The big 747 finally nosed down on the partially seaborne runway – built like a huge unfinished bridge over the foreshore – a tremendous feat of engineering which we had marvelled at from the sea. Rachel was soon through, weighed down with spares for the boat. We celebrated with a hearty local meal, and caught up on all the home news.

It was wonderful to have female company! Together she and I checked out the local market which offers a vibrant display of quality fruit, vegetables and flowers, with meat and fish sales on the perimeter, and crafts upstairs. Women flower-sellers wear the traditional Madeiran costume of yellow and red striped skirts, pretty embroidered blouses topped with black boleros, and strange little elfin-like suede boots. They blend perfectly with bird-of-paradise flowers which they sell in big bunches. Frank had stayed on board to pick the combined electronic brains of our knowledgeable neighbours and we found him deep in conference with Paul and Adrian and Des trying to fathom the Weatherfax which had been giving us problems on the trip down. A bottle of Irish whiskey had been produced, and all four were very happily ensconced putting the machine and the world to rights.

After dinner Frank told me that he had trouble urinating and was in some pain, so he went to bed. At midnight he got up and said he would go for a walk to ease the situation – he felt a bit of exercise would probably do him good. I turned back to sleep, and woke with a start two hours later to find a very anxious, ashen Frank shaking me and saying he needed to get to the hospital right away. Shocked, I didn't need a second bidding to get my clothes on and help him to a nearby taxi.

At 2.00 am the casualty department of Funchal's main hospital was very quiet, and somewhat discommoded by the arrival of two foreigners who didn't have a word of Portuguese between them. *'Passeporte?'* demanded the burly lady on the Admissions desk. We managed to get across the fact that Frank needed treatment immediately: IDs could wait. 'Prostrato!' with urgent hand signs brought a young doctor quickly, but I was barred from staying with the patient and had to sit outside the male ward – near the police booth! After about 15 minutes I managed to sneak to the door of the ward, and get a status report from Frank who was in the far bed surrounded by curtains A catheter had brought him instant relief from the pressure on his bladder – and from the dreadful pain. Within three-quarters of an hour he was released, attached to a urine bag, with no instructions other than to report to the urologist at 9.00. A taxi dropped us as near as possible to the boat, still a fair walk to the end of the sea wall. We got soaked in a downpour, and poor Frank had to negotiate five sets of guard-rails before getting to our boat – precariously clinging to the bag which by now was slipping further down his trouser leg. By the time he laid his head on his pillow he was soundly asleep, totally relieved and mercifully out of pain.

I couldn't sleep for ages: still in shock at how close we had come to a real disaster – had this happened while we were still at sea it could possibly have been fatal, as we had neither the skill nor the equipment to take corrective action – even given medical advice by radio. Frank would have been helicoptered off the boat – in severe pain – and I would have had to take the boat into busy Funchal alone. It was best to concentrate on the present – what would be the optimum course of action now? Frank seemed happy to remain in Madeira for whatever treatment was necessary rather than returning home – a difficulty anyway given the awkwardness of the bag.

A few hours later we were seen by a young urologist, who, once he was satisfied that Frank wished to be treated locally, told us he also attended patients at a private down-town clinic, near the marina, and would be able to admit Frank there on Wednesday at 7.00 am for a day of tests followed that evening by whatever procedure would be deemed necessary after the results of the tests were known. Meanwhile there were no instructions – just carry on as before, and he would see Frank in two days. I would be welcome to stay at the clinic if I liked. Back on board we brought an anxious Rachel up to date, our patient a model in non-complaining. Whatever fears and discomfort he may have had he voiced none of them.

At Mass in the sombre cathedral next morning, All Souls' Day, we were more thankful than supplicant, as the surgical procedures are so simplified nowadays. Nonetheless Frank was worried at how it would all work out, and how he would cope with his first-ever hospitalisation. Rachel and I had checked out the clinic and it seemed very pleasant, and wonderfully near the boat which would make visiting so much easier. Also the fact that our national health insurance company would pick up the tab (and at a lot less than regular treatment at home) made life more bearable for us all – as their slogan goes we could afford to be 'ill at ease'.

D Day dawned and Frank checked into a very pleasant room with private facilities – a chance for us all to shower in comfort – and a phone with which we could use our phone card with ease. After a full range of tests the surgeon and anaesthetist outlined the options between micro surgery and the traditional approach, the value of the former being that it could halve recovery time because of the microscopic incision used. Frank opted for that straight away, and when asked later if he would prefer an epidural or a general anaesthetic there were no medals for guessing which he chose – though I had warned him of the after-effects of anaesthetics. That evening he spent two hours in theatre and looked wretched when they wheeled him back. I spent the night with him, impressed by the attentive care he received from a male nurse. Frank was in poor shape for most of the next day, unable to keep his food down, but the surgery had gone well. We phoned various family members with the news, kept from them until the procedure was over, so as not to upset them at such a distance. They were devastated, but glad to know that Frank was relatively well and relieved that we were safely on shore.

A great weariness descended on me the following day – probably a reaction to the suddenness of this unexpected emergency. There were lots of jobs to be done on the boat – but somehow they didn't seem immediately important. Instead I painted our names and *Atlantic Islander*'s on the harbour wall, together with the green, white and orange flag, adding our witness to that of *Golden Apple*, and *Cú na Mara* – Irish boats that had earlier passed this way on the Atlantic circuit. Rachel stuck to her books as she was preparing for end of year Arts exams with the Irish Open University, *Oscail*.

By Sunday the patient was in much better spirits. In church

Rachel and I prayed fervently for those at home, at sea, and in hospital! Then we took a day off, visiting a nearby mountain village where the main street was lined with stalls decorated with branches of greenery and swathes of flowers, selling home brews, honeys and bottled fruits. In a clearing with a panoramic view over the whole valley huge sides of beef hung in makeshift kitchens before being boned and cubed and marinated in herbs and wine and then barbecued on long bamboo skewers over charcoal braziers. Halved chickens were also dipped in spicy marinade and laid on wire grids – the smell of cooking meat was mouthwatering – but we decided to press on. A local band played loudly, while groups of brightly clad dancers thumped heavily on a makeshift stage. We descended the curved cobbled steps of an ancient pathway to one of the sturdy *levadas* (aqueducts which criss-cross all the mountainous terrain of Madeira) carrying an abundant flow of irrigation water to the surrounding gardens. Local children directed us towards the *Boca dos Namorados* or Lovers' Pass, and we clambered higher and higher above the river, as the simple housing became more sparse. Our twisting, rock strewn path levelled off about 300 metres above the water, and then began to rise steeply up the adjoining mountain, east of the village. We remembered that the guide book had labelled this an 'advanced' hike, with the usual warnings about stout footwear and plenty of water: we were in sandals and had forgotten to bring anything to drink.

As we climbed the scenery became more and more spectacular. The village perched high on the mountainside behind us began to disappear from view, though the music could be heard for some time still. We walked up through the pine trees, until mountain mists gathered and the evening began drawing in, and then turned back the valley floor. It was a tough climb to Curral, a hard test on our hearts, but we made the last bus with time to spare, as the driver was delayed sampling local specialities!

Frank meanwhile couldn't wait to be back on *Atlantic Islander*, attending to all the never-ending tasks that fill the days in port. But he knew that it was important to get his strength back before being released in two days time. Next morning the surgeon insisted that he remain in Madeira for two weeks after being discharged from the clinic – and at least another week in Las Palmas before setting out on the transatlantic crossing. That would mean missing the start of the ARC on 19 November. Frank protested that as he was making such an excellent recovery perhaps this time could be shortened, but the doctor remained noncommittal. Maybe when we returned in a week's time for the post-op consultation he might be more lenient? We were thrown into a state of suspended confusion, unsure of what to do, and phoned a surprised and anxious Christophe to advise him of possible changes to our plans.

On release day Frank was up, dressed and ready to leave by 7.00 am. Crestfallen at having to wait for the consultant's visit, it was not until the early afternoon that he returned to the fold – and a full tide helped the trip from high sea wall, to catamaran, to *Atlantic Islander*. There were far fewer boats around, as all the ARC contestants had departed in his absence (the crew of *Annie Belle* devastated at his fate). Naturally he was quite stiff and tender, and weakened after the operation, but he was the happiest man in the world to sit in his own cockpit and watch the comings and goings and hustle and bustle of the ever-changing boating scene. A celebration dinner on board was followed by several games of scrabble that evening: we were never *so* happy to have the skipper home!!

Rachel's leave was due to finish in a day or two, but we now needed her more than ever to help get the boat to the Canaries as Frank would be unable to do heavy work. She decided to go home and work for a few days, and try to extend her leave given the circumstances. She is so lucky to have understanding workmates in Aer Lingus who fill in for her in times like these – not to mention a supportive supervisor who reacts positively to family needs.

Frank was getting a bit stronger each day, though he was constantly surprised at just *how* slow progress was, and felt very frustrated. True to form, he never complained, but must have often considered giving up the voyage. We were missing Rachel – her cheerful presence would have us laughing at small things, whereas we were taken up with the strains of wondering whether we should still try to make the ARC – Frank was determined in spirit, and frustrated that the body seemed to be going against him.

Our cheerful crew returned laden down with the heaviest bag I have ever tried to lift. And no wonder: as well as a leg of lamb and repaired equipment for the boat, she had pounds of chocolate, biscuits, wholemeal flour, post, magazines, letters, tins of concentrated fruit juice which I couldn't buy anywhere, and lots of other treats she thought we would enjoy! How she managed to lug the weight through three airports and onto the local bus I will never know. She was triumphant to have secured another week's leave which would bring us safely to the Canaries.

Wednesday, our sixteenth day in Madeira, saw us in the hospital at 8.45, where we had a cursory chat with Dr Jaoa and were elatedly away by 9.30. He had made no mention of the need to stay a week in the Canaries, thank heavens, because we had no intention of doing so: leaving today we would have to motor all the way there and would be lucky to get in by Friday – two days before the rally! We completed the last of the provisioning as we had been unable to do so until the *all clear* was given, phoned Christophe with a 'thumbs up', and left the beautiful harbour, without much regret! A huge wave of excitement, nervousness, and sheer relief flooded through us: the Madeiran Misadventure was now behind us, and who knew what lay ahead.

There was little wind, and what wind there was was on the nose – we were grateful once again for an excellent engine which carried us valiantly on course for Puerto de la Luz in Gran Canaria, 285 miles from Funchal. The sun shone and the nights got progressively warmer the further south we went, and with three of us on watch duty we got a decent six hours sleep to fortify ourselves. By now the wind-vane was working efficiently, and acted as an invaluable crew member. We christened it Brendan, after the seafaring Irish saint who crossed the Atlantic in the fifth century, and constantly praised its unstinting work. It took no food, no water, and kept us free from onerous steering except in really bad weather. We had no heavy sail changes which gave Frank a better chance to recuperate, and we ate well on the excellent Madeiran produce. It was good to put the past behind us and be thankful that things had happened the way they did, and that Frank has made such a good recovery. In hindsight it was more sheer determination to continue than physical well-being: and he would later pay the price.

We arrived into Las Palmas at the very early hours of Friday 17 November, and threw down our anchor outside an overflowing marina. A strong wind had set in, making our sleep somewhat uncomfortable, as did the huge backwash created by a fast catamaran ferry coming and going from the early hours. Next morning friends came in droves – word had got around that we were finally here! One and all were so welcoming and so concerned for Frank's health – it was almost like a homecoming!

The marina was in a state of frenetic activity – most of the 180 boats taking part in the ARC were 'dressed overall', draped in bunting which rippled in the breeze – a sea of navys, yellows, reds and whites augmented by fluttering battle flags and club burgees – under the vivid blue sky. Fifteen countries were taking part in the rally, and this being the second last day before the start most of the boats were loading provisions. Huge mounds of oranges, potatoes, onions, carrots, apples, pineapples, lettuces, tomatoes, cucumbers, peppers and cabbages were being carefully washed, dried, and stowed away, while dozens of cans of beer and bottles of water lined the pontoons ready to be packed in with the tins and bottles, jars and packets. We knew we should be doing likewise but I particularly wanted Christophe to be part of the shopping team as he would be doing half of the cooking. He arrived in darkness, hot, tired and bewildered but happy to be part of an adventure which had been in jeopardy until a few days before.

Next day, Departure Minus One, Rachel left by taxi in the small hours. I had promised to help Einer from *Merrimac* to locate a missing jib sail (my Spanish was better than his!) – somehow misplaced by the shipping company, and the entire morning was taken up with visiting the airport and making phonecalls – without success! Christophe and I eventually got to the thronged Corte Inglés supermarket by noon, and filled three trolleys to the brim with fresh vegetables, fruit, wine, olive oil, beer, cheeses, biscuits, eggs, bottled water and a huge serrano ham enough for three people for about four weeks, which should last the crossing! As we had had no success with refrigeration repairs I purchased an electric cool box, operating on 12 volts, adequate to keep the butter from melting and chill a few beers. Had Christophe known that it would cease to function after only a few days at sea, he might well have mutinied there and then! Our provisions weren't delivered until 22.00 and we stowed them as carefully as we could: there was no time for the elaborate washing and drying of fruit and veg we had witnessed earlier on other boats: supposed to discourage cockroaches. (Strange to say ours turned out to be one of the very few boats without these pests – throughout the voyage! Perhaps our once-glimpsed resident gekko took care of them?)

Tired but happy we dined very late on board – our new chef produced a first-class instant meal from gourmet treats he had brought from Paris. We were nervous, certainly, about tomorrow's

61

adventure, but the boat was well prepared and the crew ready, despite Frank's setback: he had two willing helpers, both good cooks and tolerable sailors, and together we three would get 'across'! We toasted each other and our trusty boat with an excellent bottle of Christophe's best Burgundy. Who could have forecasted the next dramatic turn of events in just a few hours time?

7

ATLANTIC CROSSING

For months after my accident occurred I kept asking myself *why?* Was I mentally unprepared for the long transatlantic haul? Was it fated that I should not complete a full circumnavigation? Did Frank actually need two strong men in place one frail female to help with the heavy work? This is the reason I like best, and the one which kept me buoyed up over the following three weeks when there was no contact with *Atlantic Islander.*

On the morning of Sunday 19 November the wind was blowing through the Las Palmas marina at about 25 knots. The skippers' briefing the night before had promised calm seas and light breeze, and had greatly boosted general confidence: we awoke to a howling in the rigging, and the clashing and clanging of hundreds of halyards against their masts. Many thought the race start might be postponed, and there was a palpable sense of tension in the air. I was extremely nervous, and had butterflies in my stomach. As the boat bucked and lurched in the wind I busied myself cleaning off the dried salt which had caked our portholes and the cockpit windows on the passage from Funchal, while Frank went with Christophe to complete the immigration formalities for leaving the Canaries. It was then I noticed the mooring warps begin to snap, and went to the bow to try to adjust them ...

The story of my damaged finger has been told – that of the Atlantic crossing belongs to Frank. His tale begins next day, at noon: 'On the way back from the airport, having left Barbara at the departure gate, my mind was reeling with worries about her injury and forthcoming hospitalisation as well as concerns about the trip we were about to make. Christophe was a brick and completely took over the final provisioning of the boat. We had to get additional supplies for the two Danes whom we now had on board. Our agreement with them was that we would purchase food for them but that they would have to supply their own beer and whatever treats they wanted. Our doctor friend insisted on driving us back to Las Palmas, and brought us to the supermarket. We also bought additional water in four litre containers as back-up to our tank supply.

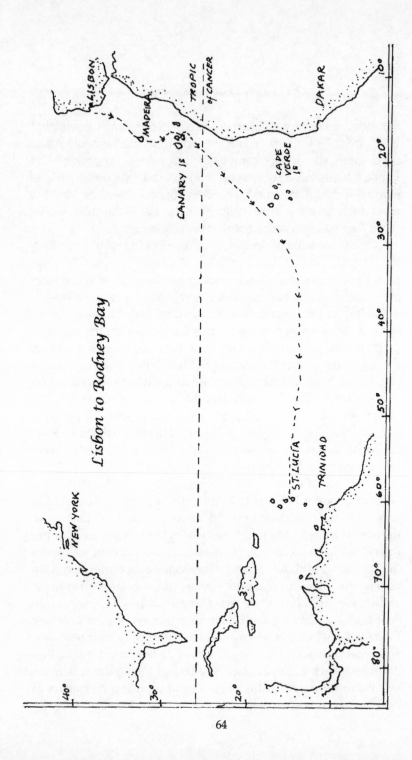

Lisbon to Rodney Bay

'We arrived back to the boat at 14.30 and sent Christien and Jurgen off to buy their supplies, asking them to be back by 16.00. Christophe and I set about final preparations. We brought the boat to the diesel dock where an excellent Texaco station is run by Don Pedro. Like other Texaco stations in the Caribbean this one fully lived up to its Q Mark. We then tied to the end of the marina and I fitted the wind-vane rudder which I had earlier removed in order to make manoeuvring easier.

'It was eventually 17.00 when the Danes returned. With them was *Red Admiral*'s skipper's daughter, Elizabeth. *Red Admiral* was the Norwegian boat on which they had travelled from Madeira and Jurgen and Elizabeth had obviously fallen deeply in love. Theirs was a leave-taking which we all suitably mocked! We eventually pushed off at 18.00 and crossed the starting line to the ARC race thirty hours later than intended.

'As there was very little wind we motored under auto-pilot. Already I was having language difficulties with the crew but figured this would lessen with time. At 22.00 the auto-pilot ceased to operate. I had established a watch rota and Jurgen started hand-steering which he did competently and confidently. We had no navigational concerns as we were well clear of land and could see the lights of Las Palmas off the starboard quarter. At midnight the wind had increased sufficiently to set sails and as I was the only one on board who knew the set-up arrangements for twin head sails I did the job with Jurgen observing.

'I then tried to get some sleep but my mind was racing. I began to worry about our cache of money (about US$500). I remembered taking it out of its secret location with the cleaning materials under the sink, as I felt it might be found there and even possibly have already been thrown out before we left as part of our rubbish disposal. (Later I made a thorough search and eventually found it in the bottom of a locker where I had put it for temporary safe-keeping – what a relief!) All of the time I was very worried about Barbara and knew she must be upset about her finger and not being able to do the transatlantic, worrying about us as we worried about her. As the crew knew little about running the boat I was called for every watch-change, and every change of wind or sails. Eventually at dawn I got up and after breakfast I gave an essential language lesson to Christophe, Christien and Jurgen on sheets, halyards, shackles, genoa and main, mizen and winches.

'We continued to hand-steer and throughout the day we had a steady breeze of force four to five. By 19.00 we had completed 116 miles on our first day which was quite satisfactory and for the next five days we averaged our best records of the entire voyage – 140 miles each day. The seas were quite rough and the crew all felt some degree of seasickness.

'On day three the infamous flashing red light returned to show that our batteries were low. We had ongoing problems with our batteries since France and I was now facing nearly 3,000 miles with a possibility of not being able to start the engine. This would result in no GPS, no radio – even the cooking gas depended on an electric impulse. By this stage I nearly had had enough. With Christophe I discussed turning back. Eventually he said the decision was mine – but to give it a bit more time. I lay in my bunk – thinking that Barbara would say I was worrying too much and getting over-anxious. Eventually at midday I decided we would continue on – there was always the possibility, although not a very attractive one, of going into the Cape Verde Islands.

'We had a group discussion in the afternoon with the Danes and we all agreed to carry on. However by 18.00 that evening I felt like changing my mind again. Christophe was very helpful not advising but urging to give it some more time. I knew that the following day would be too late but that night I had some rest and felt better in the morning. Then I went to work on the wind-vane steering. I used some 'magic tape' to hold it in position and it worked fairly well: everyone was pleased and relieved at the pressure of steering being taken off.

'Now things were getting better. The crew were over their seasickness and a good watch system was in operation. Christophe cooked a fabulous meal each evening. For the next few days I worked on the batteries and on the SSB radio. Despite having completed the radio certification course successfully my operating knowledge of the model on *Atlantic Islander* was sketchy. I had intended when things settled down to study the manual but as it turned out this was one of those dreadful tomes written by a radio expert with poor communication skills.

'On 27 November the winds had died and all the following week we had light winds or calms. We met a very large cargo ship which appeared to be hardly moving and was very high out of the water as if she were unladen. We talked to them on VHF and confirmed the weather forecast. We had been receiving forecasts each day from Radio France Inter. The programme announcer was a woman and we began to regard her as a person with whom we could communicate. Christophe of course did the translating and we looked forward each midday to the transmission which gave winds for our longitude and latitude. During week two the winds always seemed to be about 200 miles ahead of us but we didn't catch up with them.

'We kept our daily distance-covered up to eighty miles by motoring and thus providing good battery charge for that period. During one of the calm nights the sky was completely cloudless and for the first time in my life I saw stars right down to the horizon. Previously at sea I had experienced such nights but there was always that little bit of cloud or mist on the horizon. On only a few occasions subsequently did we see the same phenomenon.

'On 29 November a red-billed tropic bird darted around the boat for about half an hour, giving us the opportunity to identify it and for Christophe to photograph it. About the size of a tern, it is snowy white with a long streaming tail and of course a red bill. We had an excellent book on sea-birds and throughout the voyage this proved very useful. However birds such as petrels and shearwaters were difficult to identify because of the similarities between species and the very brief stays they made. Later I made our first radio contact with a nearby yacht, *Brigadoon*. The red light still came on occasionally, and the fridge was not operating as it blew the fuses in the invertor, and SSB contact was minimal. We got good French radio weather forecasts and managed one Weatherfax. Having four people on the watch rota was a great advantage. We operated 2-hour watches and I skipped a watch every 36 hours thus moving the rotation forward and giving me more time for repairs and navigation.

'Next day we picked up a sailing ship *Breezaway* on the SSB, and I was able to transmit to them. We requested them to relay our position to the ARC office and this gave us a feeling of relief that at least our position was now known by control HQ.

'By 1 December I felt we would succeed in completing the trip. During the calms we frequently took the opportunity to swim over the side and these dips were really enjoyable. Later I noticed more water in the bilges than usual and on checking again discovered that when the water pump was operating a significant

67

leak occurred in the water pressure tank. This small cylinder containing a pint of water is intended to maintain a head of pressure in the water system and thus avoid 'drumming' in the taps. I estimated that about 15 of our 100 gallons had been lost and decided to introduce a small measure of rationing as up to this we had been quite generous with our water usage. After every swim we rinsed down with fresh water and hair washing was very popular with the two Danes who both had abundant growth. I later learnt that this slight reduction in availability of water irked them quite a bit as they were very keen on maintaining clean and healthy hair. I repaired the pressure tank with Araldite but it subsequently opened several times and by the end of the voyage it was almost completely covered with the compound. Fortunately we had a manual pump system which avoided the use of the electric one.

'Next day the winds had picked up again to 15 knots. On 3 December we made contact via SSB with *Annie Belle*. Des Scott from Cork was on this boat and we didn't mind asking them to get on to the ARC office to contact Barbara and Christophe's wife Éléanore to inform them of our positions.

'By 6 December we had only 980 miles remaining and began to feel quite optimistic. Christophe's cooking continued to surpass anyone else's significantly. That evening we had a real slap-up feed with wine. The most successful food item on board was the serrano ham which we hung in the main saloon. From it we could cut smoked rashers for breakfast, cold slices for luncheon sandwiches, and diced ham for risotto. By the end of week two we had run out of banana and eggs. We had plenty of tinned meats which Christophe was able to spice up and make interesting. Our tomatoes, onions and cucumbers lasted the whole trip as did the cheeses and butter. In all we had plenty of variety. I used rice cakes being allergic to gluten, and Jurgen made very palatable bread when the shop supply ran out.

'We had seen no other yachts up to this but on 9 December the French boat *Bonjour* came up astern. Christophe made contact with them on VHF and was delighted to have an opportunity to speak in French. By now we were beginning to estimate our time of arrival and we all made separate guesses with a promise of beers for the closest one. As it turned out Christien got it right to within thirty minutes.

'On the second-last day we had to change butane gas tanks.

In setting up the replacement tank I made a misconnection and the gauge read empty. For a full twelve hours we thought we had run out of gas and Christophe eventually used the paraffin lamp to heat our stew and beans that evening. By the following morning I had remedied the problem but the thought of even two days without hot food was really scary for all of us.

'By now we could hear local radio on the transistor; we had winds of twenty-five to thirty knots and while the seas were rough we were delighted to be making good speed. On our second-last day we did 153 miles – one of our best days of the entire voyage.

'During the night of the 13/14 we could see the lights of St Lucia ahead and at dawn we sailed around the northern tip of the island. We had clear instructions on how to approach the finish line but with the excitement of making a landfall I was quite uncertain. Eventually Christophe spotted the finishing boat in Rodney Bay and we crossed the line at 06.33 local time. Having thanked them and received directions for the marina berth I became aware of sirens and motors around us. About six rubber dinghies had come out to greet us, among them *Annie Belle's* – blowing sirens and waving Irish flags. I was stunned by the reception and as we came to the marina they continued to serenade us waking up the other boats who added their cheers and sirens!

'By the time we got to our assigned berth I was totally confused and fortunately Paul from *Annie Belle* guided us right into the finger with his dinghy. At this stage I called instructions to the crew: "Fenders out! Prepare mooring lines!"

'"What are *fenders*?"

'Too late I realised that this was one word that we had not covered in our language lessons!

'When we were eventually tied up we jumped ashore to be greeted by a lovely local girl with a tray of rum punches and an ARC representative with a basket of fruit. Even at 8.00 am we downed the strong drinks manfully and then went to the marina restaurant for an enormous breakfast of bacon, eggs, chocolate-filled croissants and coffee. Somewhat more relaxed we then completed our customs and immigration formalities and reported into the ARC office.'

One of the first things Frank and Christophe did after their welcome breakfast was telephone us wives to announce their safe arrival! Éléanore had already consulted with me, and had flown out to surprise her proud sailor, and they spent a happy few days together before flying back to Paris.

Our reunion too was indeed a joyous one – after five anxious weeks when each of us had individually gone through traumatic experiences. Frank looked really thin but very bronzed – we clung together in the airport before stepping out into the cloying heat of the evening. In a taxi we talked nonstop, catching up on so much news, and it was quite dark by the time we reached the marina. We struggled with my heavy bags – laden with gifts, whiskey, and pre-cooked Christmas turkey! – and there, nicely positioned near the marina centre, was *home*!! The relief I felt was hard to describe. We sat together in the velvet evening, holding each other as though we were afraid of being separated again. Our solo marathons were over, and we felt we could now face anything together. We were probably never so close as on this extraordinary, tropical Christmas Eve.

We woke early on Christmas morning – 6.00 had become the norm for Frank: only in the first few relatively cool hours was outdoor work possible – after 9.00 the heat and humidity made each task take far longer. The nearest church was a good twenty-minute walk away, in Gros Islet (*groze eelay*), and we were surprised to find it copiously adorned with red and white plastic flowers (the Cork colours!) though the roadside was lined with glorious hibiscus and bougainvillea. Shiny tinsel was draped over gaudy plaster saints, and the local women and girls had their florid, frilly best dresses on, while the men were somewhat more sombrely attired. A small but very vocal choir was led by an enthusiastic lady who frequently performed out-of-key solos, and several times the carol or hymn became in grave danger of collapsing – but the congregation valiantly sang along, and most of the tunes were ones I knew.

Church can often be a place for tears, and I shed quite a few on this Caribbean Christmas morning – as a mixture of emotions engulfed me. I was really happy to be with Frank but so missed the children, celebrating without us for the first time in 27 years. I still wondered at my capability of providing the necessary support and commitment to complete this world cruise. The discordant singing heightened my inner turmoil, and the long and impossibly complicated sermon did not provide enlightenment. It was a relief to escape the garish church and to smell the sweetly scented flowers on the roadside, fresh after a tropical downpour.

Rodney Bay is situated in a curve of lush hills, with high mountains beyond them to the south and east. Formerly a swampy march, the developers cleverly dredged the swamp and stabilised a flat area behind a long spit of beach, building some choice summer homes, and providing a comprehensive commercial centre to the marina itself – with supermarket, banks, immigration offices, chandler, restaurant, cafes, bakery, bars and shower and toilet block. As a shelter for boats it is in an ideal position, doubly protected from the ocean swell, and from winds from practically all quarters. The island infrastructure is good, and the main town of Castries is only a short local bus ride away. The channel is kept well dredged, and as a result boats with a fairly big draught can come and moor alongside the ample pontoons. As we walked back from the church I could take in the full panorama, and appreciate from the ground the area which I had flown over the previous day.

While we enjoyed Frank's full Irish breakfast I studied our surroundings, and he filled me in on a *who's who* of the nearby boats. Most of the ARC competitors who had thronged the marina the weeks before had departed to other anchorages, but there was still a fair group remaining to celebrate Christmas near to amenities. Frank had met up with no less than three Irish couples, and he had had numerous invitations for us to join them for Christmas dinner. We opted to dine alone, as we still had so much to catch up on, and another invitation from the magnificent 30-metre motor cruiser berthed at the end of our pontoon we also turned down, though we did agree to join them for cocktails before lunch: I was dying to see what the inside of a luxury cruiser looked like! The crew of seven were celebrating without the boat's owners, and so had more freedom than usual.

Keeping with tradition we opened our presents after breakfast, touched by the thoughtful gifts the immediate family had given us – all lightweight so as not to overburden my luggage! Then we phoned Rachel, who was hosting the Big Dinner in our absence, and spoke to the four who were home. We were all sad at being apart, but happy that we could communicate with such ease. The previous Christmas all eight of us had been together in the big old house in Crosshaven – and we would look forward to

71

being together again in two years time.

Oblivious to our futures we lay together under a thorn tree on a nearby beach and watched a spirited horse swim with his young bareback rider, then in the cool of the evening enjoyed a quiet and simple dinner on board, before joining the poolside party where all the Irish had gathered with the crew of *Annie Belle*. The merry-making had started early in the evening, and the spirits were high as each one provided their own tipple. It was a warm and welcoming group, and we stayed chatting until the early hours. Each one missed their family back home, but all were contented to have exchanged the bitter winter for the sensual warmth of St Lucia, and were looking forward to continued cruising in similar climes. Many would stay in the Caribbean for at least another two months – we were the only ones heading north-west to Panama.

For the next few days we busied ourselves with maintenance jobs. I washed all the curtains and seat covers which were stiff with Atlantic salt. Frank finished varnishing the mahogany grab rails and hatches. We were delighted to break the chores to greet visitors, as the heat was sapping. Robin and Susan Grey from Dublin were taking a much more sensible pace to complete their circumnavigation in *Waxwing*, and it was lovely to discuss ports of call, and talk of home. Frank was still quite weak from what he told me was 'flu', but had in fact been diagnosed as dengue fever, a form of malaria. Thankfully he got a local man to help wax the 'topsides' – that part of the hull above the waterline. John agreed to sell us fruit and vegetables from his wife's garden before we left. A devout Seventh Day Adventist with four children under five, he was not ashamed to admit that he found the going tough at home, and hence hung around the marina looking for odd jobs when he wasn't working her patch of land.

We also unpacked the bikes from their bags at the stern of the boat, and oiled and greased them. The chains in particular had suffered from the surfeit of Atlantic salt. They attracted a lot of local interest, and we had many requests from potential buyers. Finally we decided to offer mine to John in exchange for produce – it had come off worst in the trials of the crossing, but the damage was only skin deep. I was sad to part with it but we knew that it just wouldn't stand the rigours of the Pacific crossing, and that here it would have a good home and many more years of useful service. I have a lasting memory of John happily paddling off in a borrowed punt, with the bicycle propped proudly in front of him.

We had a converter installed to try and make the coolbox less power hungry – it had been playing hell with the batteries across the Atlantic. An excellent young engineer from the UK had recently settled here and was very helpful to Frank in analysing some of our strange battery drain.

As departure day approached I became more and more tense and introspective, and needed to emphasise the good points in our new chosen lifestyle, to minimise my fears and self-doubt. With Frank below par, and my hand far from healed, there were many moments when I doubted the sanity of our mission. But the support and camaraderie that I had witnessed here in Rodney Bay helped steel my resolve, and my dread soon evaporated. The third of January dawned calm and clear – ideal for making our getaway from the marina. Our bills were paid, our electrics unhooked – the umbilical chord cut, and we were set to begin the final phase of the Atlantic adventure.

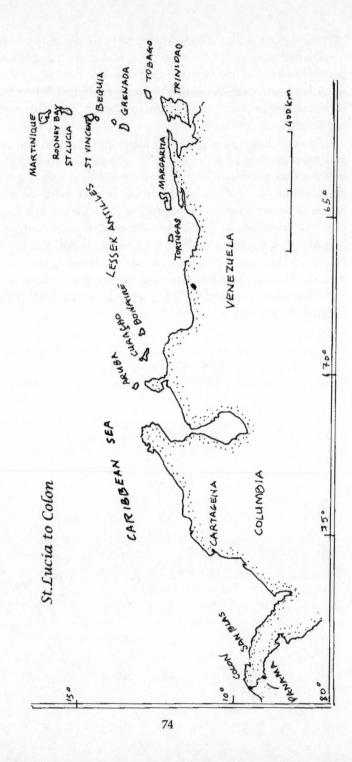

St. Lucia to Colon

8

Islands in the Sun

As we motored out of Rodney Bay I felt we were remarkably relaxed and untroubled. Frank had spent a total of three weeks there, and I had been with him for ten days. Harbour rot had definitely set in, and even though he still had traces of his so-called 'flu' it was time to be gone. We had few regrets leaving the island of St Lucia. Physically it was a beautiful place, but we had found it unfriendly and at times hostile, with hopeless service in the shops and restaurants, and a laid-back approach which bordered on total idleness. There seemed to be little life or enthusiasm in many of the people – and as soon as we left the shores we felt lighter.

The weather too sensed the difference. A stiff following breeze carried us northwards to Martinique, and we were able to fill our lungs with good fresh ocean air. I had not been sailing for almost seven weeks, but for once I didn't feel seasick on my first day out: I took no chances though and remained on deck for the entire crossing. Frank slept below for most of the morning – he had started antibiotics to try and get rid of a second bout of dengue fever – and obviously the more he slept the better.

Fort de France nestles among low hills on the western side of Martinique. It is a total culture shock after shabby Castries, with stylish shops, pharmacies, restaurants, a magnificent town hall and a splendid fortress overlooking the bay, fringed with tall date palms, and beautifully flood lit at night. Moored near us were two huge P&O cruise liners, whose passengers had spent a day ashore touring and shopping. Both left after dark, and were replaced next morning by two more! No one is letting the grass grow on this side of the channel. We checked in with little fuss at the one-stop Customs/Gendarmerie/Immigration office right by the harbour, changed some dollars, bought some excellent fresh provisions at the huge Continente supermarket nearby, and returned to the boat to have a simple meal and an early night. While Frank slept I lingered in the cockpit taking in all the sounds and sights of a busy harbour, glad to be back to life afloat. From now until Panama we would be anchoring almost everywhere, which would be great for our budget.

Next day we headed back south for St Lucia's airport, as Rachel was to join us once again. We were overawed by the beauty of the coastline and the relative lack of development due to the mountainous terrain. Seen from the sea the sheer twin Pitons – eroded volcanic cones which reach a height of 609 metres – were truly spectacular, and several yachts were anchored beneath them: but there was an all-pervading smell of sulphur which took greatly from the beauty of the place. The small town here is aptly named *Soufrière*.

There was a strong current at the Vieux Fort anchorage, and getting ashore was via a dirty stony beach where the fishermen drew up their long sturdy brightly-painted wooden boats onto raised, thatch-covered platforms. Sunken lines, floating debris, broken glass and scattered fishbones made the passage ashore hazardous, and the great rush of bodies that met us with cries of '*Skip! Skip! I take care of the boat!*' was intimidating, but as Rachel's flight was delayed by many hours we felt obliged to 'hire' one of the local lads, or risk having our dinghy stolen. She finally arrived, neatly dressed and with the her familiar overweight bag! *Now* we were glad of our paid help at the stony beach – he and his pals made light work of swinging the dinghy into the water, and the heavy bags into the dinghy – and then offered Rachel a piggyback so she wouldn't wet her trousers! She politely declined, and braved the fishbones and glass in her best style and bare feet. It was one of the more unusual 'transfers' she had experienced, and we laughed for days at the memory of it.

Five o'clock next morning saw us aweigh, motoring south into a strong current. Our destination was Bequia (*Bake-wee*), south of St Vincent. Its capital, Port Elizabeth, tucked within the lush arms of Admiralty Bay, welcomed us in the flashing form of Tim Wright, an English-born photographer who sailed here single-handed in 1986 and makes a reasonable living out of snapping visiting yachts as they come in under sail. A one-man show, he manages to steer his high powered inflatable and take excellent photographs at the same time! His spirit of enterprise is to be found all over the island, and Bequia has become a favourite for visiting yachts – there were well over 100 anchored in the bay when we arrived. We barely had the anchor down when three local youths arrived in a wooden boat, and set up the most unmusical rendition of a popular song – expecting to be paid! I told them what I thought of their music and they got the message!!

Immigration was slow but straightforward: we were getting used to the endless form filling: last five ports visited, passport numbers, boat registration number, dimensions and weight of the boat, goods to declare, contraband on board, etc., etc. – how much simpler to arrive by plane! Here at least we could declare ourselves in and out at the same time, saving a repeat visit the following morning! Frank found an excellent chandlery where batteries were cheaper than at home, and installed them that evening. This was a cramped and difficult procedure, as they were housed behind the navigation centre, almost inaccessible. Batteries were beginning to be a serious problem, as they seemed reluctant to charge, and these were the second replacements in a mere four months. How Frank stayed patient I don't know.

By 8.00 the following morning we were approaching St George's, capital of Grenada, deep in a picture-postcard horse-shoe bay – a partially submerged volcano – encircled by the now familiar but always staggeringly lush tropical forest climbing up steep hills, where up-market homes were perched high to catch any cooling breeze. Our pilot book warned of a difficult channel into the yachts' section south of the main harbour – and commented that members at the Yacht Club took delight in watching careless visitors get caught on coral. This was untrue and unkind – but did put the yacht's lookouts on their toes! Rachel climbed the mast and under her direction we carefully threaded our way between confusing marks, and breathed sighs of relief once safely inside! Our joy was increased at seeing *Annie Belle* lying at anchor, and we gratefully accepted offers of morning coffee. Immigration was an unpleasant affair with hostile officials, but later we managed to get Venezuelan visas at the nearby embassy without any trouble.

With Paul and Adrian we took the next day off work to explore the island by taxi, and swam in huge breakers on a wild, eastern shore. But back 'home' on *Atlantic Islander* our sense of well being was short-lived when we discovered that despite work Frank had had done that afternoon by a local electrician, the brand new batteries were still losing charge, flashing warning lights were blinking and the engine wouldn't start! Frank contemplated returning to St Lucia to the electrical expert in Rodney Bay, and we were thrown into a state of anxiety: we could not progress while this problem persisted. But help was much nearer at hand, as so often before.

The following morning Adrian called over to say goodbye – but when he heard of our difficulties he and Paul kindly offered to stay an extra day to help. This is so typical of the sailing fraternity – other's troubles are always put before one's own, and skills are so willingly shared. Paul was having trouble with his outboard motor and wanted to put that to rights, so Frank and Adrian (who was an electronics wizard) together spent nine hours in the intense heat trying to solve for once and for all the mystery of the power leaks. Together they set up a system which should eliminate the leak, through isolating one set of alternators and regulators and operating on the other, functional set. Now all we could do was cross our fingers and toes that this would finally stem the loss of charge.

Thank the Lord – and our good friends – next morning the engine started without problem, the batteries accepted charge, and we were soon nosing our way through the coral-scattered bay and into the swell of the Caribbean Sea. We were south-westward bound this time, for the island of Margarita, some 170 nautical miles away.

(On watch: 21.36 11°42'N, 62°26'W) This must be one of the most marvellous sailing experiences one can have. The sea is flat, spangled with phosphorescence from the bow wave, and the heavens are saturated with stars. We are directly under the milky way which stretches NS above, and in the hour before coming on watch while I lay on the deck I saw three falling stars. We are running in the warm trades with twin foresails boomed out with spinnaker poles. The main is reefed and acting as a direction/steadying fin, and the mizen is furled. Brendan the windvane is managing the helm beautifully, and we're streaming along at 5.5 knots. It's cool enough for an extra tee-shirt in blissful contrast to the steamy weather in the lagoon at St George's.

On nights such as these the beauty of the sea is almost indescribable, and the sense of peace it brings is like a balm to the soul. One forgets the problems, the discomforts, the loneliness, and becomes immersed in the magnificence of nature and the absence of external pressure. We store up the scene, like Wordsworth, to soothe future troubles.

Porlamar is Margarita's recommended port of call, near the relevant authorities and beyond the noise of the neighbouring capital Pampatar. Caught up in the 1970s' flurry of high-rise speculation as the free-port status brought more and more tourists to this rather barren island, with the drastic slump in the Venezuelan economy during the 1980s and 1990s many of these grandiose building schemes ran out of capital, and huge skyscrapers remain unfinished shells. Porlamar is still low-rise and low-key, with only a handful of yachts here – many people are put off by the complicated immigration procedures, and those who come are advised to use an agent: but we were cautioned by a Belgian from a neighbouring catamaran not to be ripped off in this way as his friends had been. $US100 was the fee charged – daylight robbery, as the actual fees amounted to about $US20. But two days later when we had spent eight hours trying to comply with regulations, we understood the logistical benefits of using an agent!

An ancient, ramshackle bus, in glaring colours with statues and pictures of the Virgin to protect us, sped us to a big covered clothes market the other side of Pampatar and cost us about one cent each. There we were immediately approached by a money changer who gave us 340 bolivars to the dollar – though the bank rate was 290! We bought 'designer' cottons at ridiculous prices, but were later glad that the international phone office took credit-card payment, as phone charges to Europe were hugely expensive. We could now have a conversation without being cut dead after three minutes. Rachel joyfully discovered that she had passed her recent exams with credit! And we were able to talk to family whom we hadn't contacted since St Lucia, and reassure ourselves and them that all was well.

The local supermarket had twenty-four cans of chilled *Polar* beer for $US5 – yes, five! – so needless to say we bought as much as we could carry – and were later sorry we hadn't made several more trips! Rampant inflation on the mainland has dried up the influx of Venezuelan visitors over the past decade, but neighbouring countries provide bargain hunters – many come with cars to stock up on the duty-free goods and provisions from Pampatar's glossy emporiums.

The next morning we motored *Atlantic Islander* to the capital to load our tanks with ridiculously cheap diesel. A UK-trained aeronautical engineer-turned-entrepreneur who goes under the apt 'handle' of *Diesel Man* had set up a first class if somewhat unusual service. As there are no berthside pumps available to pleasure craft, Rangel Zavala uses a local fishing boat to tow an 18 foot open fibreglass tender filled with sixty-gallon drums of fuel. An elderly assistant acts as boat driver and manoeuvres the tender alongside receiving yachts, where it is secured fore and aft. Then a lad of about 14 steadily hand-pumps the diesel into the receiving boat's tank. We took on 170 gallons at 25 US *cents* a gallon – certainly the cheapest fill of our entire cruise!

Rachel was on first watch from 19.00. When I came on at 22.00 she was hanging out over the guardrail, enthralled. 'Dolphins!' we shouted to Frank, and clambered up to the bow to get the best view. Each of the seven streaking bodies was totally outlined in phosphorescence – clearly visible below water and more spectacular by far than those seen in daylight. At first there had been a school of about twenty swimming close together, and Rachel had been really scared as she thought it was some strange sea monster lit up from within, but then they separated and began to cavort under the bows. We were entranced as they flashed like comets in an abandon of joy, sending spumes of phosphorescent stars into the water each time they broke the surface, their human-like breathing loud in our ears. Three hours later they were still with us, obviously enjoying their race with the boat, and then, as suddenly as they had arrived, they were gone, and we experienced a real sense of loss.

At 8.30 next morning we entered our first reef pass to *Isla Tortuga* or Turtle Island. An exciting operation in any weather, breakers pound the outer rim of coral which stretches protectively round the island sheltering an aquamarine millpond within. Through a narrow pass one must run the gauntlet between the coral heads and thundering surf: it is not for the fainthearted! We explored the low-lying uninhabited island with arid scrub vegetation alive with singing birds, a tiny airstrip, and a few deserted fishermen's huts strewn with mounds of pink conch shells. Sadly, the windward beach was rimmed with plastic flotsam – an imperishable memorial to man's insensitivity and the commercial world's lack of environmental responsibility.

Our next 200-mile leg would bring us to yet another country, our fifth in ten days, and further culture shock!! The winds were in our favour, and we got a fine push westwards with good speeds of up to 6.5 knots. Rachel and I spent most of the day cutting and sewing the Panamanian and Ecuadorian flags with the help of the international pages from an old telephone directory. It was a satisfying experience to revive the joys of hand-stitching so laboriously learnt in school 35 years ago.

Aruba's main harbour, Oranjstad, is a totally plastic, sugarsweet synthetic shorescape: most things here belong to *Toys 'R Us* guru Rob Swain and are *à la Disneyland*, swarming with ancient vacationing Americans with far more dollars than sense – and we LOVED it! There is a tiny pontoon in the pastel pink and blue pleasure port: we tied up alongside a huge motor yacht, and local liveaboards told us that our mooring fees covered use of the nearby condominium with laundry rooms on each floor, two pools, outdoor and indoor restaurants, and even an artificial beach area complete with comfortable loungers, resident calypso band, and plenty of showers! Oh Joy! Rachel and I quickly assembled two huge bags of dirty laundry (last time the sheets and towels had seen a washing machine was in Vigo, several months ago!!), grabbed our swimsuits, and headed for *civilisation*! No time to sneer at the brashness of it all – huge, efficient American machines swallowed our salty wash (at just $1 a load!) and pleasant, efficient staff made us welcome. We lounged by the man-made shore, swimming and showering at leisure, as the band played gentle, inoffensive numbers to suit the clientele. The evening buffet looked mouth-watering, but would certainly be *way* over-budget – we would find something more ethnic on the back streets later, in the *real* Oranjstad. We collected our sweet-smelling laundry and returned, restored, to *Atlantic Islander*.

Meanwhile our poor hard-working skipper had been busy extracting the final pair of dud engine batteries from their practically inaccessible home – tomorrow he would replace them with yet another two from the local chandlery. Would the power drain problems ever be solved?

Later we were visited by two young people from the Trade Winds Rally – Roger, from Kilrush, had read an article about us in the *Cork Examiner*, and was intrigued that our dog had found a new home in nearby Kilkee. We were to become firm friends with him and his pal David from Edinburgh. Throughout our cruise young people would be a source of inspiration and courage to us, and we met many fine sailors under thirty who were happy to share their experiences and know-how with us senior travellers! In many ways they linked us to our absent family whom we sorely missed, and we often valued their company even more than that of our peers.

So armed with two more new batteries, a selection of freshly laundered sheets, towels and clothing, some delicious Dutch cheese, biscuits and coffee, and good local vegetables – avocados, tomatoes, beetroots, pineapples, bananas, mangoes, oranges and lemons – we set off on what was to be a roller-coaster 460-mile ride to Panama. Ten miles offshore the cable controlling our wind-vane steering mechanism snapped, and Frank fixed up a jury rig which held while the wind was light. But in a couple of hours the wind increased to Force 6, and remained between 6 and 8 for the entire passage to Panama! It is difficult to describe the physical strain involved in steering constantly for five days and five nights of heavy weather. On watch at night it was even scarier than in the daylight, when unseen waves (up to 7.5 metres high) would come rushing up as the sound of surging water got louder and louder, and the boat would be picked up, out of control, and carried forward for several frightening seconds while the watchkeeper remained totally powerless and terrified at the wheel, before the wave's untold strength moved onwards and let the tiller bring the boat back on course. Our arms and necks ached from the strain of trying to keep on course, and many times we were really terrified of being swamped, but kept those fears to ourselves. Those off watch needed to be free of worry, until their turn came.

Yet, no matter how tired or scared we became, there were always countless things to be thankful for! We were warm and the boat was strong. Our deep and somewhat uncomfortable cockpit almost never let sea in, so regardless of the constant wash over the deck, we were snug and dry. None of us was seasick, despite the constant roll, and we never lost our healthy appetites. I had an excellent helper in the galley, which ensured a greater variety of food and more care in preparation. And most importantly, we were covering the passage with speed, and would soon have the opportunity to repair the cable at anchor. So the positive far outweighed the negative, and we remained cheerful if tired! The miles flew by, and we kept our tempers at bay. Frank got a large gash in the head from taking down the spinnaker pole in Force 7, and we made him *promise* not to attempt it again in similar conditions.

Our relief on turning finally into the Cristobal roads was not just the prospect of showers and some good nights' sleep – but also the triumph of having completed a significant part of the circumnavigation, and probably some of its most difficult sailing, competently, safely, and on time! We had a lot to celebrate, and the ice-cold jugs of beer at the Panama Canal Yacht Club tasted better than French champagne!

9

Between two Oceans

Colon is not a major tourist destination. In fact it is one of the most dangerous cities in Panama, and many of the taxi drivers carry loaded guns (as we were to find out!). It is run-down, lawless, dirty and poor, and is of necessity temporary home to all sailors who wish to transit the canal from the Atlantic side. As soon as we stepped ashore we were warned not to walk *anywhere* – and *not* to go into town. A yottie had just been mugged, his watch, all his cash and credit cards snatched from him (alighting from a taxi, as it happened!). What a welcome! With trepidation we proceeded to the Immigration Office on the Yacht Club's grounds, and declared ourselves. An extremely pleasant official told us the steps we should take to complete entry formalities and to arrange for the boat admeasurement – an obligatory requirement for all yachts and ships transiting the canal for the first time. He provided us with a map outlining the various offices within the Canal Zone area, 15 minutes from the Club. We hesitated, then asked if it was safe to walk there, and he assured us there was no problem, so taking our lives in our hands and feeling like pioneers of old we set out, all three together, to undertake the possibly dangerous and certainly time-consuming ritual of formally entering the Panama Canal! We had been advised by a cruiser skipper in St Lucia to use an agent who would complete all the formalities for us, and limit our time in Colon, but on enquiring about the cost I was told it would be about $1,000 – and somehow it didn't seem worthwhile! (The actual total cost worked out at a mere $170 – *and* ten days of our time!)

So what does an agent do to earn this cash? We proceeded as directed to a series of offices, none of them labelled – hence the map. All were located close together in the 'safe' Port Administration area, separated by railway tracks from Colon's open market and seedier part of town. Our first stop was at a very dingy cubby-hole manned by a severe lady in muslim headgear and white four-inch heels. Without a smile she demanded our passports, scanned them, and directed us upstairs, where we found ourselves in a large airy room with rows of chairs and a long counter behind which sat several extremely relaxed young girls eating sticky buns. No business proceeded until these were finished, and then we were ushered forward with the wave of a sugary hand. Postage stamps were licked, stuck into our passports and stamped, and we were asked for ten dollars each, and received hand-written receipts for same. Downstairs the still unsmiling lady scrawled her signature over the stamps – we were now holders of thirty-day visas for Panama which we hadn't realised we needed! Part I complete. Next stop was Customs, in a nearby two-storey building. The officer in charge of yachts was asleep on a *chaise longue* in the corner. Once wakened he received us cordially, and we filled out the usual forms – no cash required here. At the well-hidden office of the Department of the Marine a mother and son team ran a very laid back but profitable operation. It seemed we would need a cruising permit, as without one only 48 hours are allowed to get through the canal from time of arrival. We knew that we wouldn't be able to transit for some days as the Trade Winds Rally yachts had preference over all the independent boats (they used an agent!). More photocopies of the boat papers were required, and special stamps had to be purchased at a nearby bank. Back we went to the family group – now the daughter-in-law and very willful grandson had come visiting and things were hotting up. We completed more form-filling, and were asked for $69 – presumably that's $23 per head. We were stumped – all our dollars were on the boat as we had taken the minimum with us. We had a choice of returning to the club, dinghying out to the boat, coming back into town and completing the business, or taking out some dollars from one of the nearby banks. We took the easier option, but sadly at the only bank which processed credit-card transactions in the safe Zone Area the computer was 'down' and there was nothing for it but to walk across the railway track!

We were immediately approached by a shady looking youth telling us how dangerous the place is and that we should use him as a 'guide'. Pretending not to understand, we marched ahead chattering in Irish as though we were old-timers in Colon! Luckily there was a bank nearby, and the security guard brandishing a machine gun made us feel very safe! The staff were all most pleasant – people are not *all* gangsters here – and eventually we had a supply of dollars which Frank secreted down the leg of his trousers while I carried the empty decoy handbag, and using an old trick we sent him ahead while Rachel and I monitored from the rear! We felt like extras in a movie, but with more of a thrill. In fact we were quite scared, and didn't breathe properly until we were safely across the track again, and had deposited our cash. Relieved, we obtained our thirty-day Cruising Permit duly stamped.

Back at the yacht club, we admired the gentle Cuna Indian women in colourful native costume who sat on the floor stitching intricate *molas* or bodice fronts for their elaborate blouses: they are adept at a type of appliqué work which is achieved by superimposing several layers of brightly coloured cotton, one on another, and cutting away complex bird and animal motifs. The raw edges are then carefully stitched under with tiny fine needles, and the vibrant finished products line the entrance to the club. The women are small and squat – like Amazonian people, with straight jet-black hair and pierced noses. A lovely gentle people, we were sorry not to have had the opportunity to visit the welcoming San Blas reservation where they continue to preserve their unique culture.

Micky Donoghue, our friendly American measurer whose grandmother hailed from Cork, arrived some days later, with Jasmine, his delightful Panamanian assistant. They bustled about with a tape measure, doing complex things in the bilges and engine compartment, and making heavy use of both their calculators. Micky was training Jasmine in, as all US personnel would leave the Panama Canal Commission by 1999 when Panama assumed full responsibility. Jasmine was nervous that her job would still be there as many foresaw huge cut-backs in personnel, or rampant nepotism. Before they left the boat they were able to tell us roughly what our transit charge would be – based on our displacement weight and size – and advised us when paying the charge – in US$ cash in Gatun, we should watch other boats transiting and have some idea of what to expect! This seemed a great idea, and since it was going to cost us a taxi-ride anyway we might as well get value for the trip.

So we travelled in style about 16 km inside the PCC Zone. The Commission are responsible for thousands of acres of manicured land, beautifully maintained and landscaped, with airy wooden two-storey buildings housing administrative offices and staff personnel. There are schools, pools, shops and clubs, and an airbase within the enclave, and several hundred people then worked for

the Company. Fees (including a refundable $190 break-down secu-
rity) paid and receipted, we walked through the pleasant grounds
about a mile to the Gatun Lock, and were admitted to a glass-
fronted viewing pavilion high over the middle of the three locks,
with comfortable seats to accommodate about 100 people! To our
right back towards the Atlantic we could see a procession of huge
container ships slowly making their way from Colon to the first of
the lock chambers: when traffic is busy the double set of locks
work on a one-way basis – both sets admitting vessels in the same
direction: at noon the direction changes and all vessels come from
the opposite side of the canal: all movements are pre-arranged by
computer, and we would receive a print-out of all traffic on the
day of our transit. In the first chamber on the near side was a huge
Panmax container-ship (built with specifications to exactly fit the
canal lock chambers – 294 metres long by 29 metres wide!) being
hauled into position by four powerful electric 'mules' as these bat-
tery-driven engines are called. The difference in height between
each lock is almost ten metres, and every big ship has to be towed
from one chamber to the next as their own engines cannot be relied
upon in the huge turbulence of the very limited area of water. In
the far lock a cruise liner was making its ascent, many passengers
busy with videos and cameras recording this day in a lifetime! We
were dizzy from trying to take in the complexity of the whole
manoeuvre. As the powerful locomotives hauled the great ships
forward through the lock doors, a small catamaran on the far side
used her own power to nose forward. This gave us an excellent
opportunity to prepare ourselves mentally for our transit – which
we had been dreading up until this, knowing nothing about how
the system worked.

Back aboard we readied our set of lines (four sets of 61 m),
once again blessing Charlie Brown, *Atlantic Islander*'s former owner, who had stowed more than enough rope for our needs. With
several more days to wait for the transit, we took a bus to Panama,
the oldest city in America, a vibrant mixture of old Spanish Colonial, with balconies of wrought ironwork running round four sides
of the grander houses, and new, gleaming masses of steel and
glass. Rachel and I were tempted by low, low prices, but Frank
hauled us away and into a taxi to visit the chandlery and chart
suppliers inside the canal zone.

The remaining few days in Colon passed relatively quickly,

and by good fortune we came to know two seasoned line-handlers who had been on board the French catamaran that we observed in the Gatun Locks. Each transiting yacht must have four crew on board – excluding the PCC pilot – this leaves the skipper free to concentrate solely on navigating under guidance, while two handlers front and back keep tension on the ropes to ensure that the boat stays in the middle of the locks. We loaded up with diesel to give ourselves the necessary steam power for the big Gatun Lake and all the lock manoeuvring, and finally completed lengthy departure paperwork to obtain the all-powerful *zarpé* – the official clearance document that is absolutely essential for entering another country by boat.

We slept out on the morning of departure, and barely had Leo and Nigel on board by 7.00 when the pilot boat arrived. A pleasant, stocky, dark-haired young man stepped on board, with bulging briefcase and oilskins in hand. There was little time for chit-chat, we were under orders! Canal rules specify that the pilot is entirely responsible for the management of the vessel for the duration of the transit – his rule is law except in very extenuating circumstances, as he is the expert in this area.

'Up anchor!' Thomas ordered and Rachel and Leo manned the electric winch. No time for the usual cleaning of the decks as the dirty chain comes on board.

'Half ahead!' Frank throttles up and we make our way towards the main channel past the sleeping yachts. A sudden downpour makes us shelter below or under the coachroof – glad of tea and freshly baked brown bread. At the first lock we tie alongside another yacht, careful that the spreaders don't touch, and that we are well secured fore and aft, with spring lines keeping us steady. The rain has started again, and it is really lashing down on us all! Frank and our partner motor carefully forward behind the big container ship who shares the lock with us. Our pilots communicate with each other and with the lock personnel on two-way radios: total co-ordination is vital in these manoeuvres. On a signal from Thomas, PCC handlers 12 metres above us throw down light ropes with monkeys' fists at the ends (special knots with heavy rubber weights inside them) and we take those from the right hand wall and attach our lines to them to be hauled up and attached to bollards high above. Meanwhile our 'raft' partner misses the rope thrown to him! There is some panic while the canal's line is retrieved, and both yachts are sucked towards the left-hand wall. Leo and Rachel try to haul on our forward line – but are unable to tow the weight of the two yachts against the current – and the electric winch comes into its own. Finally all is well, the lock doors slowly swing closed behind us, and we tense ourselves for the upwelling of water that will fill this huge chamber within 15 minutes. We must keep our lines taut as the water level brings us upwards: this demands steady hauling against a lot of pressure, and Rachel and I are glad to have two strong men in control while we give the extra pull when needed. Before we know it the chamber is full, and the front gates open to allow the container ship to be towed through to lock number two. She gives a forward thrust on her engines, and we have to continue to keep pressure on our lines until her wash has dissipated. Then the PCC handlers release our lines and we pull them inboard before motoring into the second lock, where the procedure begins all over again.

Finally the third lock is reached, we are beginning to gain more confidence in our ability – and the rain has stopped. By this stage we are raised 26 metres, and we marvel anew at the magnificent feat of engineering that made all this possible a full eighty years ago! The final gates open, our container partner is released of all the hawsers, and motors under his own steam into the Gatun Lake. It's 11.00: we can't believe four hours have passed, and we suddenly feel ravenous. Rachel and I cook up a hearty lunch which is welcomed all round, and our pilot tells us that there is a good chance, if we are willing, of getting through the entire canal today! As this is nearly always a two-day passage we are certainly willing – but will the boat keep up a good speed through the 35 miles of lake to reach the next lock by 14.30?

Frank orders the mainsail and genoa to be set so as to optimise the engine speed, and we take several short cuts to improve our chances. The other yacht soon begins to fall behind, and we are secretly proud to be winning this unexpected 'race'. The wind dies as we navigate through the island-strewn lake, and we roll in the genoa. Lush tropical forest surrounds us on all sides, and we see the flash of parrots in the trees. Here and there local pandanus thatched huts peek through the bush – many of these are holiday retreats for PCC personnel. We overtake a coaster in the Galliard Cut – a long canal cut through the highest part of the canal system, the Continental Divide – which is currently being widened to allow two Panmax size ships to pass each other. Thomas keeps checking his watch, and speaking into his walkie-talkie with the pilot on the ship we hope to join at the next lock. He also constantly checks with Frank to see how the water and oil gauges are doing – no point in burning out our engine. But the 80HP Mercedes loves being put through her paces, and could go on for hours! Finally we catch sight of our goal, the Pedro Miguel lock, with our giant partner edging towards the chamber. In 'down-locking' smaller craft go first, avoiding the wash from the big ships, so this time we nose right up to the lock gates, having first taken the lines from the handlers at both sides. It's unsettling to be floating nine metres above the level of the water just ahead of you, and we feel dizzy, but it's time for Rachel and I to be fully-fledged line handlers, as we take responsibility for the starboard ropes while Leo and Nigel take the port-hand side. We get to feel the full pressure of the lock emptying this time, as we release the lines steadily while the water level drops and drops. Gates open and we motor into the Miraflores Lake, the second-last stage before the Pacific Ocean!

In the final lock we tie up alongside a tug, already berthed against the lock wall. Just as the water began to ebb the tug's forward line to shore snaps like a piece of spaghetti, and her nose, and ours, begins to drift out towards the right-hand wall. Shouts and confusion, and more line is produced, as thick as an arm: hopefully *this* will hold them in position. Secure once again the lock water sucks down 9 metres, and the giant gates open up in front of us and we motor out into the great Pacific, the suspension Bridge of the Americas etched in the skyline ahead of us.

We were totally drained, physically and emotionally, and the beers we shared around were like nectar. Our pilot jumped onto a PCC tender, and we progressed to the Balboa Yacht Club's moorings under Nigel's guidance, grabbed a free buoy, caught the club ferry ashore, and bade our competent friends goodbye and fair sailing. It has been a long, hard, exhilarating, and exhausting day: one we shall certainly remember for the rest of our lives! Our arms ached, our backs were weary, our throats dry – but we were the happiest people on earth! Today we had mastered the ups and downs of one of the wonders of the modern world, and had come through the Panama Canal in a single day!

10

GALAPAGOS

Twenty-four hours later all our preparations were complete, and we set sail into the mighty Pacific on 7 February. There were more than just a few butterflies in our stomachs. For me this was the first serious piece of sailing: 3,700 miles of ocean with one stop en route (if we had the time: Rachel's leave was up on 27 March, and the ten days in Panama gave us very little time in hand). I had no idea how I would cope with so much sea-time. We seemed terribly small and frail and alone in our little boat, setting off across the world's greatest ocean which comprises one-third of the earth's surface, and has only a small smattering of islands tossed like grains of rice on its surface. It also hides significant tectonic plates, edging towards each other and causing seismic mayhem below its vast depths. But it was more its startling colour that amazed us – an ultramarine blue of unbelievable intensity, that we had never seen so strong in the Atlantic or Caribbean.

A favourable current chased us out of Panama, giving us a marvellous start to our voyage, and in a following wind we put up twin headsails and sped along over truly pacific waters. Each day we would take a quick 'dip' for our daily wash – towed behind the stern gripping a floating line. If our speed increased too much this became dangerous, and we would discontinue the practice. For the first few days we were all very tired and slept quite a lot during the day: this was to be expected after a tense time ashore, what with anticipation of the transit and the enormity of our undertaking ahead. Extra sleep was nature's way of preparing the body for emergencies that might occur. Our self-steering wind-vane was working perfectly, thanks to Frank's repair in Colon and this gave us tremendous freedom to read, write, sew, sleep or fish, according to our whims. We maintained an alert watch as there was initially plenty of traffic near Panama. The further south we went the less shipping we saw: we were heading east of the Galapagos to keep our options open.

After three days the wind died almost completely, and we were obliged to use far more engine than we would have liked. Unsure of whether we could get Rachel to Nuku Hiva in time for work, we decided to visit the Galapagos – from there she could calmly make her way home. Now that the time pressure was lifted we enjoyed the light airs for the remaining seven days. My Valentine's day present was an extra half-hour in bed when I should have been on watch! The fifteenth of February was more of a red letter day, as we celebrated two major events: we had left Crosshaven six months before, and had now completed 7,000 miles, and we were about to sail across the equator – a first for all of us. But no one felt like getting smeared in foam: Frank caught our first Pacific fish – a delicious big-eye tuna, which we sautéed in butter with a hint of celebratory champagne! We toasted ourselves, absent friends, and our sturdy boat.

I did a lot of letter-writing knowing that Rachel could post them securely from home. I was hoping that by keeping friends informed of our doings and passing on addresses to them I would eventually be at the receiving end! In Panama I had had only two letters, though I had circulated our address there in plenty of time, as I thought! (Later I discovered that all the mail posted in St Lucia had gone astray!) This time I made a direct appeal for replies, as after five or six weeks voyaging it would be nice to have news of friends. Many sailors before us have found that very few people back home, despite good intentions, actually get down to write: perhaps the art has been lost with the convenience of the telephone? Thankfully there were always two or three faithful correspondents who kept us fully up to date with home and family news: we would have been so much more lonely without their regular contact.

Ten days after leaving Panama we were nudging close to the green and verdant island of Santa Cruz. Rachel's last night in the Pacific began with a spectacular sunset over a lake-like ocean of shifting pink and peach. We drifted, enthralled, in a windless sea. The beauty of the evening took all breath away, and to shatter this quiet with the engine would have been unthinkable. We didn't want to reach the island in the dark, so drifted in a mirrored calm until every vestige of light had faded to velvet, and the stars above and reflected round us were intensely bright. Then we motored gently through the night, to reach Puerto Ayora early on Saturday morning, 17 February. Forty shades of green tumbled down the mountain, swerved over fields, trees, grasses and shrubs, and out to the mangrove swamps at the water's edge, where the seas teemed with dolphin, turtles, and fish of all types. The greens reminded us of Ireland, but there the resemblance stopped. Boobies, noddies, lava herons and gulls wheeled overhead. The heat was intense, and the sea was aquamarine! There were several yachts at anchor in the circular bay, where low-rise buildings peeped through the deep fringe of trees and giant flowering shrubs.

Back in Panama people had said that the Galapagos were so expensive to enter, and cruising permits so hard to come by – boats had to be fumigated before entering and this added another $100 to an already hefty bill. Some of the Trade Winds Rally boats were avoiding the islands altogether, and we had been very much of two minds ourselves, though family and friends who had visited here warned that we should on no account miss them. Some sailors said it was impossible to get more than 72-hour visas: we determined to make the best of whatever was available to us, and to see as much as we could within that time. So not knowing what to expect we brought our papers to the Port Captain, situated in an impeccably clean naval barracks by the water's edge. He told us that this was a big national holiday weekend, that the President of Equador was visiting, and that he could not formally check us in until Monday, but that we were most welcome to come ashore and make our purchases and visit where we liked in the interim. We were overjoyed, as properly speaking no one is allowed ashore until cleared with Customs and Immigration. We were less thrilled to hear that none of the banks or airline offices would re-open until Wednesday, by which time we should have left the country! We did not want to leave Rachel alone here to sort out her fate unaided!

But for the moment there was little we could do except make the most of every second, and so we grabbed swimsuits, towels, camera and binoculars and set off for Turtle Beach, through arid coastal-zone vegetation – thick with huge cacti and pale green palo-verde trees, and every kind of singing bird. (Darwin's finches alone comprise forty varieties!) Huge breakers washed in on the fine coral sands, and ugly marine iguanas cooled off in the spray, blending in with the volcanic rock at the water's edge. These strange creatures are like pre-historic monsters, all spiky scales, lumbering bodies, long tails and tiny, reptilian heads. None of the birds or animals were the slightest bit bothered by our presence, and carried on with their daily activities at our feet.

Next day we went inland by local bus to visit the annual agricultural fair. Lush meadows and an abundance of trees made us feel at home – so unlike any of the places we had been for the past five months! We had already enjoyed the excellent local dairy produce, delicious milk and rich yogurt, and were looking forward to seeing some of the prize animals that produced these good things! The fertile volcanic soil had been under-utilised since the first people to settle here came in the 1800s, and a lot of cash is being sunk into dairy and food-production projects so that the islands can sensibly reduce their dependence on the Ecuadorian mainland some 700 miles away. As well as a range of quality cows we saw displays of magnificent vegetables and luscious fruits: this augured well for our restocking plans! Local people were done up in their Sunday best, and dark eyed children were healthy and happy, gleefully inspecting the prize animals and slurping huge thirst-quenching wedges of cool pink watermelon.

Monday was spent on immigration. When we explained our predicament with Rachel and the airline office they said, 'No problem! How long do you *want* to stay?'

'*Diez dias, por favor?*' we ventured boldly.

Without further ado we were stamped in for a further ten days (not from the Saturday we arrived)! Now all we needed to do was to wait until Rachel could get her ticket to Quito sorted out and then we could plan an inter-island trip. We made enquiries into boat tours round the islands, and met two Dutch girls who had been working in South America. Having tried unsuccessfully to get a berth for several days their funds were low. We offered them welcome accommodation on board until their tour materialised. They had never slept in a boat before, so this was a good preparation for their mini-voyage.

At the nearby Darwin Institute we saw hundreds of baby Galapagos tortoises which are being raised to put back into their natural environment. Lonesome George, the world's only survivor of his subspecies, lives here in splendid isolation, with big rewards offered to anyone who can supply a female companion for him – but sadly so far no genuine contender has been found.

We laboriously loaded diesel by 25-litre jerrycan in preparation for our longest voyage, bought Rachel's ticket to Quito, and made arrangements to take a 4-day cruise, which would neatly drop her off at the airport bus on the last morning in good time for her flight. By now David Forsyth and his parents, John and Carol, had arrived on their 11.8 m *Alb*. We were delighted to meet them, and to hear of their adventures since Aruba. Dave very kindly agreed to boat-sit for us when we took off – it would give him independence from the elders, and us peace of mind.

Our cruise boat, the *Española*, locally built of heavy hardwood, looked top-heavy in comparison to the sleek lines of *Atlantic Islander*, as the skipper skilfully nosed her up to a pier on the north of the island, just as the sun was beginning to set. Roland, the resident guide, helped us aboard and took our bags. We met the handsome captain, and the pleasant *marinero*, or deck-hand, a lad of about 14, and were led to our cramped quarters in the forepeak. Our cabin companion was a graphic artist from Paris, in her forties, and the other passengers were four young Germans – two female post-graduates in micro-biology, and a young couple who were passionately into photography. We dumped our gear and made our way to the saloon, aft of the wheelhouse, where the evening meal was being laid out by the chubby cook. Though his galley was much smaller than mine, he produced three delicious meals a day for twelve hungry people.

There followed a marvellous few days of carefree island hopping, motoring in the evenings or early mornings, observing a huge range of birds and animals who seemed to have no fear of us. Seals, penguins, and millions of fish would dive and drift around our snorkels as we swam in sheltered anchorages. Ashore, on sunbaked volcanic rocks, hundreds of female sealion lay around, nursing young, or slithering down to play in the turbulent rock pools, while sleeping babies in furry brown coats took up every available nook and sheltered spot near the water's edge. It was pure magic – but we resisted the urge to touch any of the little ones, using our cameras instead. Thousands of coral-coloured Sally Lightfoot crabs, like dainty little dancers, swarmed over the black rocks in search of morsels to eat, and over weird bundles of marine iguanas huddled together to share each others body heat.

Roland's little four-year-old son had accompanied us on the cruise, and manfully came ashore with us on all the excursions, despite the boredom of so much English. He never complained or whined: I couldn't imagine a guide back home bringing any of their children with them! Each day while we were ashore the skipper headed off alone on the panga (aluminium tender), and returned with fish for our next meal – thus keeping overheads down. At $52 a day we all felt we were getting excellent value, though Roland's English was not the best, and there seemed to be large gaps in his knowledge, which the German graduates stretched to the limits! It is forbidden to cruise in one's own boat in these waters – permits are occasionally given but they prohibit one from going ashore without a certified guide, so in principle one is far better off with local operators. This ensures the preservation of these unique habitats, while it causes a lot of grumbles from yachtsmen, used to having the freedom to go pretty much where they like. We felt it was vitally important to preserve the ecology of these fragile places, and were happy to pay the reasonable price.

Our cruise was coming almost full circle. On our last evening the cook prepared a huge cake – supposedly for the Skipper's birthday, but in fact a good-luck cake for us all! We had brought some wine, and shared that out with crew and passengers – it was the first time the two groups mingled, and was a fitting send-off for Rachel. Later we visited the nearby mangrove swamps by panga, and saw scores of turtles swimming by, and small white tip shark. My camera jammed in the excitement, and all the efforts of our on-board photographer to put it to rights were useless.

The best treat was kept until last. Next morning our ears were assailed by the most curious cries and chattering all around us as we landed on a totally flat island with low scrub, its entire surface covered in the pungent guano of hundreds of thousands of nesting blue-footed boobies. These large brown-and-white gannet-like seabirds have feet of Dresden blue, and during the mating season the males display in a clumsy 'dance' which shows their feet to best advantage! All around us they were prancing about in the most ungainly fashion, lifting one foot and then the other – *Blue! Blue! Blue suede shoes!* readily came to mind, but their singing was not at all in the same league as Elvis'! Nests consisted of vague sweeps in the sand, with a token twig or two to mark the spot: many contained two irregular eggs – rather like very white new potatoes – which both male and female incubate. The din and the smell were almost overpowering – but the scene was so absorbing that these irritations seemed a very small price to pay! Not one bird moved away as we tiptoed carefully between the nests. It was frustrating to be without a camera , but vivid memories of the scene will always be with us.

Atlantic Islander *under way* [photo: T. Wright].

*Wind generator operational, with
Frank's bike wrapped for the weather.*

*A tuna this size fed us for three days.
Frank in tropical garb.*

*Gatun Locks, Panama Canal. Our line-handlers help a French catamaran
in the far lock.*

Barbara fillets the catch: Ballymaloe cookbook and Snoopy mascot to hand.

San Bartolomé, Galapagos.

Rachel with sea-lions, Galapogos.

Time out from hard work of sailing.

Sudanese friends at Suakin market.

Corinth Canal – the shortest and most expensive.

Frank's four-wheel-drive in Rhodes, diesel-loaded.

Greek Kastellórizo – a short hop from the Turkish mainland. Note the minaret on the right.

Arriving back in Cork, Roche's Point.

Home at last! Frank and Barbara return to the RCYC marina.

Together again – Mag, Frank and Sue aboard Atlantic Islander.

Rachel was delivered by panga onto Baltra Island, where the airport bus was waiting to take her off. I shed plenty of tears as we waved her out of sight: she had been such cheerful company and a tremendous support when we needed it most. But back in Puerto Ayora we had so much to do – phonecalls to make, vegetables to buy, and all the last minute things that need to be seen to – there was little time for sadness. The longest voyage of our lives lay just ahead! We quickly got the exit formalities over with, but a final dinner ashore brought a bad bout of gastroenteritis, forcing us to stay one extra (illegal) night. Next day all was well, and we slipped quietly out of the bay early on the bonus 29 February, greatly the richer for our enchanted time here.

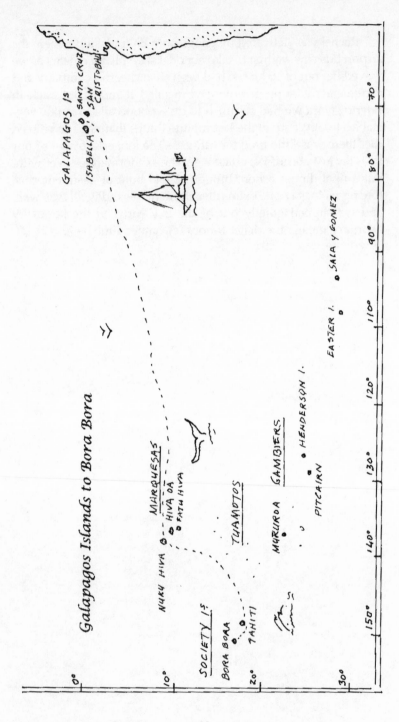

Galapagos Islands to Bora Bora

GALAPAGOS IS
ISABELLA ⊙● SANTA CRUZ
● SAN CRISTOBAL

SOCIETY IS
BORA BORA
TAHITI

MARQUESAS
NUKU HIVA ⊙
⊙ HIVA OA
● FATU HIVA

TUAMOTOS

MURUROA
GAMBIERS
HENDERSON I.
PITCAIRN

EASTER I.
● SALA y GOMEZ

0°
10°
20°
30°

70°   80°   90°   110°   120°   130°   140°   150°

98

11

PACIFIC

The Pacific Ocean – the world's largest, covers 179,668,300 square kilometres, one third of the total surface of the earth, and contains half of the world's seawater. For centuries little was known about it, and the only people to have navigated it successfully were the Melanesian and Polynesian tribes who spread from Asia in fragile pirogues – sometime between 3000 and 1000 BC. Smaller versions of these outrigger canoes are still used today in coral lagoons throughout the Pacific.

Many superlatives describe its features. The deepest depths in the world are found south of Guam, where the Mariana Trench plunges to 10,889 metres below sea level. The Tonga Trench just off the Lau Islands drops to a dizzying 10,040 metres. Think of the pressures exerted at those levels! In other places the subsea activity is so strong that new islands appear every few years. The floor of the eastern Pacific is shattered by no fewer than ten massive fracture zones, where tectonic plates collide and produce violent seismic activity off the coasts of USA and South America. Four of these are responsible for the frequent earthquakes and tremors experienced in California. El Niño, the warm eastern Pacific countercurrent that occurs irregularly every three to seven years helps cause severe floods or drought in countries on both sides of the ocean.

But it is the South Pacific that conjures up magical images to most of us. Magellan was the first European to sail these waters from east to west, and after him there was a slow progression of explorers and opportunists, seeking to extend their European empires. France and Britain were to outdo each other in the 'discovery' and annexation of lush tropical islands, with devastating consequences for their inhabitants. A nineteenth century onslaught of missionary zeal combined with everyday European bugs to which the islanders were devastatingly vulnerable, and steady doses of lethal sexually-transmitted diseases, decimated the peoples and the cultures of these outstandingly beautiful islands.

Captain James Cook painstakingly skippered his research vessel *Endeavour* to these uncharted waters in the 1760s, without the benefit of proper compass or any navigational device other than sextant, and brought back to England tales of paradise on earth. Writers, artists and poets flocked here to experience the romance of the South Seas, particularly to French Polynesia where the missionaries had not entirely wiped out the native habits. The accounts of writers like Stephenson, Melville, and Loti, and in particular the paintings of Gauguin brought home to Europeans and Americans the exotic, mysterious, childlike appeal of the Coral Islands. Later accounts were given by Somerset Maugham, Rupert Brook and Jack London. In fact such a flood of adventurers came to French Polynesia that in 1939 the French Government introduced a requirement that all visitors not in possession of return tickets should pay a hefty repatriation bond. This was intended to discourage would-be settlers slipping in on small boats: but more of that later!

3,020 miles separate Puerto Ayora in the Galapagos and Taiohae (pronounced exactly as its spelt – *Ta-ee-oh-ha-ey!* – with a lovely Polynesian lilt) in Nuku Hiva, the capital of the Marquises groups of islands and the most remote part of French Polynesia. It was a little hard for me to imagine a journey so long by anything other than a plane! Yet up to this our average monthly sailing was 1,100 miles, and across the Atlantic Frank had made a distance of 2,640 miles in little more than three weeks. We had no schedule to stick to, other than the broad requirement of being in Australia sometime in July. Our time was our own, and we would be at the mercy of wind and current.

Unlike Captain Cook we have excellent twentieth-century electronic navigation systems – our small GPS is the size of a large calculator, weighs a few ounces, and linked to a compact antenna, acts as a powerful receiver, obtaining position data from no less than 24 orbital satellites circling the earth every 12 hours at a height of 10,900 nautical miles. We tended to use the unit in its simplest form as a position finder, while plotting our course manually on navigation charts, once or twice a day – and more often in dangerous waters. No one would put to sea on extended cruises without having some knowledge of celestial navigation, as *in extremis* fragile electronics cannot sustain water immersion or aerial damage. We were fortunate to have no such breakdown.

So we left the Galapagos with indelible memories, and surprisingly little fear or trepidation. The sun was shining, the swell minimal, the breeze light and the current in our favour. It seemed like an auspicious beginning to our long journey. We were well stocked with fruit and vegetables, bread and free-range eggs, tinned butter, coffee and tea, and endless tins of fish, meat, fruit and vegetables. We had 'sucky sweets' for cheering up night watches, and enough wine from Panama to ensure a glass or two with dinner every night. Our fuel and water tanks were full, all the boat gear in good condition, and we ourselves were rested and fit after our cruise on the *Española*. We had lost a valuable crewmember, and the night watches would take some getting used to – but provided we didn't hit really nasty weather we should be well able to manage.

As young parents we had relied a lot on Dr Spock's famous manual on child-care, giving us vital information on illnesses, behaviour, developmental psychology, and all the unknowns that go with parenthood. Now Dr Spock was replaced by Jimmy Cornell's *World Cruising Routes*, a bible for all long-distance yachtspersons, which covers 400 cruising routes world-wide, outlining prevailing winds, currents, mileages and optimum times for passage-making. We had read it from cover to cover several times, and studied it as we travelled on each successive leg of the voyage. Cornell was very positive on the Galapagos to Marquesas passage, though he did advise that the optimum time to benefit from the south-east trade winds was between April and August – and we were setting out in very early March! He also mentioned that currents are favourable but says that the trade winds are more fickle in the South Pacific than in any other part of the world. The occurrence of the infamous El Niño countercurrent can play havoc with all trends. So with this much information and some advice from people who had made the passage before, we set out into the unknown!

For the first few days we took things easy – luckily the light winds allowed us to do that, and we absorbed a lot of sunshine, hand-steering for two hours each every day while the engine ran to charge the service batteries. I got over my usual day or two of queasiness, and we tried out various watch routines, finally settling on the three-on-three-off pattern (19.00 to 22.00, 01.00 to 4.00) which we maintained for the entire Pacific and for the rest of the voyage.

There was remarkably little to be seen in the vast ocean around us. A few seabirds, some flying fish, and one coaster after six days

– bound for Chile and very helpful on the radio. A school of small whales thrilled us on the fifth day – the large male was about four to five meters long, and the youngsters were leaping exuberantly into the air – our hearts leaping with them! Frank caught the first fish of the passage, a delicious skip-jack tuna, and we had fresh fish for two days – nothing can compare with its delicious taste after tinned food! Things were going well though we weren't averaging much more than eighty miles a day – it would be a slow trip. On day seven a flashing red light told us that the four-hours engine per day was doing little for the service batteries – they were still not getting sufficient charge to keep up to requirements, and this after all the work Frank and Adrian had put in in Grenada. He spent the next two days testing and trying to figure things out, then changed over to the second alternator and regulator that they had neutralised as he was fairly sure they were still in working order. The blinking red light went out for a few hours, then returned that evening! Now it was a case of cutting back to absolutely essential electrical requirements: who was prepared to sacrifice what? Frank always kept the GPS on day and night – I felt this was unnecessary as we only need one or two positions per day to navigate successfully. The coolbox we could do without – we were used to soft butter and could survive without cold beers. My computer was another matter – I felt I couldn't live without it, as I had started the book and my diary would have to be maintained: with the savings from the GPS I could surely afford to charge my batteries every second day? Frank agreed, but I quickly made copies of everything just in case the worst came to the worst and I had to resort to pen and paper! We turned off the electric pumps – we could just as easily hand-pump our water – and the bilges were also hand-pumped. At night we could navigate without lights – provided we kept a good look-out for shipping, and lit up when anything was around.

So we quickly changed our energy consumption levels to a very manageable amount, and got rid of our red light. We started to use our petrol generator to charge my computer batteries, and I longed for an additional energy source. We knew that our problem was far from solved – but we might have to wait until Australia to have it fully checked and there were a lot of miles to cover before then. Yes, it was frustrating to keep running into the same setbacks – but if Frank was down I was usually able to see the bright side – and *vice versa,* which kept us going through some of the tough times. For a while Frank contemplated going 370 miles back to the Galapagos to have some repair work done, but that was just not an option as far as I was concerned. To make matters worse we had two nights of torrential rain, and contrary winds followed by no winds, when the sails flapped wildly and we made no progress. We were wet and miserable – and *mad* to be doing this crazy voyage.

Then the sun shone. We got some sleep, ate well, and felt brighter! We were both back to full health, we had managed this far: the weather would improve, the trade winds would set in – and fabled Polynesia lay ahead! Then we discovered that the water taken on in Panama was tainted, and even coffee tasted foul – we would have to collect rainwater for drinking. It galled me to think of all we had wasted the past few nights! Bread that I baked was fermenting from the inside because of the bad water and the heat, and all our bananas had ripened together and were falling onto the deck ... It was hard to remain cheerful – *but* we still had our health, and the Polynesians were waiting with sweet-smelling flowers in their hair ...

On Sunday 10 March two lazy turtles swam by the boat, and later we saw a small family of whales, elegantly displaying their magnificent tails as they dove into deeper water. How could we feel low? There was no wind, and we hand-steered all day. (No one so far could fix our electric self-steering which has to be used when we motored in light winds, so the visit from the whales gave us a needed boost). Neither of us enjoys being tied to the wheel hour-on hour-off for twelve hours, and we would usually lie hove-to overnight rather than demand twenty-four hours from ourselves or the engine. That evening there seemed to be hope of meeting the trades – but it dwindled fast and next day we were motoring again. We saw our second boat – a French yacht bound for Hiva Oa in the Marquesas, searching in vain like ourselves for wind. We knew by the daily radio net that all the Trade Winds Rally boats had headed far south, which proved to be a wise decision.

Frank caught a big dolphin fish – or dorado – and I poured a few drops of alcohol in the gills – a tip given by a young couple in Puerto Ayora. This prevents all that mayhem on deck when the poor fish is flailing around for his life: he suddenly becomes quite still and stupefied, and can be left in a bucket to be subsequently gutted. I hated having to kill such beautiful creatures, especially when fellow dorados looked on – they seem to congregate in the shade of the hull, and even Frank felt guilty slaughtering one of their number, though he loved the thrill of catching them and the excitement of the chase! He had lost many lures and traces, and a quantity of line, to big fish that got away: we soon followed another yottie's tip of cutting up old rubber gloves and mimicking the squid-like expensive lures that are the normal bait here.

All the second week and into the third the sailing was particularly frustrating. No wind during the day, wind from every direction at night. Frequent torrential showers meant we had good supplies of delicious drinking water, collected on the sun awning and channelled down via a clever canvas funnel into whatever containers we could muster. Frank put up spinnaker poles and took them down about thirty times, always sure that the trade winds had come, then disappointed half an hour later when the breeze died away. Spirits were low, so I planned a celebration for St Patrick's Day: we would have bacon and cabbage and the nearest thing to parsley sauce. I'd make a cherry cake too, and we'd compose a tape to friends back home.

The patron's day dawned cloudless, a welcome change after the mixed weather we had been having. It was also windless, which was no surprise, and the sea was so inviting that we let the boat drift, and took turns to scrub off goose barnacles that were growing all over the hull – we had attacked them severely in Puerto Ayora but they were back with a vengeance! We said our Sunday prayers, and read some of them in Irish from an old missal I had won as a schoolgirl! This must have done the trick, because after dinner the wind freshened from the south-east (shouts of joy!) and Frank was keen to get the twin headsails up immediately though it was now blowing fifteen knots – the agreed borderline for single-handed pole work. He persisted however: he had been waiting for these winds with even greater anticipation than I, and after eighteen long days and nights they had finally arrived: he didn't want to waste a second!

And so it continued for the next fortnight. Our daily average jumped from 70 to 100 miles per day, and we slowly became accustomed to the famous down-wind roll, which initially made sleeping quite difficult as one struggled to stay firmly in the berth at night. Cooking and food preparation was also a logistical nightmare as onions rolled round the worktop, and the oven would not stay still, but I soon adapted to the constant lurching from left to right. Wedged into the cockpit I tackled new covers for the deck cushions which were clothed in sticky leatherette, more suitable to northern climes. This took a long time by hand, but the results were worth the hours of effort involved as we eventually had comfortable seats to sit on!

On 22 March, after three weeks and a day at sea, we passed the 2,000-mile mark, giving an overall average of 87 miles per day. Some Trade Winds Rally boats were already in Nuku Hiva, while we had another 1,020 miles to go – possibly another twelve days. For some strange reason this fact made me very depressed, even though we had worked out all the figures beforehand. I felt we had taken the longest route, didn't have enough information, etc. etc. – and placed *most* of the blame on Frank. We had a flaming row, he calmly pointing out that we would have gone south except I didn't want to use too much motor. (One of the Trade Winds boats had had to take on emergency fuel supplies at sea!) By getting our feelings out in the open we at least cleared the air, and I felt a lot better afterwards. We had continually been improving a generally very good relationship, something we both really valued as it could be so easy to go the other way and drift apart by bottling up negative feelings. Small irritations can appear very great at sea, when the body is tired from being flung about, and the mind isolated from friends to act as sounding boards. On land one can go and take a good walk, or dig up weeds, and get frustrations under control, but on a small boat there are no such relief valves available, and it takes a lot of patience and understanding to live so closely together in trying situations. This is why choosing the right crew is such a difficult task, and why husband-and-wife or family crews generally work best. With the weather so warm we wore very little clothing – just two of us together demanded little modesty, and we felt we had the world to ourselves. This helped our sex-life considerably, and despite the frustrations and short-lived rows, much of this time at sea was like an excellent second honeymoon!

A large fishing boat called us up on the VHF – they were a Spanish crew from Bilbao on a US registered boat, fishing for tuna near the Marquesas and now heading homeward after six months absence. They were delighted to chat in Spanish over the radio –

and hearing that we had been in their home port en route gave them a big thrill. They offered us anything we needed – fresh steaks, ice, beer – but the logistics of picking up supplies from the water were too complex for us, and we reluctantly declined with thanks.

That night we saw an incredible sight in the northern sky. Near the end of the 'handle' of the Great Bear was a star with a huge ring of brightness round it like a cloud – which stretched back to form a tail of about thirty or forty feet long. It is pretty well impossible to gauge the length or size of objects so far away but this covered quite a large swathe of sky, and remained there all night, and for the next few nights. We felt overawed: at sea the nightly heavens are always breathtakingly beautiful with the vast milky way gleaming in a huge arc overhead, and hundreds of millions of stars shining brightly with no lights to detract from their brilliance, but this was as strange as a huge UFO, and we were very much in awe of it. Much later we heard it was the comet Hyakutake. I always expected comets to be dashing through the sky with the speed of falling stars – never something static like this! Hale-Bopp did not seem half so spectacular when we returned home.

Suddenly the equinoctial storms arrived, and we were forced to hand-steer continuously for three days and nights as the winds were too high for the wind-vane to cope with successfully – in the direction in which we wanted to go. This meant continual vigilance at the wheel. A day later all our batteries went down yet again, and we didn't even have a compass light! We searched for torches only to find that each one was defective in some way! Frank managed to fix up a jury system which just about held together, but after each dark hour at the wheel our arms were stiff, and our necks ached from keeping an eye on the badly-lit compass and the wind-direction gauge, to avoid backwinding the twin head-sails. How long could we keep this up? We switched to a two-hour-on, two-hour-off system at my request, and would snatch an odd hour's sleep during the day to make up for the lack at night, but the demands on just two people were very great, and we constantly fantasised about having a third person on board. Thank the Lord, on the fourth night the wind veered and eased enough for the wind-vane to cope with, and we were back on course once more, and into a manageable routine.

By the thirtieth day at sea, our fresh supplies were beginning to run out, and I tried to stretch out the last few eggs by making pancakes every few days – this provided a hearty breakfast for two from a single egg! Home-made marmalade was welcome on freshly baked bread, particularly as the butter supply was finished. I so longed for a full, uninterrupted, 8 hours in bed – and for a cold beer. Temperature never fell below 28° even at night, and this contributed greatly to fatigue. We wondered how we would survive this heat in a sheltered anchorage! I was in a strange limbo, wanting the shore and fearing it – difficult to put in words. Frank was really anxious to get to the phone and let the family know that we were alive and well – this journey had been too long for him, and he hoped to be able to put behind him the persistent worries of the battery troubles once we reached terra firma.

On the morning of Good Friday, 5 April, 36 days out of Santa Cruz, we finally made our landfall in paradise. The longest, most difficult leg had been successfully completed.

12

POLYNESIAN PARADISE

Taiohae nestles in the embrace of a semi-submerged extinct volcano. We approached in a violent rain-storm when its beauties were veiled in mystery, but earlier dawn-lit glimpses of the verdant mountains of Nuku Hiva promised something special. We nosed cautiously into the horseshoe bay: unlike most of the South Sea islands the Marquesas have no coral reef barriers to negotiate, and are therefore an ideal initial landfall after a long and wearisome passage. The clouds lifted, and we could make out scores of masts tucked into the north-western corner of the deep bay. David and his parents, and Roger were there to welcome us: it was so good to see them, compare notes on our long journeys, and get information on where to check in, collect mail, and what were the 'must sees' on this glorious island. We then had time to take in the staggering beauty of the lofty mountains that surrounded us on three sides – huge waterfalls glistened in their folded depths, and a profusion of glorious flowering trees clothed their lower slopes and swamped the small, shore-side village in a wealth of colour and a sweet, delicate perfume. Flame trees, flamboyants, yellow-flowered cotton trees and velvety frangipani, hibiscus the size of saucers in every possible shade adorned each garden. Shiny lush breadfruit trees with their pale green, pimpled fruits like small melons nestling in lush foliage, towered over citrus trees bearing huge grapefruit (pamplemousse) the size of soccer balls. Lemons, limes, mangoes and bananas also grew in profusion beneath the shade of lofty coconut palms. There was so much green after weeks of blue and grey it was almost too hard on the eye. All round the northern rim of the bay ran a golden beach, with breakers foaming onto it in places, and gentler waves at the extremities. We would soon learn that successful 'dry landings' had to be carefully planned and executed!

Anxious to phone home and let them know we were alive and well after a five-week silence, we extracted our wizened, sun-ripened rubber dinghy from its plastic case, pumped it up, and threw it overboard. Then we lowered the heavy outboard motor with the help of a gantry system from the mizen boom. We had no problem beaching the dinghy on this initial run, and our first duty on land was to check in. On our way to the Gendarmerie we met two Danes whom we had befriended in the Galapagos. They were sailing 6.7-metre *Pluto* round the world *without* GPS, their wives back in Copenhagen busily working to keep them in the limited comfort to which they had become accustomed! They told us that as it was Good Friday all offices and shops were closed, so we would have to check in on the morrow. We investigated the lovely local church and found out the times of Holy Week ceremonies, before going back to the nearby hotel, the Keikahanui (*kay-ee-ka-ha-nu-ee*) Inn. The name means tattooed warrior – the Marquesas are famed for the artistry of their tattooists, and formerly it was customary for each man to be tattooed all over the body. An American, Rose Corser, had sailed here in the early 1970s, fallen in love with the place, and with her now deceased husband opened what has become the unofficial Yacht Club of the Eastern Pacific. A big stack of mail awaited, and we made a quick ultra-expensive reverse charge call to Rachel, who then phoned back (£50 for five minutes, we later learnt!) with updates on all that had happened during our period incommunicado. Later I curled up gratefully in the cockpit for a mammoth read, emotionally catching up with home news. How far away we were from loved ones, yet so closely tied as each writer painted local happenings in a unique and personal language. I would read these precious letters over and over in the months to come.

Next day we were checked in efficiently and pleasantly at the spotless, computerised Gendarmerie, with no request for a repatriation bond. In the afternoon we had a visit from a nearby boat flying a US flag. Brendan and Frances turned out to be as Irish as ourselves, though living in San Francisco for several years. A good deal younger than us, they had brought their family – a dog called Jacko – on a year's trip through the Pacific. It was tremendous to hear the 'lilt of the Gael' and learn all the local tips – they had come from Hawaii some weeks before. Frances brought breadfruit and huge pamplemousse – gathered at the side of the road! We promised to bring her to Easter mass next morning, and to return to *Elan* for breakfast.

By the time we reached the Cathédral of Nôtre Dame next morning it was already full to overflowing. Rows of Japanese 4WD vehicles were lined up in the ample parking space, and the latecomers were streaming in in their colourful Easter best – men, women and children all wore flowers in their hair. The Marquisans are a hefty race of people – the men have fine physiques but the women tend to be quite stout. The church had been transformed with garlands of gardenia – the famous *tiare tahiti* – draped over the magnificently carved crucifix, above the simple stone altar, and round a beautiful wooden carving of a Polynesian virgin and child. The scent of flowers was almost overpowering, but a pleasant breeze fanned it through the aisles and out the open windows. Near us stood the children's choir, lead by a dynamic, smiling teacher, and a small group of men played guitar, banjo and keyboard. A procession of young girls with flowers in their waist-length gleaming hair brought a long gardenia lae to the altar, laid in on the floor in a large rectangle, while others filled the space with strewn petals. Baskets of fruit and more flowers were laid on this, together with implements used in tending the gardens – hoes, spades and rakes. The priests embroidered robes were carried forward and left on the altar. Then the singing started, as every one of the 700 or 800 people in the cathedral raised their voices in the most electrifying harmonies – it was like nothing we had ever experienced before, and I could feel the hairs rising on the back of my neck. Some of the tunes were easy to hum along with, others were extremely complex – all were sung in natural multi-part harmonies that seemed to come spontaneously from everyone. For almost two hours we were entranced, moved, and uplifted! Two new-born babies were baptised, and welcomed into the family of the church. Their parents and god-parents were obviously thrilled to be such an integral part of the most important liturgy of the year, and the babies were quiet as angels. At the consecration a single wooden drum was sounded, the tempo and volume rising dramatically and then fading away to silence. I shivered, thinking of human sacrifice practiced here until the last century, and the strange compelling link between eating human flesh and taking the symbolic body of Christ.

Back on *Elan*, Brendan's special French toast was delicious, smothered in Mexican honey – a fitting follow-up to such an uplifting morning. Fortified in spirit and body, we spent the afternoon tackling *Atlantic Islander*'s filthy topsides: after the long voyage it was murky and dejected: we soon had it looking like new. Roger would dive to take care of the underwater work for us, so difficult when armed with only mask and snorkel.

All of Monday and part of the following day was spent on the alternator, with John and Eric,* both motor experts, giving nobly of their time. A compromise solution was found which should get us to Papeete, where a full test could be carried out. Their helpfulness was really touching – a camaraderie and sheer generosity of talent that we came across so often in the sailing community. That night we treated John and Carol to a superb lobster dinner *chez Rose* – successfully negotiating the breakers on the beach. The previous night we had been capsized and soaked in our best attire, and had dripped dry in Rose's dining-room, so this time we took no chances, and went in old clothes, our good things in a waterproof bag!

Each evening as the sun went down, handsome local boys would come out to practice in their beautiful pirogues – the outrigger canoes which used to be made from carefully dug-out trees but are now of light fibreglass. These are paddled by teams of either four or six oarsmen – or women! – wielding ergonomic paddles at extreme speed. Watching them in the fading light against the backdrop of the glorious mountains, under a immense canopy of brightening stars, brought the romance of the South Seas sharply into focus, and we had to pinch ourselves to confirm that we were really here!

We longed to stay, and postponed our departure as long as possible. Frank received attention for a swollen elbow at a nearby hospital, and we explored some of the surrounding area. But after nine days we could find no further excuse, loaded diesel and petrol by jerry can, and sailed out of Taiohae Bay on Sunday 14 April, our lazarette overflowing with roadside fruits including a huge branch of bananas which cost us $7 and comprised over 100 individual fruits! (I chronicled their demise on our next passage!)

We headed south-west for the Tuamotos, an archipelago of seventy-eight islands scattered widely over a great arc of ocean, known in Tahitian as *The Dangerous Archipelago* because of the difficulties they pose to navigators. Many are atolls, ring-shaped, low-lying islands encompassing shallow lagoons, formed by successive deposits of coral. While Nuku Hiva is more than 800 nm from Tahiti, Rangiroa, the biggest of the Tuomotos, lies at a more

* *Eric Forsyth: awarded the American Cruising Club Blue Water Medal in 2000 for his extended voyaging.*

reasonable distance of 230 nm from the administrative centre of Polynesia. Thus they receive far more visitors, though still remaining very undeveloped. Negotiating a safe passage between them would have been a nightmare in times past, but today, with excellent charts and the redoubtable GPS it is simply a matter of taking the optimum course in given wind and current conditions.

Our first few days back at sea were sunny with moderate winds, and we progressed slowly towards Rangiroa. On the fourth day the winds picked up, and Frank *almost* caught a huge dorado – it seemed like forty lbs! Luckily it got away! I made mango chutney as the Marquesan fruits were not likely to last. We experienced quite a few squalls and monitored possible landfalls. On the sixth day we were in sight of our goal, and approached the main pass, but the winds were strong and the skies overcast, with a powerful current sweeping across the passage: Papeete seemed a safer landfall. We contented ourselves to see the fabled atoll with its many magical *motus* (islands on the reef itself) from without rather than within.

On the morning of the ninth day out of Nuku Hiva we were on target to reach Papeete in excellent conditions: the famous Point Venus was off our bows, and we knew that the capital with its main reef pass lay to the east. It was here that Captain Cook carried out his observations which, it was hoped, would help calculate the earth's distance from the sun. Unfortunately, poor weather foiled his attempts. We knew where we were – but certain things just didn't seem to add up. There were scores of masts to be seen in the bay near Point Venus, despite the pilot's insistence that this was a poor anchorage. Perhaps we were mistaking our location? Another position fix from the reliable GPS confirmed we were where initially presumed. We longed for a local returning boat to lead the way! Then we spotted a black mast coming from the shore – *Elan*! We called them on the VHF – they too had been confused, and had mistaken the entrance and almost hit the reef! They warned us to keep well off, and we followed them towards what did seem to be Papeete's skyline. Until one is very near the reef, marks and buoys are extremely difficult to spot, and Brendan was not going to have another close shave. We had read of the extremely strong cross- current in the pass, and finally lined ourselves up for the attempt: local craft had eventually materialised in the shape of two passenger ferries to nearby Moorea – one a hydrofoil who took the pass at about twenty knots! We got into top revs, and were astounded at the breaking waves just a few yards from us on left and right – and beyond them fishermen *standing* in shallow water. Our throats felt dry as the current took hold and Frank wrestled with the wheel: were we on the correct side of the green mark? Brendan ahead seemed to hesitate – we did not want to lose way. He surged forward, and we followed, spewn out into the calm lagoon as we breathed great sighs of relief. We threw down our anchor near *Elan*, and with their help ran a long line to the shore to tie round a strong cotton-tree. We were thus able to pull our dinghy ashore and back without need for oars or engine! It was an excellent solution – and because of the protective reef outside the harbour, there were no breakers to negotiate!

Papeete is a bustling, cosmopolitan capital with modern buildings and all amenities – a total contrast to sleepy Taiohae. Cruise liners call every few days, and daily ferries shuttle to the outlying islands. Anxious as usual to complete our entrance formalities, we were waylaid by Brendan and Frances, who were eager to hear how our passage had been and to compare notes with them. They had made it to Rangiroa and thought it was lovely, but a really tricky entrance and exit took a lot of the good away. Eventually we got ashore and went to visit *Alb* who were all happy to see us in one piece. With their crew of four they hadn't missed a single island, it seemed, and made excellent time on passage, flying maximum sail and spinnaker day and night. Moored with the other Trade Winds boats at the down-town promenade, they were just across a busy road from the Post Office and lovely wooded Bougainville Park, where lady gardeners proudly maintained a huge display of bougainvillea of every hue. Already here for a few days John knew all the local lore, and as we were by now too late to check in, they brought us to one of the 'colourful' haunts nearby – a dark and cavernous pick-up bar for transvestites and transsexuals! It certainly was a new experience for us greenhorns to be chatted up by a well-developed 'lady' with a cleavage far better than mine! Her feet were the only giveaway – large and manly! Most of the 'girls' hanging around outside were a sight to behold, in the skimpiest of minis and the highest of heels, displaying truly amazing legs – they were more beautiful than most of the stunning 'straight' Polynesian women. Transvestitism is widely practiced and accepted in Polynesia, and has been for centuries. What is sad is that it has now been corrupted into prostitution – thanks to the cooperation of sex-hungry tourism and military presence combined with Gallic laissez-faire.

In contrast, the buzz and life around the roulottes – mobile eateries parked each evening in the large carpark near the liner wharf, featuring mainly Chinese and Italian cooking – was exciting and inviting, and the excellent food on offer was good value for money. Most of the dishes were prepared to order on barbecues, and were fresh and delicious. Many dessert vans were tempting with *crêpes* of every type, and luscious ice-creams. We ate well while absorbing all the local colour, and our pockets were not much lighter – a rare thing in Papeete!

Next day Frances and I went to investigate the colourful covered market, about 15 minutes walk from where we were moored. Mangos, pineapples, bananas, plantain, rambutans, melons and pawpaws, pamplemousse, oranges lemons and limes were on colourful display, with yams, taro, breadfruit, tomatoes, peppers, spinach, chinese leaves, cauliflower, potatoes, celery, spring onions, leeks and unknown greens providing wholesome choice for our bare lockers. Ginger, garlic, parsley, onions, chillies and piles of powdered spices helped flavour the local ethnic and Chinese cuisines. A local specialty was cinnamon which scented the entire building, and together with vanilla and other local spices were sold in charmingly presented baskets by flower-crowned women. High-quality craft-shops offered beautifully made shell jewellery, mother of pearl buckles, exquisite batik *pareos* and fine art works. It was good to have another woman to talk to, and share the frustrations of sea-borne life, as well as revel in its good side! Frances confided that she might be pregnant, after many years of marriage, and was anxious, naturally. I reassured her that it would be wonderful. Months later we were thrilled to hear of the birth of their son soon after reaching home.

Later Frank and I headed to the immigration centre to formally declare ourselves – though the Gendarme in Nuku Hiva had already forwarded all our details on computer. We thought that on that account formalities here would be at a minimum. Not so. The usual pile of blank forms were handed over to be filled in yet again, by a very pleasant, elegantly uniformed harbour policeman. We filled in the blanks, consulting with each other on our ten last ports of call. With so much travelling this can be a difficult thing to recall on the spot! These were relayed to a non-uniformed official who laboriously typed them on another form, and asked us had we paid 'The Bond'. Thunderclap! I immediately cited the fact that none of the 38 Trade Winds Rally boats was asked to pay such a bond, that we were members of the EU and that the bond contravened our rights to free movement, etc., etc. What would happen if we refused, or were unable to pay, I asked. 'Leave the territory within four days, and do not stop at any other island', was the stern reply. Many clever yotties have fake airline tickets as a sensible alternative to this ridiculous and costly procedure – difficult for us to organise 13,000 miles from home. We slumped away, defeated. Having come so far we did not want to be forced to leave Polynesia in a hurry. But we vowed that if our £1,400 was not accepted by credit-card, we would have no choice.

Next morning Frank organised the bond transfer while Frances and I investigated another anchorage with better facilities ashore. When he told me later that the bank had charged an additional non-refundable $70 my lid blew! Nothing would calm me, and I stormed to the local newspaper office to blurt out my story to anyone who would hear. A very attentive reporter, who had excellent English, listened to my tale, and then produced that morning's front page. 'End To Repatriation Bond' blazoned the headline, and the story went on to explain that as of the day before the requirement to pay a bond was abolished for all EU citizens. I was absolutely dumbfounded! He suggested I write to the High Commissioner – I asked him to first verify the story with the Commission as newspapers often have their facts distorted. He did. His contact in the Press Office confirmed. We were getting somewhere: justice was in sight. Next morning I brushed up my rusty French and typed an impassioned plea for *liberté, égalité, fraternité*, the cornerstones of the French Constitution. I welcomed the fact that these principles were now being acknowledged in relation to visitors to Polynesia – but why then had we still been forced to obey a now-defunct law? Surely the police and bank personnel must have been aware of the situation? I hand-delivered my letter to the Commission's Press Office, and was told to return on Monday when a reply would be ready. Somewhat pacified, I walked back to the port.

We had read of the legendary singing and even more renowned millenary at Papeete's main Protestant church, Le Temple, and we shamefacedly went to gawk rather than to pray. The hats lived up to their reputation, and viewed from the gallery above looked like a scene from *My Fair Lady*. There were confections in straw, lace, cotton and felt, adorned with bows, feathers, tulle and taffeta, fruits, flowers and even stuffed birds. All the ladies wore them, and most of the older girls, while the menfolk were resplendent in best dark suits. Obviously this was a wealthy congregation, and the style was Polynesian chic – French with a dash of warm abandon. The preaching, however, was overlong and the singing too short for us – we had to rush to catch a bus to the out-of-town folk museum where the bi-annual Sports Day was being held.

La Musée de Tahiti et ses Îles sits in a glorious location by the ocean's edge, in sight of the lofty outline of neighbouring Moorea. In a parkland of tall coconut palms, local fare was being taken from an underground oven – fish and breadfruit cooked in banana leaves, taro leaves boiled with coconut cream, and delicious baked chicken. This was doled out onto banana leaf plates to visitors and competitors alike. When all were fed the real fun began. Teams had come from the farthest outer islands to compete in a unique quartatholon: javelin throwing, coconut husking, tree climbing and the much-lauded fruit carriers' race. Handsome competitors strode round the grounds, wearing not tracksuits but colourful cotton pareos, tied around their loins like floppy nappies – and garlands of leaves and flowers in their hair. They reminded us of the Greek athletes of legend – and this was no tourist display but rather a serious inter-island contest. First the javelin throwers lined up – four to a team – and aimed their flimsy bamboos with pointed metal ends at a coconut speared on top of a forty foot pole which could be raised and lowered by a simple balance device to retrieve the hits. The youngest competitor was about fourteen – from the remote Gambier Islands in the south where javelin throwing is practiced from primary school upwards! It seemed impossible that anyone could hit the hard, unyielding target, but there were several 'bulls eyes' which were greeted with loud cheers! When the last shot was fired, and the javelins gathered and tallies taken, all repaired to a sandy enclosure near the beach to compete in the *décoquillage des cocotiers*. Each man was presented with a dozen coconuts in their hard green outer shells. A sharpened stake and a large stone were the only implements to be used. Propping the stake against the stone and holding it in position with his left foot and across his right thigh at a slant away from his body, the competitor would then drive the hard nut onto the sharp part of the stake with both hands, forcing cracks into the shell, while at the same time tearing it away from the inner, hairy nut. I was worried that they would stab their hands or let the stake slip and damage their thighs or more vital parts of their anatomies – but these young men could hull the dozen unyielding nuts within minutes. Time was carefully taken by three uniformed judges, and the outright winner was a finely muscled, magnificent youth with flowing hair, a tiara of twined palm leaves on his head, and instead of the bulky pareo, a loincloth of pale green cotton, modestly complimented by matching *slip* – briefs to us. He beat the others by about four minutes! He was also the fastest to shin up the coconut tree – barefooted as they all were, using feet and knees to reach the nuts at breakneck speed.

The final competition was the most spectacular. Earlier in the afternoon I had watched as six-foot long, six-inch thick bamboo poles laden at each end with ingeniously fixed bunches of coconuts, bananas, palm leaves and flowers, were carefully weighed by the games officials, and shorn of their fruits until the required weight was achieved: it seemed such a pity to upset these works of art! Now their beauty had been restored with additional leaves and blossoms, and the contestants lined up: the strongest men from each team as these burdens weighed 30 kilos. The route was a stiff 1,000 metres around the museum buildings – the heat of the day had dissipated somewhat and that at least would help them. On the signal the bamboo poles were hoisted onto one shoulder, and the men took off, straining visibly under the weight of their loads. Barefoot they ran on the grassy path, dodging trees and bushes as spectators made way for them to pass, carefully balancing the bouncing poles with one hand as they were urged forward by team-mates and spectators alike. Cameras whirred and children cheered as the last and oldest competitor limped to the finishing line: just to compete was an achievement in itself.

Prize-giving followed – with bags of sugar being included with the medals and trophies – as well as flights to other islands. Then one of Tahiti's best dance troupes, with classical grass skirts and magnificent woven headgear, took their places near the beach, and with a backdrop of one of the finest sunsets we have ever wit-

nessed, performed their exotic vibrating dances, with hip swaying and arm shaking, and wailing, haunting music. The women's
hair was down to their waists, and they wore coconut-shell bras
in deference to modern-day modesty. It was a day we shall never
forget!

The Trade Winds boats were beginning to leave, and next
morning we found a couple of free spaces on the downtown marina. There Jean Luc, a local electronics specialist, provided a new
regulator, which finally provided the solution to the battery-
charging problems which had dogged us since the Atlantic. We
invited him to dinner some days later, and learnt a lot about life
in Tahiti – he came here when he was six, and returned to France
to go to college, working his way round the world for the next
eight years. He found nowhere he liked more than Polynesia, and
returned for good to set up his successful business. Like most people in Papeete, he works long hours, being on the job by 7.00 and
never finishing before 19.00. For this he makes good money, and
spends his weekends visiting other islands in his fast motor-boat
which he co-owns with his father.

We were surprised to learn that it is not illegal to grow or use
marijuana, but it is strictly illegal to sell it! Another interesting
French approach to a potential problem.

After the relief about our electrics all that remained of unfinished business was my rendez-vous with the High Commission Press Officer. Surprised to be met hastily in the corridor, rather
than in his office, I was in for quite a shock. My contact had passed
on my letter, but in fact the newspaper had been incorrect in its story,
despite the earlier confirmation. A law proposed in January, but held
up by a rightest MP, had been passed, and French citizens were now
free to enter without paying the bond – all others were still required
to do so. So much for the EU!

I was totally deflated – I had been misled by people who
should know better, and had made a complaint based on incorrect
information. I now had to redraft my original letter, pleading fairness and common sense towards visitors. I went to phone the jour-
nalist – he was away on assignment until next week! Suddenly
my case seemed to be swallowed by bureaucracy – but I determined not to leave things hanging like this. I wrote to Hugh
Coveney,* a friend in the Irish government, giving him the details,
and delivered an up-to-date review, together with a copy of my

letter to the High Commissioner, to the newspaper to await my contact's return. It was interesting that boats who checked in after us were *not* asked to produce either return ticket or bond. This didn't help our bruised sense of fairness. I hoped the story would be published, and would gain some sort of public sympathy and provide embarrassment for the government. We would have to wait for an outcome – but meanwhile there was little more I could do. We completed marina-based jobs, washing down the boat, thoroughly cleaning and re-filling the tainted water tank, and preparing for our next leg – via several Polynesian islands to our final Francophone destination, Bora Bora. We bade Frances and Brendan an emotional goodbye – our paths would not cross again as they were returning to San Francisco, and set sail once more.

To many people Moorea is the most beautiful of the Society Islands. To us it was like heaven after the frustrations and noise of the capital. In the fjord-like Opunoho Bay, sacred mountains towered over us on both sides, and only two other boats were anchored in its calm waters. We nudged deeper into Robinson's Cove, where a brightly painted dug-out pirogue was pulled up on a tiny arc of sand, under swaying coconut trees.

It rained quite heavily overnight – washing the decks for us! By 7.30 next morning we were ashore, packed lunches and water bottles in our backpacks, striding out through a lush, mountain-ringed valley redolent with the smell of pine and alive with its soughing. This area of rich volcanic soil was heavily populated in the eighteenth century but now is almost totally deserted apart from an agricultural research station set up to study suitable crops and animals for local production. Blonde Aquitaine cows and calves were feeding in the dewy grass, and fat contented sheep occupied other, shadier fields. We continued to rise into the area of ferns, and counted at least a dozen varieties on the steep roadside banks. Our quest was the Belvedere, a look-out point which gave us an unsurpassed vista over mountains and bays – our boat a tiny speck below! A thoughtful roulotte was doing a roaring trade in morning coffees and crèpes, and we indulged gratefully – it had been a long hike since breakfast!

We descended to a sister bay, named after the intrepid Captain Cook. This is the more popular anchorage, as there are some

---

* Later tragically drowned while five of his seven children were completing a circumnavigation to raise £1 million for charity.

shops and restaurants here. Today the magnificent four-masted sailing cruiser *Windsong* was lying peacefully at anchor while her passengers did a tour of the island. By the time we got to the shoreside we realised that we had a lot more walking to do, and as we wanted to leave by mid-afternoon we decided to get a bus back – several had passed earlier. A local cafe owner told us there was no regular service – those we saw were school buses, or cruise tour buses – we would have to walk or get an expensive taxi. We decided to hitch, and picked a safe spot. A taxi stopped (we had not hailed *him*) and very kindly took us for nothing – typical of these friendly islanders.

The walk had tired Frank out completely, and he fell into yet another bout of dengue fever. I became seriously worried about his health, and the wisdom of us continuing the voyage. He had lost about 6kg weight, and was constantly falling prey to boils, sores, and fatigue which required at least ten hours sleep. I blamed anxiety, heat, excessive exercise, and departing from his gluten free diet as the most logical causes, rather than the malaria-like dengue. I depended too much on him, and became depressed if he was not in full health. I was about 3kg lighter than usual, very conscious of my hand injury, and prone to moodiness and mood swings. As there was no immediate solution to the problems we kept most of our negative thoughts to ourselves, and passed a lot of time in anxious silence. Thankfully we were now on a series of short hops from island to island, rather than a long passage, so night sleep was guaranteed.

Huahine is not as geographically spectacular as Moorea, but it has one of the most important collection of historical sites of all the Society Islands. Leaving Frank on board I had energy enough only to visit about half of the sixteenth-century lagoon-side temples at Maeva. At the beautifully restored Fare Pote'e or communal meeting house built on stilts over the water, its walls of woven split bamboo, and the roof of pandanus thatch, I was bitten by a dog – one of a pack of mixed parentage in the 'control' of a local youth. Badly frightened by the thought of rabies I yelled at him to get the dogs off the public area, and shortened my visit as I was keen to treat the slight wound as soon as I could. The hospital in Las Palmas had given me a giant shot of anti-tetanus – but should I have had a booster? I didn't feel ill – just hot and bothered. Thankfully I did not suffer any after effects – but was determined not to go walking on my own in the future!

We left Huahine next morning, and made the short trip to Raiatea by noon, with a strong following breeze. Against our better judgment we anchored in an exposed bay on the windward side of the island, to seek out a much-praised restaurant, as it was my birthday. It was closed to non residents, so we had to make do with tinned food on board! At midnight we woke to howling winds. Rain was falling heavily and everything was rattling and clanking. Frank went on deck to check things – and discovered to his horror that we had dragged our anchor several hundred yards and were practically on top of a tiny UK boat which had tucked itself well into the bay. Hastily I got the engine going while Frank windlassed up the thirty feet of anchor chain. It was a nightmare to try and negotiate through the long bay with not a glimmer of light anywhere, conscious of two dozen highly expensive charter yachts we had seen earlier moored in the middle of the bay. Thankfully we negotiated our way round them, attempted to anchor once more – this time with twice the weight of chain. Firmly secure, we had to agree that the day had been pretty much a failure – but we resolved to treat ourselves to a special meal at our final Polynesian port of call.

The most spectacular way to arrive into Bora Bora must be by plane. A hexagonal reef surrounds the highly mountainous volcanic island in shallow aquamarine waters, isolating it from the ultramarine Pacific Ocean. A single pass in the reef permits boats to enter the sheltered lagoon, where world-journeying yachts lie peacefully at anchor. As the plane descends, thatched huts, swaying palm trees, and eight-men pirogues become visible beneath, and the tiny airport's runways seem to be part of the surrounding coral. We made our approach through the foaming reef, and headed for Bora Bora's Yacht Club, nestled into one of the world's most seductive settings. Built in Polynesian style, right over the fish filled waters of the lagoon, with breathtaking views of the bay and outlying motus, it is open on three sides to the cooling breezes from the bay. Pennants from Yacht Clubs all over the world flutter from its high, thatched ceiling, and we were happy to hang the Royal Cork's among them. Most of the Trade Winds Rally boats were at anchor nearby, and we renewed friendships once again. After a few nights' blessed sleep Frank was able to build up strength for the next long leg.

Before we left we celebrated our joint birthdays in style. The Moana Beach Hotel has regal Polynesian ambiance, with simple woven rattan walls, hung with local pandanus and tapa matting, and glorious chandeliers made of copra. Set on a squeaky white palm-fringed shelving beach, some of the hotel's thirty bedrooms are perched on stilts right on the reef itself. Their glass-covered coffee tables built into the floors give unrivaled views of the myriad fish and corals below! We donned our best outfits, travelled by taxi (a real luxury), and feasted on a delicious seafood buffet – the most opulent we had ever seen. Afterwards we took our places on beachside chairs to watch an exhilarating dance show, where the sensuous *tamouré* was beautifully presented by a young adolescent girl of about twelve. More hectic adult versions followed, with mesmeric wiggling of oiled hips glimpsed through rustling grass skirts – gyrating at incredibly high speed while the upper torso remains almost still, arms raised over the heads, and waist-long shining black hair crowned in fragrant flowers. Such was the seductive beauty that caused the *Bounty*'s crew to mutiny, Captain Cook's men to be loath to leave, and countless poets, painters and writers to linger on in these paradise isles. Though the dancing is now mainly performed for tourists, the tradition remains beautifully intact, restored after its banning by the various Christian proselytisers in the last century. Thankfully tourist interest, and tourist dollars, have helped keep culture alive. It was a truly fitting end to our visit in these entrancing, far flung, magic islands!

Next day we learnt that a front page article had appeared on the local paper, highlighting our displeasure at the unfair imposition of the repatriation bond, and I felt that some good would eventually come of our protests. (In 1999 the requirement was thankfully waived, not before its time.)

Spiritually, culturally, gastronomically and physically delighted with all we had seen and experienced, we were sure that this had been the highlight of our wanderings to date. We collected our infamous 'deposit' and bade enchanting Bora Bora *au revoir*. We sincerely hoped that at some future time we would have the good fortune to return again to magical French Polynesia.

13

SOUTH SEAS CONTRASTS

Sunshine, cooking, varnishing, fishing, sewing, baking, contemplating – such was our life afloat: a wonderfully simple rhythm not unlike monastic life, with the stars for night-time companions, and the warmth of the sun to keep morale high. Like monks, we tended to pray a lot, though not in formal words. Rather in wonder at superlative sunrise and sunsets, in thanksgiving at having survived another night alone on the wide expanse of ocean, and in petition when the wind howled and the waves rose. Without newspapers or TV, with limited radio and reading material, the simple yachtsman divides his or her time between manual tasks and meditation, sleeping and eating, early mornings and midnight vigils, deprivations and feasts. Much time is given to the 'inner man' – and from this comes great peace and satisfaction. The single-handed sailor must be closer to a shore-based contemplative than any other person afloat, but even couples tend to spend much time in other-worldly, companionable silence.

We had hoped to visit Rarotonga in the New Zealand-administered Cook Islands, but as the Trade Winds Rally group would more than stretch the limited anchorage there, we decided to bypass this celebrated spot and head instead for Nuie, a former Cook Island, now independent.

Good winds were bringing us a little too far south, but we were happy to have wind at all, and would use it to the maximum to cover as much of the journey as possible by sail alone. We could always correct with the engine later in the passage. We were averaging 100 miles a day – which for slow *Atlantic Islander* was not bad at all. After seven days of fair weather we suddenly found ourselves in the Inter-tropical Convergence Zone, the ITCZ, where winds and seas do unexpected things – ranging from nil to storm force in a matter of minutes. On 21 May we hit one of the worst storms of our lives, with winds of up to sixty miles an hour whipping the seas into a frenzy. Huge waves lashed down on us, tossing our 14.5 tons about like a piece of flotsam. The howling of the wind in the rigging really scared us half to death, and we felt out of control. With just a tiny sliver of mainsail to keep direction, we

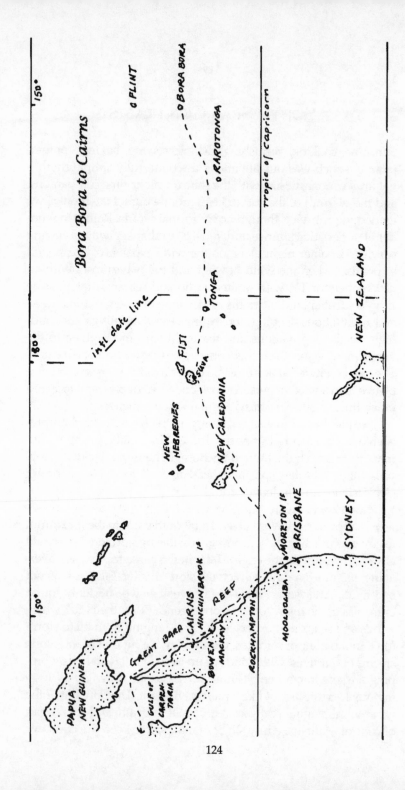

Bora Bora to Cairns

ran before the wind, heavy ropes streaming out behind to prevent the waves from swamping us. I prayed like never before. Actively reciting well-learnt words aloud helped block out some of the fear, and brought a sense of hope. It was impossible to sleep off watch with all the noise and turmoil, and I could not stay alone in the aft cabin, afraid that the next huge crashing wave would drown us: if we were to end our lives I wanted to be close to Frank.

Together we spent all night in the saloon, wedged in on the settee, as every bulkhead creaked and shuddered. Watch-keeping consisted of reluctantly leaving the safety and warmth of the saloon, and struggling out through the hatch every twenty minutes or so, switching on the deck lights and confirming that all the deck equipment was still in place, and there were no ships on the diminished horizon: we used a kitchen timer to prevent us forgetting or dozing off. It was a long long scary night: we were completely at the mercy of the forces of nature. It was a sobering time to reflect on other storms we had witnessed, when the children had been such a concern. We thanked the Lord that at least none of them was with us now: the danger was only to ourselves. We prayed and prayed for the frenzy to ease. During the day it was practically impossible to prepare meals, or use the toilet, as we were buffeted and thrown around the boat: one hand firmly grabbing any handhold we could find. Our tempers were short – but we concentrated on preventing accidents, and limited our activities as much as possible. By some great miracle we suffered no damage whatsoever, and that evening when we heard on the radio net that some of the Trade Winds boats had been knocked down (turned onto their sides with masts in the water) in this storm – we were even more grateful to have escaped with mere bruises.

After twenty-four hours the wind abated, but the seas were agitated and confused for another two days. The storm had driven us too much off course for Nuie, so we laid track for Tonga, hand steering for hours on end. A glorious sunset more than compensated for the frenzy that had gone before. In thirteen days at sea we experienced only four days of favourable winds: four had no wind at all and five had totally contrary wind! The passage was taking much longer than expected, and I was really missing the family back home. David was completing his final university exams at this time, and there was no way of getting in touch to wish him luck.

On the seventeenth day we crossed the International Date Line, and deducted twenty-four hours from our lives – a unique experience though nicely cancelled by this being a leap year! Sailing over the second deepest piece of ocean in the world gave us an eerie feeling. The Tonga Trench plummets to a dizzying 10,040 metres – and we dared a very quick spooky dip, holding tightly to our safety line lest lurking leviathans snatch us below! Next morning we began to see land, and thankfully entered the safe harbour of Neiaf'u, capital of the northern Vava'u Group, a few hours later.

Tonga has never had the major injection of European, Australian or American capital that has helped or hindered so many of her neighbours: no great building projects, harbours or industries have been initiated, and the country's scattered islands sustain a fishing and farming community, with limited though expanding tourism, mainly diving and sailing. Neiaf'u is the main cruising base, some 280 nm from the capital Nuku'alofa. Only 1,500 nm from Australia, Tonga is easily accessible, and is a short flight from New Zealand.

It would be hard to find a greater contrast to heavily subsidised, sophisticated Polynesia. Neiaf'u has the old-world, pioneering feeling of some outback town, with clapboard stores and raised wooden pavements, dirt streets which ooze with mud in the rain, locals huddling together in the shade, and bands of brown pigs with striped or spotted offspring rooting at every unprotected garden. Despite obvious poverty, school children wear smartly pressed white shirts and clean trousers or skirts, and all have huge smiles and beautiful teeth. They chattered in animated groups near the shops, released from religious-run schools. There was the usual opulent bank, wholly out of place, some spacious stores selling a little of almost everything, and an excellent cafe which unexpectedly served great filter coffee and good simple food. The phone-centre was hard to find, basic, and crowded with local people, but it was so good to talk to the family after eighteen days at sea. And to complete our joy the local hotel had a thick bundle of welcome mail for us – fifteen letters in all. I read and re-read to my heart's content, and immediately got down to typing replies.

Sunday's mass was even more dramatic than the superb Easter morning in Nuku Hiva. Here, in contrast, the Catholic church was quite dilapidated. We could understand why when we watched the congregation assemble – all in their very best attire but clear-

126

ly extremely poor. Children were barefoot, and some of the adults, but most of the women wore ill-fitting, hand-me-down high-heels which clacked loudly on the concrete floor. Many had traditional pandanus mats folded in half and wrapped around their waists. These give the wearer a bulky and imposing appearance, and are only worn for important occasions. Finally the congregation was gathered together, and then the singing started. It was electric – full of spontaneous harmony and up-beat rhythms – nothing like the timid, wishy-washy hymns we know back home. Everyone sang with all their heart, and the music rose up and transformed the simple church, and flowed out over the town and the sleeping bay below: we were moved almost to tears, as once again we thanked the Lord for bringing us safely ashore.

We spent a week relaxing and recuperating from the hard conditions at sea, and made new friends ashore. Three young crew were boat-minding for some of the Trade Winds Rally, and we listened entranced to stories of adventure. Callum and Lucyanne, Scots social workers based in Sydney, had hitch-hiked from Australia to Moscow, entering Nepal under forged papers: it would have taken weeks to hear their full story! Harriet was taking care of *Hilda*, skippered by Graham and Mary, a charming couple in their late sixties who were friends of the *Alb*s. It was good to be with young people again, and we invited them to dinner. We hoped to attend a typical Tongan feast together, but unpleasant bureaucracy from the immigration people made it impossible for us to depart at the weekend, and we left a day early with a less than happy impression of officialdom though reports from others who cruised the islands were one hundred percent positive.

Fiji lay some 250 miles to our west, and we completed a slow but uneventful passage in six days. Rusted hulks of shipwrecked freighters dotted the surrounding reef, making us additionally anxious as we attempted to find and run the extremely narrow entrance to Suva, the capital. Safely inside we were overjoyed to see an Irish flag flying from the stern of a Freedom-rigged, 36-foot ketch, aptly named *Saoirse* (Freedom). We couldn't believe our eyes: the second Irish boat we had seen since leaving Crosshaven ten months before (it would turn out to be the only one we would meet until Piraeus in Greece). Orla and Gearóid had left Ireland a year before us, on their extended honeymoon, and planned to be home a year after us – the sensible four-year odyssey, allowing time to work in the Caribbean, New Zealand and Australia. They are a charming and competent couple, and we were so thrilled to hear those good Irish accents again. It was more amazing to learn that Gearóid was from our hometown Limerick, and that Orla had spent a long time in Cork! We would pass many memorable evenings with them, swapping adventures and exchanging ideas.

Fiji had known various European masters, and the principal city of Suva was modern and vibrant, with a colourful Indian population originally brought in by the British to work on the coffee plantations, and eventually represented in all walks of Fijian life – not without resentment. After serious disturbances in the 1980s all government and other positions of importance are barred to Indians, who confine themselves to shopkeeping and non-governmental clerical work. Officialdom here was reasonably straightforward, though 'gifts' *were* sought by the Harbour Master and we were obliged to tie up to an unfriendly, dirty commercial dock on arrival. (More sensible skippers simply anchor at the yacht club on the outskirts of the town and present themselves to the Harbour Master on foot.)

Swaying palm trees shaded the pleasant yacht club gardens, where excellent food and cheap, cold beer was served. A good washing machine and large area of clothes lines thoughtfully strung up under a roof were luxuries, as rainfall was frequent and thorough. In the nearby bustling market an arrow pointed to the upper level with a large sign for 'GROG!' (Australian for alcohol) On inspection all we could see here were huge piles of what looked like dried roots. We learnt that this was the ubiquitous, mildly narcotic yanquona or kava which is prepared and consumed every day in Fiji – an essential ritual like Japan's tea-drinking – and now getting popular worldwide.

Wanting to see some of the interior we travelled upriver by flat-bottomed boat – like a Shannon ganloe – shooting the rapids through a tree-lined gorge with rushing waterfalls on both sides. Herons fished by the river's edge while eagles soared overhead. After 20 km we reached a village, perched on a knoll about twelve metres above the river, and learned it had been totally flooded during the 1993 typhoon. All the tiny square houses stood on stilts and were made of split bamboo walls and modern galvanised roofs – but the village meeting-place had traditional pandanus thatched roof, and was delightfully cool. We took off our shoes and sat cross-

128

legged on the comfortable pandanus mats while the chief's son prepared the ceremonial kava. The roots of the pepper plant had already been finely ground to a powder with a stone pestle and mortar, and left to soak in water for several hours. Our host dipped in a muslin cloth and wrung out the mixture into a four-legged stone vessel known as a *tanoa*. From there he filled a half-coconut shell or *bilu* and passed it to Frank. The chief and our guide clapped three times and shouted *Bula* (Good health) while Frank downed the liquid in a single gulp as custom demands, returned the bowl, clapped and shouted *Bula!* Next it was my turn, clapping and shouting before accepting the hollow coconut, and swallowing fast. It looked and tasted like dishwater, but was not repugnant. Our tongues were slightly numbed, but otherwise we felt no ill or good effects, even after a second and third cup – much to the host's delight! We wondered at the similarity of the Gaelic *búla bas* (applause) so far from the Emerald Isle! A welcoming speech was made and translated, and we made appropriate gestures. Then some village women in long cotton skirts and colourful blouses came in bearing plastic plates laden with local food – prepared in a *lovo*, a pit oven outside – before laying out rather mediocre local craftware for us to purchase. Later they 'danced' in a unique style: sitting cross-legged on the pandanus mat they wave their arms, sway their upper bodies, and sing together, with accompaniment from the men on guitar. It's quite a soothing experience after the exuberance of Polynesia, and particularly charming when the tiny children join in, carefully imitating their mothers! An obvious love of children exudes from all these island people, and we were never to see a child cry or be scolded anywhere in the so-called Third World.

On our last evening in Suva we had several farewell drinks with Orla and Gearóid. Once more we were sad to be leaving new-found friends. Each of us faced the constant possibility of not completing the next leg of our journey, and who knew if they would ever meet each other again? At least the likelihood of seeing *Saoirse* in a year or two was very strong, and we promised to keep in touch meanwhile. So several beers and a few whiskeys the worse for the wear we returned to *Atlantic Islander*, clambered up the boarding ladder, and went to bed – conscious of another big day on the morrow.

After breakfast I went to fetch the dinghy from its usual location at the stern, but it wasn't there. An ache of anxiety hit me with a hammer blow as I remembered that neither of us had properly tied it up the previous night. Our inflatable was vital to us – more important than a car to land-based folk who can always get a bus or a taxi instead. Without it we had no way of getting ashore other than by swimming, no way of bringing provisions, water or diesel to the boat: in short, we would be permanently stranded on board except at marinas, which were few and far between – and expensive. Thanks to a borrowed spare which Gearóid kindly provided – he sensibly had two! – Frank searched every nook and cranny along the reef, but to no avail. We were certain now that we had little hope of finding the dinghy – but would report the loss to the police as a matter of form so we might get some compensation from our insurers. Meanwhile, where were we to buy a replacement? Worse, at what cost? We had neither tender nor outboard – nor oars, and would have to start from scratch.

At the police headquarters, to our amazement and delight, a dinghy *had* just been reported found – drifting during the night – so provisioned with enough dollars for a fair reward, we were sent to a sub-station out of town, where were warmly received by some splendidly uniformed officers. Fiji's magnificent police force wear cream wrap-over skirts (*sulus*) with saw-tooth hems which fall just below the knee – these are worn with a smart navy shirt, shining black patent belt with elaborate buckle, and tasselled epaulettes and woggle. Unlike the usual *sulus* this one is cut on the bias in front, so that the edges just come together at the hemline, but are well doubled at the waist, ensuring modesty with flexibility when chasing criminals!! We were treated with courtesy, and eventually brought in a police van to an area somewhat inland. We were led along tidy paths through a beautifully kept village green with tiny, immaculately clean concrete houses and a large chapel, an ancient hollowed-out tree trunk hung nearby to call the people to service. Past the village the path became narrower and slippery and there was very little housing, though we knew we were heading in the direction of the sea. A small boy joined us to lead the way. He was the grandson of the woman who had reported the missing dinghy.

Finally we reached a clearing and found ourselves on a carefully tended lawn with a small galvanised hut in the far end, some flower-beds near an outside latrine on our left-hand side under huge shading trees overlooking a mangrove swamp about nine metres below. Standing near the hut was a man in his fifties, missing most of his teeth, his arm protectively around the edge of our battered rubber dinghy. The policemen chatted with him in staccato, and once we confirmed that this was indeed ours, we enquired whether the outboard motor and oars (and our shoes!) might also be here. More rapid speech, and slowly but surely all the missing items, except my 'best' sandals, were secured from various different places round the hut – hidden for safe-keeping, the man said.

We were overjoyed, and shook hands with our saviour and with the police, who left to join their companions. We handed over a wad of dollars, and the villager seemed satisfied – his wife who had reported the find (somewhat against his will, we thought) was still in town with their daughter. We were beginning to gather our things together when the ladies appeared, and I hugged the mother who had been so honest. Their daughter remarked that they had seen us in town that morning, and I wondered how she possibly could have know who we were. The answer was on her feet – and mine. The sandals I had left in the dinghy were a match to the pair I now wore – though in better condition! I *couldn't* ask for them back! She told us her mother had been fishing in the early hours of the morning, and had found the dinghy free-floating off the inner reef. She towed it behind their wooden canoe, and brought it upriver where her husband and son had cut the safety lock and removed the heavy outboard motor so as to drag the dinghy up to the house for safety, as they feared it would be stolen. We were so touched by the honesty and humour of the women – which didn't seem to emanate from the man of the house. I only hoped that he would share the reward money which we would have preferred to have given to the mother. But an exchange of addresses would lead to further opportunity in that regard.

Bit by bit we trudged boat, engine, and oars down the steep ridge to the muddy, shallow river below, and with tears in our eyes made our way by paddle and engine off into the bay, really touched by these honest people who obviously had so little, yet were cheerful and good-hearted in the extreme. Children ran down the steep bank waving to us, and we felt more at home than we had ever done on our trip.

131

Next day we made our departure, just as many of our friends from the Trade Winds Cruising Rally were arriving. We were elated with our good fortune, and an excellent forecast bode well for the second-last passage in the great Pacific Ocean. All along the fringing reef here there are rusted hulks of commercial vessels who misjudged the pass, and are impaled forever on the sharp, shallow coral. Markers and buoys are badly maintained in widely scattered island communities, and entries and exits in this part of the world are extremely difficult. We held our breaths until we were clear of the crashing waves and steered a course to avoid westward and southward islands in our path. Suddenly, from nowhere, a blinding thunderstorm erupted, and we were deafened by cataclysmic, quadraphonic thunder. Driving rain distorted the simultaneous lightning, reduced visibility to nil, and the needle on the wind-guage stayed at the maximum reading. We were really scared, but thanked the Lord and all those who keep us in their prayers that we were clear of the pass, and had only a shortened mainsail and no genoa set. Frank battled to reef in more main, and I saw my carefully crafted Fijian flag, Union Jack laboriously worked onto its upper quarter, whipped off the shroud and whirling into the storm. The winds continued to rise and we recorded speeds of 40 knots, never below 30 during the night when we changed to two-hour watches as hand steering was imperative to avoid the dangers in the channel. So much for the good forecast! We got practically no sleep that night, but by morning we were left with no wind at all and had to motor, exhausted, at the wheel. Nighttime brought the gales back – what were we facing? It was impossible to go back, and difficult to continue.

On our fourth day at sea the winds had lessened completely, and Frank finally managed to get some elusive weather faxes after weeks of nothing. He called me below decks for a conference – something that had never happened before. In front of him was a flimsy weather chart, and beside it a key to the various symbols. He looked very serious, and I quickly discovered why. On the chart, just south-west of our path were wind speeds of 50 knots and over – hurricane force, coming towards us – while outside all was calm. We decided not to take evasive action until the next fax came through in a few hours time. Meanwhile we fretted and fussed – how could such weather be around when we had no foretaste of it – nor any telltale signs in the sky? Where could we run to? We were equally far from New Caledonia and Fiji: we would just have to head north should the worse come to the worst.

The next fax showed even stronger winds – but miraculously further south. Still we fretted and still the immediate weather was perfect – calm seas with just a slight breeze. We decided to keep on course for Noumea, capital of New Caledonia, and added several extra prayers to our nightly quota! The following morning the picture looked far more normal – and during the day Frank suddenly realised with relief that we had in fact been receiving the aeronautical charts, with wind speeds shown at 250m altitude! We felt such fools – but happy ones! Our winds however remained contrary, and we averaged only 60 miles a day, taking eleven days to complete 700 miles. We reached the dangerous, but well-marked pass into the reef off south-eastern Nouvelle Calédonie on Sunday 30 June: the Pacific was rapidly shrinking beneath our bows.

We found an excellent marina, competently run, where the immigration and customs procedures all happened on board, once one was comfortably berthed! We talked with the extremely pleasant French immigration officer, who was nearing fifty and looking forward to returning to France, though the government offers all sorts of perks to ex-employees to remain in the territory and enlarge the French presence. This is the richest of the Pacific Islands (outside New Zealand and Japan) – after New Guinea which is really in a category of its own. Bauxite has replaced timber as a vital export, and tourism is fairly advanced. However, internal strife between the indigenous Melanesian Kanak people (43% of the population) and the superimposed French majority has led to widespread unrest in the island as a whole, and one gets a really sinister feeling in Noumea, where prosperous buildings rub shoulders with vacant lots roamed by workless, disaffected Kanaks.

We stayed only long enough to reprovision and fill our diesel tank. Friendly yotties who, like those we met in Tonga, were perfectly happy with this part of the world, and spent the annual hurricane season in American Samoa, spoke highly of the cruising pleasures we were missing out on by dashing away so soon. But we were conscious of family commitments: David had passed his final exams and was due to graduate in a few weeks time, and I really wanted to be back in Ireland for that important event. And

Cathy and Sarah would be awaiting us in Australia – how could we dally with such a reunion in the offing? The conquest of the Pacific was a mere ten days or so away, and we focused on our entry into Brisbane as a Roman consul might dream of his triumph!

By 4 July we were underway, for once without the usual queasy stomach: were we at last becoming less apprehensive about setting out into unknown waters? How long would this last Pacific passage take? I was so impatient to be with the family, and each day I eyed the mileage with hope and determination – though knowing full well that our progress lay entirely at the whim of the wind. Luck was at last on our side, and the elusive south-easterly trade winds finally set in. We were keeping up a marvellous average. On 9 July they got a little too frisky rising from a comfortable 16 knots to between 25 and 30 knots, and I wrote on watch:

The wind is howling steadily. Every now and then it gets louder, and shakes all the rigging, building to an intensity that makes me terrified of what might happen next. Sheets rattle, and a shrill, deafening whine builds up in the running rigging. A big wave shudders the entire boat, and the very reefed genoa flaps violently from side to side. The next wave hits the boat like a ton of rock, and sheets of water run down the decks, sloshing backwards and forwards before they escape slowly through the drain holes. Down below the cups and pots and pans rattle violently in the cupboards, despite being wedged tight with cloths and clothes. Halyards rattle against the masts, and the cabin supports groan alarmingly under the extreme stress. In quiet moments between waves water noises bubble against the windward hull, and our freshwater sloshes loudly and thwacks in the stainless steel tanks below the floor – making a sound like a shaking steel drum. Every inanimate object below and above decks seems alive, with a will of its own.

Luckily the winds abated by morning, and the storm for once had driven us much nearer to our goal. Air temperatures had plummeted and we were now getting regular readings in the low 20s (after months in the low 30s!) with squally rain showers – we had to drag out the old plastic cockpit hood, hidden months before in the depths of the lazarette under ropes, sails and vegetables. This snapped on securely and kept us both warm and dry. We had thought we wouldn't need it until Biscay!

We reached the shallow shoals of infamous Moreton Bay well in time for a pre-weekend clearance by the custom authorities –

an important consideration as overtime incurs huge surcharges –
on Friday 12 July, and motored carefully on an elaborate dog-leg
course to the mouth of the Brisbane River, tired but jubilant.
Atlantic Islander had successfully crossed the world's two greatest
oceans, carrying her crew to safety. Here lay *terra incognita aus-
tralis*, proud family members, and well-earned time ashore!

14

Down Under

Australia's Health and Customs requirements are more stringent than any other country's, and we were somewhat in trepidation when tying up to their wooden jetty. We knew that no vegetables, eggs, milk or dairy products, cereals, pulses, pork meat products, fruits, gourds, wooden artifacts, nor a hundred other assorted goodies were permitted into the country, and we had been busy devouring the ends of our fresh stocks before arriving. As Australia is such a unique, isolated and disease-free environment, the government is at pains to keep it so, and hence these stringent, enforced regulations. (Who hasn't been mildly insulted when sprayed with disinfectant on arriving by plane?) Duly checked and cleared (by a young officer whose grandmother – yet again! – came from Cork!) we headed up-river past magnificent homes with their private docks and sleek motor yachts.

As we neared the city, banks of glass-fronted skyscrapers reflected the changing hues of a slow, spectacular sunset. This was a far more vibrant, modern Brisbane than we remembered from eight years before, and to a couple who had not seen a skyscraper since Panama city, six whole months ago, it seemed like somewhere futuristic and fabulous – a dream world. We were heading for a new mooring experience, as the light fell, and with it an increase of tidal flow. Just off the city's Botanic Gardens stand a triple row of wooden posts, driven deep into the fast-flowing river's bed. These are one of the yachting world's best kept secrets, as for AUS$15 a week one can tie up to them and spend as long as one likes at one of the city's best addresses, in the heart of the downtown district, with showers and toilets a short dinghy ride away. Trees, flowering shrubs and plants provide a serene backdrop, and just across the river lies the pleasure land that in 1988 housed the Expo buildings. It was almost dark as we approached to size up the situation: one needed to tie a stern rope onto a ring on one post, while quickly latching a forward rope to the post downstream, without letting the boat drift into any of the many other yachts tied to neighbouring posts. We were both tired and felt unable to manage the contortions involved, and having already spied a tiny marina nearby which, to our amazement, had several empty berths, we headed there, and helping hands took our lines and tied us securely. No officials would OK our stay until Monday, so our kind new neighbours lent us their spare entrance key, told us where everything was, and invited us to join them for dinner. But we were too overwrought with tiredness and excitement to talk to strangers, and needed to find a phone right away and call my brother.

We excused ourselves, and putting on as many layers as we could find against the winter cold, headed into a bustling Brisbane Friday night. Having no currency was not a major problem – plastic was king everywhere except the phone booths and John forgave a reverse-charges call in the circumstances. Not expecting us until Monday, he was so excited to hear we were already settled he was prepared to drive 100 km immediately to see us. We hastened to deter him – we wanted to be fresh and relaxed when he came. We were exhilarated at having reached the other side of the world under our own steam, despite difficulties and set backs: this was my proudest moment of the voyage, and being so close to family made it even more emotional.

When John and two of his clan arrived at our temporary abode next morning he was amazed at how central and up-market a place we had found. A nearby McDonalds with a great river view provided easy nourishment for young and old, as we reminisced and caught up on each other's news. Our girls were off on a jaunt to Sydney, and would not know of our arrival, but after Sunday mass we came back to the boat to a wonderful surprise: they were awaiting us on the quay!! Cathy had been away for more a year and a half in Cambodia, and Frank had last seen Sarah nine months ago. After much hugging and kissing and sizing each other up, we were all soon chopping salads, shaking dressings and cutting breads and cakes for our augmented group of nine!

There were more tears, hugs and kisses when my sister-in-law and eldest niece arrived a few hours later – *two* bottles of champagne were opened and we toasted each other and all absent family and friends – especially Frank's and my parents, who would have been so proud of us. The sun was shining but the winter air was chill for us, accustomed to the tropics, and despite the crowd in the saloon, and the joy of the occasion, we were glad of our thermal vests.

The security people had been trying to move us on all week-end, so it was good to be legitimised at the marina on Monday, and be free to come and go without compromising our neighbours who had been initially so kind and welcoming! We raided the bookstores, buying up navigational and travel literature, whoop-whooping our way through shelf after shelf! It was like paradise regained, after all the months away from such luxury! We gaped at the crowds, the cars, buses, taxis, coaches, all the commercialism of the consumer society: like country bumpkins come to town on their annual visit, we were awed by this hive of activity, this determination to spend, spend, spend – and were swept into its embrace, until caution cried – Halt!

The girls brought us back to our senses. Cathy felt it was high time that strict budgeting was implemented – the ad hoc methods hitherto applied would have to go. From now on every penny was to be strictly accounted for! We knew the wisdom of this, and leaving the girls in charge, we repaired to the peace of John's home in Toowoomba, where night-time temperatures several degrees lower made us huddle together in a real bed, after a good hot bath! The warm welcome more than compensated. Our stay was too short – but things needed doing on the boat and I wanted to get back to Ireland. So a week after our triumphant arrival we were on our way down river, with two willing and able crew members, ready for whatever adventures lay ahead. The girls were quickly baptised with twenty hours of the roughest weather we had encountered, finding sleep in the cramped, pitching forepeak almost impossible. Once out of Moreton Bay and into the quiet waters of the Mooloolah River all was calm, and the friendly community there offered help and companionship during the two weeks of *Atlantic Islander*'s stay at Lawrie's Marina.

Back in Cork, Dave's graduation was an event to remember with glorious weather (so much warmer than Australia!). Friends and family were agog for news, and I recounted highlights for attentive audiences! I spent almost as much time travelling as I did at home, but it was well worth every flying hour, and I returned to 'The Project' refreshed and renewed.

Atlantic Islander sat high and fairly dry on the hard standing as the girls and Frank scrubbed and scoured prior to painting the hull. The propeller was shining bronze – with no trace of a barnacle to be seen. No one had been idle in my absence, and inside and

out was polished and re-varnished. Cathy had totally transformed the saloon table which had become scuffed and scratched
– and was now smoothly gleaming. This was at the height of the
Olympic Games, and we watched gold-medalist Michelle Smith
claim a bronze. Much later Michelle's glory would be as tarnished
as our propeller had been.

Once the boat was safely back at her berth, the girls and I now
tackled the much easier chore of provisioning: I wanted to purchase enough basic tins to last us until Ireland, as this was our best
chance. We were only a ten minute walk from an immense shopping centre – with two excellent supermarkets. Franklin's No Frills
summed up the cheaper of the two's philosophy in a succinctly
Australian way – the girls had wisely tried and tested some of the
plainly wrapped goodies in my absence and pronounced them
excellent. So that was our first destination, and we loaded three
trolleys with *no frills* basics, which we pushed back to the marina
with many a laugh. Why do supermarket trolleys the world over
have minds of their own – particularly when they leave the smooth
terrazzo of the malls? We were a public danger on the roundabout
– but luckily there was little traffic, and our most tense moments
came in negotiating the steep marina ramp at low tide!! A further
three loads next morning, and hours of coding (marking symbols
on the tops of the tins to facilitate accurate retrieval) and stowing
in three layers, with mixed varieties to ease selection, before our
task was complete. Frank protested that we would *never* eat all
that food – but I knew better, and for the present we had four
mouths to feed! Sacks of potatoes and onions, boxes of oranges and
apples, and general vegetables found homes in the airy lazarette,
and soon the boat was shipshape. Frank's bike, which had made
it this far, was discreetly dumped – too rusted to ever ride again.
I made a full set of covers for our badly marked fenders. Surplus
material – an ingenious tube of black ribbed jersey – became Sarah's
'Fendi' dress, which was later to gain much acclaim back home!!

We were anxious to have the wind in the sails again as we
headed north toward some of the most marvellous cruising grounds
in Australia. Our crew were keen to do some serious sailing, sun-
ning and swimming, hoping for warmer temperatures as we
moved nearer the winter sun. Fraser Island, 70 miles north of
Mooloolaba, is the world's largest sand island (120 km by 15 km)
and protects the shallow Tin Can Bay and Great Sandy Strait,

popular spots for fishermen and bird watchers. This is tricky ground for a keel boat, but with excellent charts photocopied from local friends, we had a safe and exhilarating passage towards the northern end of Fraser, which at this time of the year is famous for migrating whales.

A strange aspect of Australian cruising is that more than 95% of those involved tuck themselves into safe harbours, marinas or anchorages before dark, and the local coastguard radio shuts shop firmly at 17.30 – to resume at 07.30! We found this really quaint after all our hundreds of nights at sea. Shortly out of Urangan (a busy whale-watching port) when all aboard were asleep, I was at the wheel, passing the brightly lit port of Gladstone. Suddenly to seaward I spotted two lights heading directly for us, and barely made out two speedboats, very anxious to be home as it was *long* after curfew, One nearly hit us beam on at about 15 knots. The skipper just didn't see our masthead light, and I had to flood the decks with every light we possessed to get him to alter course – just in time. For my pains I got a string of language that would make even a sailor blush – and all I could do when the adrenaline had returned to normal levels was laugh. Idiots like he would not learn anything by being reported for dangerous driving. And an MCP Aussie idiot with a fast boat is hard to match!

John flew into the nearby town of Rockhampton, just north of the Tropic of Capricorn, to join us for a week's cruising from Roslyn Bay. Further north is a huge area of coastline and mountainous interior cordoned off by the military, and therefore of interest to him as he had never been able to explore it by road. Only one anchorage is permitted on this stretch of virgin coastline, and we spent two marvellous nights at lovely Pearl Bay, surrounded by Huon-pine-clad craggy slopes, loud with birdsong. We watched osprey swoop to snatch fish in their talons and soar back to their twiggy eyrie to feed young, and listened to the strange cry of the friar bird, while grey herons loped by on heavy wings. Having a knowledgeable ornithologist with us really improved our enjoyment.

A gentle overnighter brought us to Brampton Island, a five-star resort which welcomes 'trippers' and yotties alike, and has an excellent network of nature trails. This was 15 August – the first anniversary of our leaving Crosshaven, and we celebrated with ice cold hotel beers as we watched a majestic sunset over the resort's beach. Excellent snorkelling makes this a favourite island, and we stayed two nights, before heading back to the mainland to let John fly home – this time from Mackay, where he had first worked in Australia. We wouldn't see him again for at least two years, and possibly a lot longer. Now we were back to a crew of four, and Cathy was making rumbles about leaving us until Darwin, as she wanted to return to Cambodia to see her boyfriend. It was now very unlikely she would be with us for much of the voyage home.

We meandered further north – passing the over commercialised Whitsunday Islands in the dark. We had cruised here in 1988 when things were somewhat quieter – now we were in search of fresh pastures. Down-to-earth fishing harbour towns like Bowen were packed with hardy seamen, cattle ranchers and vegetable growers, and had excellent provisions and fuel. We had to shelter here for two days, initially tied alongside a 20-metre aluminium racing machine from Perth called *Risky Business*. Here Cathy arranged her Phnom Penh flights, and took off on the local bus for Cairns, wisely not trusting us to get her there in two days!

We sailed through the spectacular Hinchinbrook Passage, overlooked by the towering mountains of Hinchinbrook Island, and found a glass-calm estuary where we cast anchor and investigated the mangrove swamps by dinghy: it would have been a sacrilege to disturb the calm. The still air vibrated with the sounds of swamp birds, and the mesmeric popping of the mangrove roots as they soak up and process salt water, turning it into valuable nourishment for the glossy evergreen leaves.

Next morning we picked up a nice breeze which strengthened as we approached tricky Cairns harbour, and made for a really exciting entry. This is *the* capital of the Great Barrier Reef business – scores of high-powered craft roar off each morning laden to the gunwales with divers from all parts of the world. We berthed in the busy commercial marina, and were amazed at the constant activity. We often wondered how long the Barrier Reef could stand this level of penetration, but a knowledgeable pilot we met later told us that different sections are successively visited, like rotation farming, giving breathing space to the coral. After we arrived home we heard the horrific tale of the young honeymooners who were 'lost' on one of these dive expeditions – due to miscounting. They did not survive.

We purchased half a case of inexpensive 'bubbly' to toast to 'events' on board – and we reckoned there would easily be six before we reached home ... our twenty-ninth wedding anniversary on 2 September; re-crossing the equator; Christmas morning; reaching the Mediterranean; leaving Gibraltar; and the final one for the first glimpse of the *bán cnoic Éireann – O!*

Our coastal hopping was now at an end, and in order to rendezvous with Cathy we would have to head non-stop for Darwin. The first part of our passage as far as northernmost Cape York entailed four days and nights navigating through the narrow shipping lane inside the Barrier Reef, which must be one of the busiest channels we have ever sailed. *Now* we could well understand why most yachts in this area do day sails only, anchoring near shore each evening. This is an area of dense reefs, and the narrow well-marked channel dog-legs around myriad dangers and shoals and demands total concentration. With a crew of two it would have been almost impossible – four would have been ideal. But we three managed very well, doing two-hour night watches followed by four hour's sleep. It was necessary to memorise the chart rather than run below to study it every few minutes, so heavy was commercial traffic in both directions – and each time there was a particularly narrow passage between reefs we invariably found ourselves sandwiched between large ships travelling in different directions! Luckily we were through after ninety-six hours, and could breath sighs of relief once we rounded the remote Top End, the northernmost tip of Australia, where extraordinary currents in the Albany Passage gave us speeds of up to 14 knots – the all-time record on *Atlantic Islander!*

Frank had the almost impossible job of replacing a broken bolt on the wind-vane rudder while under way – this entailed perching himself on the stern ladder in pitching seas, removing the defective bolt, repositioning the heavy, awkward rudder onto the steel 'stock' and working a new bolt through. I had noticed something different about the rudder the day before – but forgot to mention it. There were no recriminations: the ever-patient skipper did not complain. The rest of the voyage to Darwin passed uneventfully, though we had some really big seas once through the Gulf of Carpentaria, where the weather was perfect despite all the dire warnings we had read! We were now truly in south-east trade winds, and the famous down-wind roll took quite some time to get used to, as there was no totally safe place one could retire to on board. Once I was flung out of my berth, and both mattress and I ended on the cabin floor – despite my lee-cloth!

We reached Cullen Bay Marina early on Saturday 7 September – nine-and-a-half days out of Cairns. We were several tins lighter as there had been little luck with the fishing, and our wedding anniversary 'champagne' on 2 September had tasted delicious! Cathy arrived next day when we were well and truly in our snug berth, with electricity plugged in and all systems operational: the cool box was working, electric kettle boiling constantly for tea and washing, various batteries charging at every available socket, sewing machine droning through repairs, and even the TV connected to review recent video footage. Ours was an unashamedly modern boat, its umbilical cord our vivid yellow electric cable, and man and women happily at work!

Darwin was a big surprise. We had expected a fairly hick town, here in the back of beyond. The Northern Territory is the least populated state in Australia, and is home to several Aboriginal tribes, where tourist visits are restricted. It is also one of Australia's most controversial states, and while we were there the legislature had just passed the Euthanasia Bill, which was causing a furore all over the country. The capital is a city of wide, tree-lined streets, plain but functional buildings, and pleasant suburbs. There is a healthy cultural life here, and a degree of sophistication which surprised us. Darwiners would not live anywhere else, contrary to general belief, and seem genuinely proud of their non-pretentious city. But beneath this satisfied air there lies a malaise just below the surface, as more and more dispossessed Aboriginal people come to be aware of their history and the unforgivable injustice that was done to them. This was the first time we had seen native Australians in any force – huddled in empty sites drinking from cider bottles, or crowding into 4WDs going back to their reservations. The lines of demarcation here are very distinct: between whites who have and the indigenous Australians who do not have – but will want their fair share as they become more and more politically aware. Native Australians are causing a lot of necessary debate by totally refusing any development in their vast reservations, to the frustration of miners and fortune seekers. The next few decades will be decisive in Australian history, as whites come to terms with a disgraceful history, the memory of which they have up to now tried to suppress.

Before we left we threw a big drinks party for all the boats we had come to know here. Litres of sangria were merrily consumed, and our dustbin/washing machine stood good stead as a beer cooler, filled with ice. Soon our ten days were over. Sadly we said goodbye to Sarah who had to return to medical college. We made our last easy telephone calls home, and called John and family to thank them once again for everything. We completed all the pre-passage checks and were satisfied that the boat was in good shape to continue into the other half of the world, and on Cathy's birthday, 17 September, one year, one month and two days after leaving Crosshaven, we set forth towards the Timor Sea: South-East Asia lay unexplored before us.

15

INDONESIA

Most of the Australians I spoke to were totally negative about Bali. 'Its been *ruined*. You should have gone in the early 1960s. Don't go now – you'll regret it!' But Bali was the main reason I'd come this far, and I *wasn't* going to sail past it! Ever since I was old enough to travel I had wanted to go there. Tony Wheeler's successive *Shoestring* and *Lonely Planet* guides were lavish in its praise – though increasingly dismissive of the brashness of the original hippie drop-out spots like Kuta and Legian.

Many yachts from Darwin head directly for Benoa, one of Indonesia's few recognised Entry Ports and Bali's main port, thus avoiding the expensive and time-consuming procedure of obtaining an Indonesian cruising permit, which is valid only for two months. Others take part in the annual Darwin to Ambon race: Ambon is an island north of Timor and arranges all visas at minimum cost and fuss. At the time of our trip it was a peaceful place. The race is an ideal entré to Indonesian waters and yachts can cruise in comfort westward to Bali. We were a little unclear of our situation, but did have a valid cruising permit which had cost us a total of $US240 – or at least we had a photocopy of the permit: the original was *hopefully* with an agent in Benoa.

Our sailing life was beginning to get exciting. We were in an area of uncertainty. Pirates roamed these waters, and hundreds of boats were stolen every year. It was comforting to learn that modern pirates were after valuable cargo and not the slightest bit interested in impoverished yotties' stashes of gin or corned beef, but one never knew ... maybe someone needed a getaway vessel – that left plodding old *Atlantic Islander* off the hook – her absolute highest speed was eight knots! There were plenty of faster boats around! However, the extra edge of fear added spice to our journey to Indonesia. We knew there would be poverty and that we were arriving like the conquistadores of the seventeenth century – though unattractive to the pirates we were wealthy beyond the wildest dreams of the villagers we would sail past. Would there be envy? Theft? Would there be the same feelings of malaise that we sensed in St Lucia? We had never journeyed in South-East

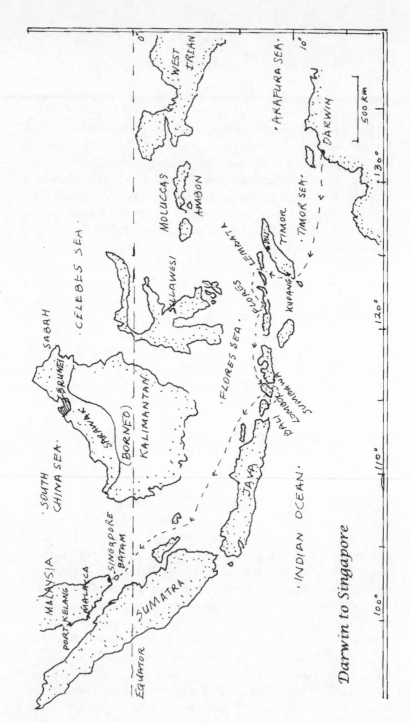

Darwin to Singapore

Asia: three nights in Bangkok and a short bus and boat ride to undeveloped Ko Samet in 1988 had not exactly exposed us to Asia. We were glad Cathy was with us, a seasoned ex-pat with 18 months' Asian experience behind her! She would be our guide and minder!

Little wind meant lots of motor, and the four huge fish Frank caught in the eight-day passage were kept fresh and delicious as our energy-hungry cool-box was supplied with engine power: not a single tin was opened! It was a gourmet trip, and we sailed towards Kupang, West Timor's capital. A visa issued here would cost us $100 and would be valid for one month only and impossible to extend. We thus decided we would sneak past the port and not declare ourselves, but as we tried to slip through the narrow approaches to the town we were radioed by a friendly Australian boat who had already been boarded by customs officers. They suggested we should make anchor and prepare to receive the said gentlemen. This was not at all the way we wanted to do things, but there was absolutely no alternative. The officers were extremely pleasant, did minimal checks of our papers, and suggested we leave a 'gift' for them with Jimmy, the main shipping agent in town. We acquiesced, and dinghied them ashore, in quite a muddle as to what to do next. It was by now too late to declare ourselves, and Jimmy when contacted suggested we continue on to Benoa next morning, once we had obtained some fuel which he could arrange. His charge for service and information was $20, which was a lot cheaper than going through 'official' channels, and we thanked him and exchanged addresses before leaving to quietly cruise the eastern islands of the Nusu Tenggara group (South-Eastern Islands in Malay). Technically speaking, as we had not formally entered Indonesia, we wouldn't be legally admitted into the country until Benoa, but we might possibly get a chance to slip ashore discreetly in some of the quieter places. So still the thrill of adventure prevailed!

And that sense was heightened as we sailed up the Flores Strait and anchored at dusk between two smouldering volcanoes, whose sides were gashed with flames: it seemed as though the mountains were issuing runnels of fire. We tucked ourselves into a sheltered anchorage close to a sleepy Muslim village, with a sacred mountain on either side of us – their profiles majestic in the blood-red setting sun. We woke to the sound of a thousand cock-

147

erels outdoing the wail of the muezzin, our nostrils filled with the smell of wood smoke which rose in slow spirals from the sides of the lofty peaks of Ari Api and Mount Boling. We were about five miles from Lamalera, one of the last places on earth where men still go after whales in dugout boats, using nothing more than harpoons – but these brave fishermen have a reputation for not welcoming yachts (whom they may rightly feel carry lesser mortals into their area!). As the holding there is not good we had reluctantly decided to leave them undisturbed.

Already we had seen many evocative wooden sailing boats, *'o'er cargoed, bending low'* – their lug sails now colourful woven plastic in place of the pandanus cloth of old. Hauled up on the beach in front of us, or in intricate wooden pens, were small dugout canoes with out-riggers, while hardwood-planked trawlers, looking like well-used galleons, were carefully moored in the slightly deeper waters near us. As day approached there were signs of activity everywhere – children running along the road to school, men in fezzes chatting near the beach, dogs barking, older girls leading goats to fresh pasture, women gracefully walking to market with great bunches of cabbages or coconuts perfectly balanced on proud heads, fishermen heading off to sea for another day, gliding quietly out the careful channels to open water. We lingered, entranced, all day, pottering and cleaning, soaking up the strangeness and beauty of it all, and spent a second night. We didn't go ashore, and while passing fishermen waved and smiled no one came near us, though a knot of men gathered in the spreading shade of a great tamarisk, observing us well.

On the neighbouring island of Flores Cathy and I decided to make a clandestine overnight visit ashore to 'climb' Keli Motu, sacred mountain of the dead, 1,403 m above sea level: we would complete most of the ascent by local transport! A long journey in a ramshackle, bone-shaking bus was enlivened with marvellous scenery: we rose over the northern chain of mountains through lush tropical forest and past intricate rice paddies tucked into every available nook near water. Higher up, the hillsides were terraced to keep the coconut palms intact, and healthy cabbages, cos lettuce and tomatoes were tightly packed in tended fields. A rice-filled plateau stretched to the village of Mone nestling at 1,047 m under the shadow of the peak.

We quickly found a delightful losman or guest house on the

outskirts of the mountain village and for a few dollars had our-selves a tiny bamboo hut on stilts – with concrete-floored toilet and shower room attached, and minuscule verandah overlooking a paddy field. (This was my first experience of the squat toilet so favoured in eastern society – with mandi or water tub rather than the western paper dispenser – it is a good system which takes a bit of getting used to!) The air was pure, and everywhere rever-berated with the sound of rushing water. We walked past a clear waterfall where the village people, in carefully segregated sec-tions, completed their own bathing and domestic washing. Then we followed a slippery path to a small village above Mone, where a lovely young girl invited us to see her *ikat* weaving, and to share a cup of green tea. The art of weaving fine tie-dyed cotton threads into intricate shawls and sarongs is particular to Nusu Tenggara. Using natural dyes from tree bark, huge concentration and skill is required to map out designs, and then tie and dip the appropriate sections of the vertical warp which is strung on a frame before weaving through the west. An excellent sales lady, our young host-ess showed us her family's work, then introduced us to her tall mother whose teeth were rust-stained from chewing mildly nar-cotic betel leaves. We purchased some shawls for a very reason-able price – Cathy was well used to the hard bargaining which they really enjoyed!

At 4.00 next morning we were collected by an open-sided truck and deposited near the summit in darkness. As we walked faint glimmers of brightness began to lighten the night, and we could see the outline of the higher peaks all round us. By the time we reached the summit, every shade of pink and red was streak-ing the sky to the east. Below us were three lakes – the triple cal-dera left by erupting volcanoes and filled in by rains. As the light increased the waters within each changed colour in the most sub-tle way. In one grey turned to peasoup green, and then to aqua-marine, while another seemed to go from deep brown to russet red. Meanwhile the sky was becoming riotous with colour, and finally the crimson sun peeked above the sea below, reddening the ground around us. The dawn chorus of ten thousand birds commenced – first sleepily and then more loudly and clearly: a universal sound spectacular in this awe-inspiring location. We reluctantly returned on the truck to the vibrant local market and bought vegetables and fruit, before rejoining our faithful skipper.

Some nights later near Sumbawa in the Straits of Alas, we anchored off a deserted island, near a beautifully kept 16.5m Canadian ketch, and were invited to share roast beef – an offer we couldn't refuse! It was *Starfire*'s skipper's birthday, and we had last met the charming, knowledgeable couple in Darwin. Cathy and I hastily assembled a dessert and dressed in our best as befitted the occasion. We dined like kings on a feast of roast potatoes, roast pumpkin, roast carrots and roast meat! A book-swap finished a delightful evening, and promises to meet with Trish and Kaspar again in Benoa.

Next evening we found ourselves off the isolated south-eastern tip of Lombok, the island due east of Bali, where a simple Muslim fishing village was preparing itself for nightfall, glowing golden in the setting sun. There was no electricity to carry TV signals, no noisy radios, not even a generator to mar the stillness of the balmy evening – just the odd oil lamp burning in some of the mud brick thatched homes. Children laughed and chickens squawked, men gathered under a tree near the tiny mosque with tin dome, people relieved themselves discreetly on the shore below. We sat mesmerised, feeling guilty for having our own source of electric power to light up our evening, and postponed our meal until darkness fell completely. Just then we had an unexpected visit from four young men on a powerful aluminium boat – trying to give us some important message which we found hard to decipher as they had not a word of English, and we knew about two in Malay. Finally we figured out that they wanted us to move to the other side of the bay, as this was a pearl farm and we needed to be kept under surveillance! We were loath to navigate through the floating cages in the dark, but they were insistent. Next morning we had inquisitive visitors before dawn, and were soon taken ashore to meet the entire workforce of the Japanese/Indonesian concern, and to enjoy a spicy but delicious breakfast of nasi goreng (fried rice) and excellent local coffee.

On 9 October we finally reached the place that had made me decide to set sail and travel more than half the world, the legendary island of beauty and grace. Bali is a small island, 100 km square, with three million people, mainly Dharma Hindu (the rest of Indonesia is predominately Muslim). According to my guide book, religion and life are totally intertwined here, and about 20,000 temples dot the landscape, hives of activity during festivals that occur in several places on the island every day of the week. Art, dance and song are integral parts the ceremonies, and daily life is carried out under the protection of gods and spirits. This has evolved into a uniquely rich and vibrant culture. We took advantage of the arrival of Cathy's boyfriend Shailesh, leaving the lovesick pair to mind the boat while Frank and I went ashore to find out whether tourism had made negative inroads on custom and belief.

Local buses brought us to Ubud, an inland village where arts and crafts thrive, equally sought after by locals as by tourists. Here part of the former Royal Palace has been turned into a delightful hotel, by community effort and thereby not losing its soul. We found a nearby guest house where the owner offered a Balinese feast once a week – and we were lucky to have arrived on the right night. We took a simple room there in the tasteful visitors' compound, and joined a group of about eleven in the eating / cooking pavilion which was open to the temple-side of the enclosed garden, and beautifully decorated with flowers. Kutut our host then took us on a mini-tour of the compound, explaining the various requirements of strict Balinese architecture. Three generations of his family live here, each one quite secluded from the others because of the system of courtyards and upper levels. The magnificent family shrines are shared between all, as is the kitchen area – all spotlessly maintained. The garden was fragrant with bougainvillea and frangipani, and several lily ponds were home to large fish. Magnificent carved demons, gods and gargoyles, wore red hibiscus blooms fetchingly placed over their ears! Cool, welcome shade was afforded everywhere, from overhanging eaves and luxurious plantings.

The feast was quite special, graciously served by family members. We sampled two soups, two types of chicken saté, duck pâté in banana leaves, and about six or eight vegetable dishes presented in woven baskets lined with banana leaves, all with specially ground spices and seasonings. Brem (rice wine) was served together with hot tea in long glasses. Each of us felt truly like guests of the family rather than mere tourists, especially when, after delicious coffee flavoured with vanilla, Kutut reminded us gently that it was time to retire! In Bali one is up with the dawn.

Ubud is the most important centre of Balinese dancing, usually performed in a religious context. Here at the Royal pavilions serious young girls of about six, clad in brightly coloured sarongs and modern teeshirts, were being put through the ritualised paces of the Legong Keraton (Palace dance) by elder dancers in their early twenties. Full concentration is put into the stylised slow symbolic movements where facial gestures, hand positions and foot movements – very like their Thai counterparts – tell the story of princesses and gods. Not all the dances are stately like the legong – many are full of comedy and burlesque, and all tell much loved tales known from generation to generation, featuring gods and kings, demons and witches – the stuff of sacred pantomime. Music is provided by the rather cacophonous gamelan orchestra – an all-male affair with complex gangsa which is like a bronze xylophone, combined with cymbals, gongs and drums. To our ears it is clashing and not at all relaxing, but it certainly adds drama to dance and religion.

Next morning we took a series of small buses – bemos – to Bangli, situated at 400 m high. We passed through magnificent mountain vistas, and gloriously green paddy fields with all stages of cultivation from planting to harvesting to burning the stubble. Bali is internationally famous for the quality of its rice, and one can clearly see why. Only once did we see any form of mechanised equipment – and that was a tiny cultivator. Almost all is done by hand, and whole families help each other when it comes to the more difficult tasks. Gathered dried bundles are beaten on pandanus mats to shake out the grains, which are then spread on smaller mats to complete the drying process. Rice cultivation is the primary activity of the entire rural population, and it is a totally communal enterprise, as well as a religious one. Shrines dot the paddy fields, and usually an out-of-town temple will be dedicated to the harvest. In Bangli we stayed at the rather run-down palace, now a *Fawlty Towers*-type of guest house, still managed by the local prince whose fortunes are somewhat reduced. We were the only western guests apart from two young German backpackers, and were thrilled to discover that the local temple was holding its main religious festival of the year – an opportunity for us to witness an integral part of Balinese life first-hand. In the afternoon we watched the associated cockfight where lots of money was changing hands. Initially I thought it was a performance of the kecak (monkey) dance, as there were waves of monkey-sounds coming from the packed audience: several hundred men were urging on the cock of their choice to mortally wound his opponent. Luckily I was unable to see the actual slaughter, but the animated faces and swaying, oohing and aahing of the men was magnetic: like watching the reactions of TV viewers of a particularly gripping thriller. Together they surged their heads forwards or jerked them back, as the fighting got particularly rough. It was mesmerising in a brutal sort of way.

Later we visited the temple, attired in compulsory sarongs and using our Cambodian shawls as cummerbunds. The ceremonies were in full swing, and the gamelan was banging away as a large group of people knelt in prayer while a procession of women bore elaborate offerings of fruit, flowers and coloured rice cakes on their heads and placed these on the decorated altars. Tight-fitting long-sleeved lace blouses in bright yellow or cyclamen were worn over slim sarongs of vibrant silk, and bare feet glided over the warm granite of the open-air temple floor. A local teacher, resplendent in white high-collared jacket and silk sarong, invited us and our German fellow guests to partake in the rituals, and kneeling on the hard stone before the main shrines, we followed his instructions, joining our hands over our heads, and receiving a succession of different flowers and blessed rice. A shorn, white-clad priestess then came and shook blessed water on us, and three times offered us a spoonful to drink. All the time the gongs clashed loudly behind us, and incense spiralled through the evening air. We felt quite out of place, so ill-clad in our makeshift clothes amid the colour and style of the local people, but we were honoured to have been made welcome, and knew that these Balinese deities would help our progress through the long voyage ahead. I prayed sincerely for ourselves and our family so far away, wishing they could have shared some of this lavish ritual with us. We retired in a daze to our somewhat dingy though highly ornate quarters.

We returned to *Atlantic Islander* happy in the knowledge that Balinese culture was indeed alive and well. Over the next few days we sampled some of the more touristy nearby treats including a shortened performance of the famous Ramayana ballet, magnificently danced by a dedicated young troupe from Ubud, and staged in a nearby shopping mall. Cathy persuaded me to hire a car for a day and the driving was not as chaotic as I feared. We managed to attend an exotic cremation ceremony – even more colourful and intricate than the temple feast in Bangli. I longed for the opportunity to stay here for months to begin to know the place! But all too soon it was time to be on our way once more, and well stocked with the best of provisions we headed for the Gili Islands off north-western Lombok.

We had a good overnight sail and witnessed a glorious sight from dawn on as up to 200 fishing boats returned to their tiny villages under sail! It seemed just like a regatta, but this is everyday working life for thousands of Indonesian fishermen, catching mackerel for the markets. Here the boats were heavy wooden dugouts, with bamboo out-riggers bound carefully to elbowed stays. The masts are bamboo, with booms a hinged piece of bamboo permanently attached to the foot of the mast, and polyamide sail bound onto both in an elegant inverted triangle. In the evening we took a stroll ashore, and admired some boats close up at a neighbouring village. Total poverty was evident except at the mosques: over fished waters yield little harvest which must be exchanged for rice as none grows in the barren soil, though bananas and coconuts and wild taro are plentiful. The small children here were so friendly calling out multiple hellos until we were blue with answering, but the men were surly and wary. Few women were out and about – this is strictly Muslim territory, and three muezzins vied with each other electronically each morning at 4.30 praising Allah.

Next day Cathy and Shailesh left the boat to make their own tour of the area. Cathy would rejoin us briefly in Singapore before returning to Phnom Penh: she was in love and would not complete the voyage with us. So once again our numbers were reduced to the core crew of two, and we set sail on the 1,000 nm passage to Singapore. There followed eleven days of torrential rainshowers and strong winds interspersed with calms – quite trying conditions which necessitated constant sail-trimming and alert watch-keeping. We had become accustomed to the luxury of additional crew, but despite the conditions we were able to enjoy our privacy once more, and the time seemed to fly by, enlivened by all manner of sailing vessels plying the seas between some of Indonesia's 13,000 islands. Indonesia's population is 170 million people, many of them abjectly poor, and it makes huge sense to use free and abundant wind power for their trading. Here sail is so wonderfully alive and essential to the local economies. We re-crossed the equator on 21 October, and celebrated with cherry brandy at 7.00 – it was just too early for champagne!

Batam is a small island south of the Singapore Straits, a trump card in Indonesia's bid for foreign dollars, as it attracts more and more wealthy Singaporeans seeking peace and quiet. Here Cathy and Rachel joined us, and with their help we motored through the teeming harbour roads where hundreds of huge container ships, tankers, coasters and smaller craft seemed to cover every square foot of water. It demanded solid concentration to cover the mere 15 or so miles to the newly opened Raffles Marina on the south-western tip of Singapore Island, where we spent the most luxurious week of our entire passage. This was a five-star marina/yacht club, with sumptuous 'member's rooms' and spotless leisure facilities. At £22 (for four!) per night this was seriously affordable luxury. Who says yachting is so expensive? A free shuttle service to the speedy trains made the city centre near, and we shopped, dined and did the tourist with great gusto. We luxuriated nightly in the hot tub beneath the palm trees, and felt like sultan and sultanas! But all too soon it was time for the girls to leave once more, and once again we bade fond farewells.

16

MALAYSIA TO PHUKET

On 16 November we headed into the busy, dirty Malacca Straits, a vital shipping corridor carrying international cargoes into and out of Singapore, where scores of local Indonesian/Malay transport crisscross back and forth between Sumatra and Malaysia. Having lost contact with all the other boats we knew, we decided to navigate the straits in daylight only, as the sheer density of shipping combined with the number of bamboo fishing traps make night-time sailing hazardous in the extreme. The traps are ingeniously set into the relatively shallow waters so that shoals of fish are carried by the current into a narrowing funnel, and onwards to a wider enclosed area from which they cannot escape. The fishermen can then take them in nets at their ease.

Slowly and carefully we worked our way up to the lovely *Besar* ('Water') Islands, an ideal anchoring point for visits to fabled Malacca. Here we met an Australian couple who gave us valuable information on how to get to the mainland. As we were anchored at a resort island with good ferry service to bring local staff back and forth, and a 'tourist service' run by enterprising boat owners who would take anyone *any*where, *at a price*, we learned it would save us a lot to take the regular 'native' boat. Armed with the facts we were ready for the next morning's ferry, a heavily-built open wooden longboat with beaten tin roof to keep the occupants dry. The wizened driver was more than pleased to be paid in dollars as we had no local currency, not yet having officially entered Malaysia, nor been to a bank. As there was no pier on the island for the boats to tie up to, clever manoeuvring brought the high pointed bow onto the beach, and a long plank was leaned against it, and with help from the shore-based assistant we were soon aboard with the returning night-staff from the hotel. We travelled at at least 14 knots, blowing out great bursts of filthy exhaust, to try to keep ahead of a rival boat laden with tourists! As we approached the mainland, long banks of mud dotted with mangroves stretched out towards us, and we were soon in a river estuary with about twenty makeshift wooden jetties providing handy exit points for similar boats – obviously destined for other points in the islands, up river, and along the coast.

In Malacca we were able to sample all the colours of a poly-glot society, from the former Dutch Christian area of the city, prettified for the tourist, across the nineteenth century docks where Malay labourers still unload sailing cargo boats by hand, into the teeming, cacophonous, Chinese quarter, where sweating black-smiths hammer out iron nails in intense heat, while noodle sellers ply their steaming goods from bicycles, and packed antique shops rub shoulders with gaudy coffin-makers whose range of paper effigies of everyday things to be burnt with the dead hang from dusty ceilings. Mosques, temples and churches share neighbouring plots, and here at least all creeds seem to be working together in harmony. We visited one of the beautifully preserved Chinese shop houses, owned by a millionaire rubber planter at the end of the last century, Baba Nyonya Heritage House, which has a delightful display of furniture and costumes of the period, and puts on an excellent guided tour. The Baba Nyonya were descendants of the Straits Chinese who married Malaysian brides, and developed a unique culture well documented in the museum.

We took a short cruise up the Malacca River, with an enthusiastic, colourful guide whose English, unfortunately, was practically impossible to understand. Ugly iguanas slunk up the muddy river banks, and city dwellers lived practically on the water, with tottering wooden houses built on sticks, Indonesian-style. Beyond these the new suburbs rose in inelegant concrete – certainly more impervious to the frequent rain, but lacking all character. We motored past temples and gardens as the river crawled northwards in tortuous loops, under pedestrian bridges and impossibly choked roads: Malacca is Malaysia's second busiest tourist destination, mostly seen by day-trippers in big air-conditioned coaches, and its eighteenth century road systems are totally unable to cope with this diesel-laden daily influx.

A carved wooden head in an antique shop window took my breath away. I am not a collector, and to date had bought nothing more than the vibrant mola lovingly stitched by the San Blas Indians in Panama, an ikat shawl from Flores, and a few baskets in Lombok and Bali. There was something special about this wooden carving, but we returned to the boat without it. That night in bed I regretted not having bought it, and next day I went back alone to find out some more about the figurine, visiting both main museums and learning little. One of these is in a 300-year-old Dutch home, while the other is in a beautifully reconstructed fifteenth century palace of the Sultan of Malacca, made entirely of teak without a single nail. Excellent dioramas depicted courtly life of the time, and there was a wealth of costumes and elaborated headdress, but none like that of my warrior. I felt he was more Indonesian than Malay, and he still called out to me. So I found again the crowded antique shop, talked the pleasant Chinese assistant down to half her original asking price, and for $25 brought my warrior prince back on board *Atlantic Islander* where he was carefully wrapped in unused mosquito netting – a talisman who would find a special niche in the house we would build on returning to Ireland. With him we carried some of the magic of this historic city where Chinese, Malay, Indian and European have mingled and mixed, fought and died over the past 400 years.

Two days later we reached the bustling container port at Port Kelang, gateway to Kuala Lumpur. When the harbour at Malacca became silted up in the last century, most commercial shipping moved to Singapore, and goods were transported by land into Malaysia. It obviously makes sound economic sense for the Malays to have their own major port, and this is rapidly going ahead with state-of-the-art facilities for commercial and pleasure traffic. Here we finally cleared into the country – by now we had become far more *blasé* about going ashore 'illegally' – and sampled the comforts of the delightful Royal Selangor Yacht Club, founded by the local sailing prince, the Raja Muda. We just missed the start of the annual Raja Muda Cup, which comprised a week's racing up the coast to the duty-free island of Langkawi: we had initially been interested in taking part, with many of the Trade Winds Cruising Rally group, but then decided that it would be too much of a rush, with a hectic program of races and social events, so we were now free to enjoy the excellent club facilities at our ease without a carnival atmosphere. Delicious food (meals for £1.50 – but beer the same price!) was served in an airy, open-sided dining and lounge areas, and a good pool, friendly staff, and easy train access to bustling modern Kuala Lumpur made this an ideal place to linger, while the twenty-four-hour free ferry service made commuting to one's boat so much easier in the river's fast seven-knot current.

Our guide books lavishly praised the great, wild Taman Negara National Park, comprising over 4,000 square miles of undisturbed 130-million-year-old tropical rain forest, and this seemed our ideal opportunity to take a few treks there. We made enquiries on an initial visit to Kuala Lumpur, and decided that two nights away would just about allow us a tiny glimpse of this unique place. We arranged for Roger to keep an eye on *Atlantic Islander*, and set off on a series of train and bus-rides, and an overnight at a convenient town where we stayed for the first time in one of the excellent Chinese hotels which are a spotless alternative to expensive western ones and a huge step above local-style cheap accommodation. For £11 we had a squeaky-clean bedroom with en suite shower and toilet, and delightful hosts who insisted on driving us to our connecting bus next morning. A half-hour's ride brought us to the river station from where supply boats plied a two- to three-hour journey twice daily to the National Park headquarters upstream.

This time our craft was a 12-metre, narrow hardwood boat into which we carefully sidled to sit on rugs on the flat bottom, one behind the other, with wide planks set vertically across the interior acting as comfortable back rests. The bow was loaded with goods and supplies, and we were low in the boat, helping the essential balance as we negotiated an endless series of rapids against the fast-flowing current. The engine was a 70hp outboard, skilfully manoeuvred by our able boatman, and we had an exhilarating, if bone-shattering ride, meeting several boats laden with local river-side dwellers – Orang Asli – going to market with their wares. Sometimes we passed people bathing in the river, or poling by on simply constructed bamboo rafts – an extremely difficult task in the fast-flowing waters. Lush tropical forest towered over us on both sides of the broad, rushing river, and kingfishers darted flashes of gold and aquamarine. Occasionally we glimpsed monkeys in the trees – and nowhere was there a building in view – this was virgin territory, disturbed only by the whine of our outboard motor.

As it was the beginning of the wet season, when in former years the park would be closed to visitors, there were few people about, and we were able to negotiate a price on a spacious riverside bungalow – with a *real* bath: the first we had seen since Australia months before! Cheaper accommodation across the river was too dirty for us to consider, and here we were in relative splendour for £30 – well worth every penny, as we were actually

159

within the park with listed trails on our doorstep, in a beautiful jungle setting. Humidity was about 95%, and the temperature in the lower thirties, which sapped a lot of our energy, and we were thankful for shade beneath the magnificent rain-forest's giant hardwood trees. Recent heavy rains had made the tracks slippery and we negotiated with some difficulty – we were not properly shod and when I found leeches between my sandalled toes I was ready to go home. Thoughts of *African Queen* came immediately to mind, and Frank pulled off the horrible, slimy creatures: *why* hadn't I worn socks? Tired and frustrated at my own stupidity we slumped by the river and watched two sensibly-clad trekkers throw off their heavy socks and boots, and outer clothes, and plunge in their underwear into the strong flow. We envied them their youth and common sense, and resolved to swim here tomorrow, having walked better prepared.

Exhausted, we sank into clean twin beds at 18.00 – to have a short rest before dinner. We didn't wake until dawn! After breakfast we tackled the marvellous canopy walkway, an ingenious series of rope bridges suspended between the tallest trees. The base is strengthened with long hardwood planks laid on linked aluminium ladders and provides a sturdy if shaky walking surface, with strong rope handholds a bit above waist height – the whole contraption sheathed in cotton fishing net for extra security. One climbs to a height of about 200 feet on a sturdy stairs build around the initial tree, then slowly and swayingly works one's way from tree to tree at the canopy level, with good views of monkeys above, and all the plant and animal life below. It is humbling to think that this ecosystem has been in existence for 300 million years – while self-important mankind has been here for a paltry 150 thousand or so.

The river pool was delightfully cool and refreshing, despite the lack of clarity, and unbelievably fast-moving. We caught the afternoon ferry and bolted downstream in half the time it took to arrive. Eight hours later we were safely back aboard *Atlantic Islander*. A day later we were heading north again, with Langkawi our destination. We met a lot of strong headwinds – ideal for those returning southwards from the Raja Muda Race! – and were forced to shelter in Lumut where the Malaysian navy have a big dockyard. Later we tucked ourselves into the southern part of famed Panang Island, but had no time to explore this delightful place, an excellent airline connection spot, with temptingly cheap flights to many Asian capitals.

In five days we were at the extreme northern outpost of Malaysia, off the south-western Thai coast. The Langkawi Group consists of 99 islands, the main one being beautiful Langkawi, mountainous and highly indented, with the free-port of Kuah an attraction to visitors, local and foreign. After a tough sail we slipped gratefully into one of the most beautiful anchorages in the world, a tiny sheltered bay with towering tree-clad mountains on three sides, and calm green water beneath. It was so lovely that we stayed for two nights, just soaking up the beauty, and gave away our somewhat jaded offshore jackets to a pair of fishermen who spent many hours of darkness in a tiny boat in the pouring rain with nothing to keep off the rain. They were thrilled, and no doubt the envy of their neighbours when they returned, fish-less, to their village. As often as we could we gave useful bits and pieces to fishermen and other boat people along the way – but never cash as we did not want to encourage a begging mentality, the last thing any poor country needs.

Kuah itself had been drunk dry by the recent visit of the Trade Winds Cruising Rally, and we could find no more than a single box of Australian wine to carry us to the Mediterranean – though we knew that Djibouti would have good alcohol supplies. (Yes, believe it or not the 40 litres of Brown Brothers Red given us four months ago by my brother John had run out – quite a few litres lost through a punctured inner sack which had sadly flowed into the bilges unnoticed.) We did, though, manage to replace my camera with a very competitively priced instamatic, which made the visit more than worthwhile, and once again we loaded up with cheap diesel and provisions.

Two day-sails brought us to southern Phuket, where we spent two nights at a friendly, family-run 'marina' – actually a collection of buoyed moorings, to complete immigration procedures and get the lie of the land, before moving to Phuket Boat Lagoon, a stylish marina development built in the middle of nowhere, where a narrow channel had been dug through the dense mangrove swamps and shallow bay to enable keeled boats to enter – but *only* on the top of the tide.

We quickly teamed up with resident boats, and learnt the tips on where to eat, how to get into town, where to buy what, etc., etc.

161

– the invaluable supply of information that is readily shared and passed on from boat to boat. Better still, our immediate neighbours, a German couple in their fifties, had just sailed *down* the Red Sea and had the answers to so many questions from all those about to sail *up* that they decided to present their information at an informal gathering in the yacht club hotel. From that we gleaned all sorts of useful tips and advice which stood us in good stead a few months later. We cleaned and cleared, and prepared our little aft cabin for my uncle's arrival. A celebrated architect in his late seventies, he had spent much of the last 15 years helping down-and-out drug addicts in Calcutta – initially with Mother Teresa – despite a plastic hip and sometimes dodgy pacemaker, and had been thrilled to escape his misnamed *City of Joy* to join us here.

There followed a magical ten days of glorious cruising in what was certainly the most stunningly beautiful area of the voyage! Phangnga Bay was made world famous in the James Bond movie, *The Man with the Golden Gun*, but the number of cruising yachts here is still small. There is an abundance of sheltered anchorages, tucked under spectacular, overhanging limestone outcrops, many hundreds of feet high, with lush vegetation clinging to ledges and nooks, and powder white sands shelving gently into warm aquamarine water. Visiting a new spot each day we would generally drop anchor around four, allowing time for a leisurely swim and sunbathe before the evening sundowner on deck as we listened entranced to stories from Andy's rich and colourful life.

Reluctantly we returned to the marina on Christmas Eve, to be near telephones and religious services, for communication with home and heaven at the festive time. On Christmas Day we shared a lunch spot with one of our screen heroes, Peter Ustinov. A day later we bade Andy a tearful farewell at Phuket's small airport, greatly enriched by his visit, but unsure when we would see him again.

17

TOWARDS THE PEARL:
Indian Ocean and Sri Lanka to Maldives

Forfeiting the lauded wonders of New Year's Eve revelries in Patong Bay, when upwards of 200 yachts gather together to celebrate a fireworks display put on by the tourist-thronged resort (a hideous eyesore of jerrybuilt high-rise apartment and hotel blocks and endless seedy bars and discotheques), we set sail on 30 December for the 1,190 nm passage to Sri Lanka. At last we were getting back into the trades, with winds of 11 to 14 knots on our tail, and big seas giving us that annoying down-wind roll. It was almost impossible to do any exercises on deck, as a hand was needed always to steady oneself, and even deck showers were trickier than normal. But we certainly weren't going to complain at having the wind astern, and Brendan the wind-vane did a perfect job of steering for all of the 11-day passage, keeping well clear of the Nicobar Islands where remote tribal people are protected/isolated by the Indian government. One of the Trade Winds boats foolishly visited here and was detained for several days by the army.

It was early morning on 10 January when we approached Galle Harbour, in southernmost Sri Lanka. We had had only three changes of sail in the entire passage from Phuket! Because of a state of war with northern Tamil Tigers, there are severe restrictions to free passage in the country, and as we were entering a military zone, we were obliged to endure endless visits from various sections of the police and army, many of them looking for 'gifts', and to hours of paperwork 'facilitated' by a local agent. All thirty-eight relatively wealthy rally boats had arrived, and with them heightened expectations of gain among the locals: we were thus all looked on as golden geese with limitless funds for local entrepreneurs to tap. This was the first time since Panama that we had felt used (apart from the bond saga in Polynesia) and it left a nasty taste in our mouths. However, once over the morning's officialdom, we were free to roam ashore and leave the heavily guarded confines of the port area. A local hotelier had erected a temporary tour office for the benefit of the rally group, and had wisely hung magnificent posters of the inland sights which Sri Lanka had to offer – we were bowled over by the drama and beauty of the island's man-made and natural attractions, and decided there and then to treat ourselves to at least three nights ashore, on tour. On the voyage from Phuket I had read up a little on the country, and learnt that it was about the size of Ireland with a population of seventeen million, chiefly Sinhalese Buddhists, and that the Hindu Tamils formed roughly two minority groups: those who had come from India hundreds of years ago and were mainly in the north, whose armed wing were the Tamil Tigers, and those primarily of lower caste who had been imported to the tea, rubber and coffee plantations a century ago. These were not involved in the present struggle. A small Muslim sector are involved in commerce, while much of the political and business life is dominated by Burghers – people of Dutch or Portuguese ancestry – who are in general mistrusted by the Sinhalese.

Galle itself is an historic town, very much in Portuguese style, with commanding seventeenth century ramparts still intact, and sturdy colonial buildings losing their former glory as successive layers of paint peel under the relentless sun. A walk here was best at sunset, rather than in the searing heat of midday, so we limited our exploring to the sweet-smelling bakeries, bought bread and eggs and fruit and vegetables, and caught a tiny three-wheeled tuk-tuk taxi back to the port area – it was too hot and dangerous on the road to walk the short half mile.

As always it was wonderful to catch up with friends among the rally group, and among the 'independent' boats, and the rest of the day was spent hearing each other's news and sharing the latest yottie gossip. A nearby 'colonial' hotel acted as contact point for faxes, and mail-drop, and though we were disappointed at getting no letters we were able to receive a phone call from home, and catch up with all the family news.

The best thing about reaching harbour after a long passage is the promise of a full night's sleep. Just as we were nodding off a loud explosion shook the bow of the boat. We feared that the Tamil Tigers must have infiltrated the port area, and were firing at boats indiscriminately, but as there didn't seem to be any sense of panic about, and one solitary patrol boat was calmly plying back and forth between all the visiting yachts, we tried to relax and get back to sleep. This proved impossible as the blasts recurred every hour. Next morning we learnt that the small naval launch drops depth charges every night to discourage saboteur divers: we would just have to get used to sleeping through them!

Once again Rachel was able to join us, this time with a friend. When they had been issued with crew passes by the authorities, we organised a marvellous four-day tour of the island, which sadly coincided with another bout of dengue fever for Frank. Highlights included the National Park at Yala, where we saw families of elephant take dust baths and water buffalo snoozing in muddy ponds. In the celebrated tea-growing area around the former capital, Kandy, terrace upon terrace of immaculately tended, rich green bushes rose up the sides of steep mountains, with rushing streams and waterfalls all around. Splashes of vermilion, orange, scarlet and purple hinted at the brilliant saris worn by the mainly Tamil tea-pickers who are an essential part of this almost totally hand-produced industry.

In Kandy itself we stayed at a B&B run by a former mayor of the city who had spent many years in London and was a gracious host. From the balcony there was a spectacular view over the town and the lake, and the famous temple where Buddha's tooth is revered by Buddhists and Hindus from all over India and Sri Lanka. The optimum time to come here is during the full moon in July/August when thousands of dancers and fifty to sixty caparisoned elephants parade through the streets of the town, as the reliquary of the tooth is displayed to assembled devotees. While Frank rested we girls visited the temple in time for the evening service – or puja – when the sanctuary was briefly opened so the faithful could pass it with a prayer, amid the booming of gongs and the blowing of horns. Ceremonies here are performed with noise, colour, and clamour – all the senses are affected! It seems so different from our quiet, restrained services back home!

Kandy to Sigiriya via Dambulla is a journey of about 120 km, but on roads reminiscent of the outer reaches of Connemara in the 1950s, this journey took us all of a day to complete – with a few memorable stops. Frank was still quite unwell, but managed to doze in the minibus, despite the jolts and bumps, horn blowing, wheel screeching and sudden braking. The first-century BC cave-temple at Dambulla entailed quite a climb in searing sunshine, and Frank remained in the relative shade of the bus, while we were enthralled at the 150 magnificently carved and painted Buddahs decorating all five chambers near the top of a huge mound reminiscent of Ayers Rock.

Standing 183 metres above the surrounding plain, the nearby vast ochre monolith of Sigiriya was favoured in 480 AD by a local prince as a fortress site on which to build a summer palace. He is reputed to have walled up his father alive, and was being hunted by his half-brother, so needed a deal of security – but the story goes that having built a magnificent home on the top, with fresh water pumped to a huge hollowed tank from the plains below, he foolishly descended to attack the righteous half-brother, and was drowned in one of the artificial lakes below when his elephant took a wrong path.

We stayed near the base at a luxurious hotel, to give Frank a chance of a good, air-conditioned night's sleep, and next morning the ladies headed off early on foot (our driver had slept in for the second morning in a row!). The hotel manager was reluctant to let us go unescorted, but time was of the essence, and we managed the early stages of the climb without problem. The final part is along an almost vertical slope of rock – about 60 metres high – via narrow groves cut out of the face. Luckily there are iron bars and railings set into the stone to steady one, but signs of rust everywhere tend to diminish one's trust in the system, and we sincerely hoped we wouldn't have to descend by the same route!

The scene at the top made every moment of the climb worthwhile! Here 1.6 hectares of brick and stone foundations indicate the vast size and strength of this wet-season palace, and a huge rock-hewn pool (27m x 21m) collected enough rain water to keep all the palace needs well supplied. And what a view there was over the flat plains below, and the water gardens at the foot of the rock. We could see the swimming pool of our hotel, not half as fine as the luxuries evident here 1,400 years ago! We sat and gazed in amazement, and presumed that neither prince nor nobles would have had to ascend as we had done, but were hauled up by basket – an early form of elevator which would also have served to move supplies and animals to the summit.

By now the tour crowds were beginning to build up and we were glad we had had the early start. Our subdued driver, Sanjo, came to meet us, and whisked us back for a welcome breakfast. Frank was feeling somewhat better, and we were soon underway – at breakneck speed – for the longish journey back to Galle, with a stop in Colombo for western goodies at a luxury supermarket.

We reckoned Sanjo must have had a date back home, because his driving became more and more reckless on the busy main road between the capital and the south, and we were barely allowed time for a very necessary pit-stop en route. Sri Lankan roads are really like few other, as they are notoriously badly paved, narrow, and used by pedestrians, sacred cows, goats, cyclists carrying several passengers or huge, precariously balanced loads, ox-carts, donkeys, three-wheeled taxis, ancient filthy lorries spewing diesel fumes, ramshackle buses heavily overladen, and the occasional car or minivan used by government people or tourists. Motorists drive on their horns, totally insensitive to the needs of all other road users, and seem to relish close encounters with oncoming vehicles and pedestrians. Even the calmest western passenger finds difficulty in sitting in the front seat, wondering when a crash will take place, and we continued to rotate seats!

Road repair work is carried out in the main by women or children – we watched big groups on the roadside break stones to gravel size pieces in the searing sun, wearing wide straw hats and cotton scarves to eliminate some of the dust and fumes. Workers' babies are often laid under trees nearby, and fed when they cry or comforted by older sisters. In the wet season bridges are often swept away and alternative crossings have to be made using gabion walls. Everything is done by hand, and takes forever. We were saddened by the extreme poverty we saw everywhere, and were once again struck by our privileged position of wealth and mobility, and conscious of the universal need to seek just solutions to world want.

Uneased by the injustices ashore, it was time to escape once more to the realms of the deep. We provisioned on excellent fruit and vegetables, tea and sugar, eggs and bread, milk and cheese, and a few tins of inferior corned beef. We tried to buy locally grown produce, shunning luxury foreign goods except for what we considered essentials like butter or tinned meat. At least in that way we were contributing to the wider local community, while keeping within our budget. We knew that we paid more for goods than the locals did, but in this case we hoped that the shopkeeper might pass on some of his easily won surplus.

Our next voyage – the second in the Indian Ocean – took us south-westwards to the Maldives, worlds apart from Sri Lanka. We were eager to leave the dirt and oppressiveness of Galle harbour, and with crew of four, happily took our leave on 23 January for an easy 5-day passage to Malé, capital of this Muslim republic which has a very pragmatic approach to tourism. Most yachts en route to the Red Sea visit the northern part of the archipelago of 1,000 islands, thus avoiding paying agents' fees and making official entry declarations. But as Rachel and Audrey were to fly back from here, it was essential to have them enter legally with passports duly stamped. At US$100 is was one of the most expensive entry/exit payments we had to make, and that did not include a cruising permit, but at least we had legitimised ourselves and once again helped the local economy! In compensation the price of diesel turned out to be 25 US cents per litre – delivered to the boat! Malé itself was spotless, tout-free (what a luxury this after Sri Lanka!), and excellent for provisions, particularly fish. The local boats are like wide, shallow Viking long ships, with glorious curved prows and swan-necked tillers. They are called *dhonies*, and are used for cargo and fishing, as well as passenger ferries to all the seventy-odd tourist islands. A huge effort is made here to keep tourism and local culture totally apart, and it is very difficult to get permission to visit any of the non-tourist islands. The people are exceptionally nice, though it is mainly Sri-Lankans who work on the resort islands. The picture-postcard aquamarine against ultramarine surrounds every little motu, and Malé itself is just a denuded, extended motu, about five miles from the airport which is built right onto the reef, where arriving planes seem to land directly onto the ocean!

The girls left us to spend a few days at a dive-hotel while we took a brief overnight near an atoll resort with excellent snorkelling. We were once more back to the crew of two, faced with a passage to Aden of 1,800 nautical miles, and then a slog of 1,200 miles into the wind in the Red Sea. I confess I was very tempted to stay with the Trades and continue to the Cape of Good Hope – but we didn't have charts and it would have been folly without them. There were a few moody days, when small rows grew out of all proportion, but we stuck to the old adage and never let the sun go down on our anger. Living in such close proximity for nineteen days with nowhere to escape to, and suffering from very heavy periods and resulting PMT, I was sometimes inclined to illogical and cruel outbursts, which I always subsequently regretted.

I discovered weevils in the flour and rice, and had to jettison several pounds of both overboard: that did not improve my mood. But soon we caught excellent tail winds once more, and I began finally to start the knitting which I had promised myself for months. I had had a great scheme to knit tiny Aran cardigans as baby gifts – possibly to sell among other yotties. It was only months later that we learnt that at exactly round this time Cathy had become pregnant, and this initial effort thus went to our first granddaughter!

I caught up with my writing, Frank with his reading, especially preparations for the Red Sea, and we thankfully suffered no damage other than one burnt bottom (mine!). Surprisingly soon the nineteen days had passed, and we were nearing the rocky desert shores of Yemen. We had travelled from lush tropical mountains to coral atolls, and were now facing the great arid vastness of the Middle East. The Indian Ocean was successfully behind us, and Europe was almost in sight. I longed now for the calm, soothing green of Ireland, for people and things beloved and familiar: it was time for going home.

18

Unexpected Adventure – the Red Sea

Aden, our ninety-sixth port of call, was recovering from the strains of war. Most of the buildings were pierced with bullet holes and many were in ruins. Behind the straggling town rose steep, arid mountains, and we could make out bands of long-eared brown goats running freely through the streets, and women clad from head to toe in flowing black robes – with just a slit for their eyes. The men were less uniform – some in white robes, some in partial western garb. A dozen yachts lay at anchor, and many of their names were familiar through radio contacts over the preceding days.

Our initial impression of the place was soon softened by the warm welcome given us by the port authorities, who seemed genuinely glad to see us, and later by Omar, the recommended taxi-driver, who gave us a free tour of the city, pointing out the several mosques and a Christian church (now secularised). I was anxious to find the post office, as we were expecting a packet from Rachel, containing essential batteries for our main GPS which had given up the ghost shortly after Singapore. We had been unable to find replacements anywhere. But there was nothing for us, and we hoped they would arrive in the next few days as they would be vital should our back-up fail.

We were surprised at the number of men with bright red hair, and Omar explained that it was the custom to use henna. He pointed out great piles of it for sale in the market, together with *Qat* – the local opiate. He was a great believer in the second substance. He brought us to the neighbouring town where we visited the Egyptian embassy to secure visas (advisable *before* entering the country), and then to a westernised supermarket run by friends of his. It was close to 13.00, and having made our luxury purchases, we were invited to join the owners and Omar for lunch. In a trice a tablecloth was spread on the spotless marble floor of the shop, and customers stepped carefully by! Our hosts spread out a delicious array of roast chicken legs, spicy pink rice, cold chips-and-tomato mixture, and rich ratatouille with lots of aubergines, as well as rotis and salad. No one seemed the slightest bit surprised

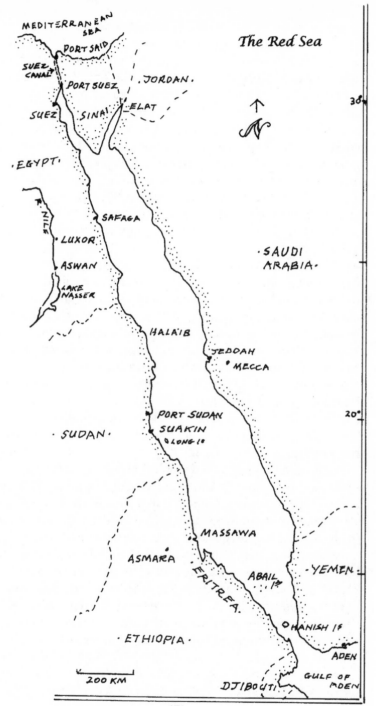

The Red Sea

MEDITERRANEAN SEA
PORT SAID
SUEZ CANAL
PORT SUEZ
JORDAN
SUEZ
SINAI
ELAT
38
EGYPT
N
R. NILE
SAFAGA
LUXOR
ASWAN
LAKE NASSER
SAUDI ARABIA
HALAIB
JEDDAH
MECCA
20°
PORT SUDAN
SUAKIN
LONG I°
SUDAN
MASSAWA
ASMARA
ABAIL I°
YEMEN
ERITREA
ETHIOPIA
HANISH I°
ADEN
GULF OF ADEN
200 KM
DJIBOUTI

to see us all eating in the midst of the shoppers! I was very anxious lest I offend by hand or foot – we were now firmly in Muslim territory, where hands are strictly segregated for personal hygiene and food: only the right hand may be used for eating and cutlery is not employed. However our hosts *did* seem to use both hands when tearing bits off the rotis – so all I had to bother about was not pointing my cramped feet at anyone – another no-no! It was awkward for those not used to eating on the ground – but it was worth every bit of bother to be exposed to such hospitality and spontaneity – the warmest we had received *anywhere*. None of the banks would advance cash against our credit card, but Omar found a local hotel clerk who was happy to facilitate us to the tune of $250, which thankfully covered the cost of our visas, cheaper here than in Egypt itself.

I had made a vow to socialise as much as possible in Aden, as it was weeks since we had spoken to another person face to face, and we needed to widen our circle of friends. We invited people aboard for drinks, for morning coffees and finally for a never-to-be-forgotten dinner! Local butchers were displaying marvellous legs of lamb in the town market, and huge sheaves of mint and excellent vegetables – a miracle in this barren outpost – were also available, so I invited four people from nearby boats to join us for dinner. John had received a very early redundancy from the British army, and had soloed his 26-foot Halcyon *Violetta* as far as New Zealand. Since Australia he had been joined by Fred, a quiet-spoken American who had worked in Guam, and was looking for a boat of his own. Richard and Jacqui, a delightful British couple in their late twenties, were sailing back to England from Australia, where they had worked for several years to buy their boat, *September Ripple*. They would continue the circumnavigation after a year or two back in Blighty. I set to with gusto to make mint jelly to accompany the roast joint, then went to buy the lamb. Before I could protest the butcher hacked a lovely leg into several pieces with a huge cleaver. That should have been a warning! The resultant 'roast' was as tough as boot leather, and had to be chewed and chewed – obviously it should have been boiled! Our guests were more than understanding, and the famous roast lamb became quite a joke.

Our next rendez-vous was in Cyprus with Rachel and David, so we could not linger in Aden. Reluctantly we had to leave without our GPS batteries, but one of the Trade Winds boats promised to collect anything that arrived for us, as they were remaining a few days longer. Our topsides were filthy from an oil spill that had occurred the day before we arrived, so we followed *Violetta* and *September Ripple* to a beautifully clean anchorage about 15 miles west, where we were able to swim and scrub the boats for a day or two, bringing them back to reasonable cleanliness. We were all nervous of what lay ahead, and had agreed to remain in a group of three. We were so pleased to have the cheerful company of competent young people, who reminded us of our own family back home, and they were probably glad to have parent substitutes near at hand, whom they could advise! As events unfolded, we were the ones who benefited most from their friendship.

When we could find no further excuse to delay longer in this peaceful anchorage, we left together on 26 February, heading directly for the southern entrance to the Red Sea. We had discussed the best options for passage-making, and knew that the first few hundred miles would have to be completed in a single passage as there was no suitable shelter en route. The Perim Islands at the southern end of the Red Sea were out of bounds, and many others further up were in a state of war as neighbouring countries claimed them. All African borders were no-go areas, and Saudi Arabia in principle was less than friendly towards yachts. The centre channel was overcrowded with commercial shipping, and therefore dangerous to navigate, and the reefs off the western shores were tortuous and potentially lethal. However, our endeavours were made easier by Stephen Davies and Elaine Morgan's excellent pilot book completed when they cruised the Red Sea in 1993. This was everyone's bible, and was referred to every day on the local amateur radio net, the *SiOui*, ably run by Tina Olton, which proved invaluable to us as it gave daily weather reports from boats further north, as well as up-to-the-minute comments on the safety of anchorages, navigational dangers, current political attitudes towards yachts, and help services among participating yotties.

Safely through the Bab al Mendeb Straits before darkness fell, we were now in the Sea of Dread. The winds were predictably from the north, and we had a hard time tacking back and forth. My laptop's transformer died just out of Aden, and from then on I had to keep all notes by hand. Our main GPS was out of commission and should anything happen to the back-up we were really in deep trouble. But, thankfully, we had a group of fine competent friends sailing the same area, and both our radios were working well. Just before reaching Aden we had spoken on VHF with a French ship some 105 miles away! (Normally the maximum range is 30 miles.) We reached our first anchorage off Southern Eritrea – the Abail Islands – on the last day of February, in good time to negotiate a tricky passage through the reef. Already there were the *Ripple* and *Violetta*. Later we were joined by *Alb* and *Hilda*.

Next morning the winds began to pick up, but I was really eager to step onto African soil. All around us was rock and sand, and the mainland stretched into mountainous desert, layered shades of ochre and grey. I donned my plastic sandals and swam into a narrow rocky beach on the nearest island. The volcanic rock was sharp and inhospitable, and a great number of sea eagles clearly resented my presence, swooping threateningly overhead! I beat a hasty retreat back to the boat, and none too soon, as our companions were in the process of hauling anchor and getting away before being dashed onto a lee shore – the wind had swung right around and the island no longer offered shelter. With 25–35 knots we sped up the inside channel, helping Brendan the windvane by hand steering as he wasn't inclined to keep direction. Loath to waste a following wind, we headed for Eritrea's entry port, Massawa. Two days later we arrived, and found the town heavily shelled in the recent war for Eritrean independence. Former emperor Haile Selassie had had a fine summer palace here, where he was kept under house arrest until his death in 1975. On a direct ferry line to Jeddah, the port for Mecca, Massawa has always been an important departure point for Muslims making the *haj* or pilgrimage to Islam's holiest shrine.

Situated round a wide, deep bay, the town was one of the loveliest we had seen, despite the ravages of war. None of the buildings were higher than two storeys, and were nearly all built of mud bricks. Desert sand had blown onto all the streets, and the waterfront bars and coffee houses had wide verandahs where white-robed men discussed the latest politics: many had crude Coptic crosses incised onto their foreheads. Extremely tall, slender women pluck the front of their scalps to elongate beautiful features. It is said that the legendary Queen of Sheba came from this region, though she may have been Yemeni. Having passed from Turks to Egyptians to Italians in the past 400 years, Massawa has had a bewildering history, but remains mainly Christian, and Italian is still widely spoken. People were friendly and cheerful, despite decades of war and deprivation. The market was not highly stocked, but had good fruit and vegetables. And to see the shape of women again after the over-clothing of Aden was indeed a pleasure.

We arranged for a small minibus with driver to take a trip to Asmara, Eritrea's capital. Up until quite recently an Italian-built railway carried passengers on a tortuous journey through the coastal mountain chains – but this engineering marvel had been completely torn up in the 1990 war, and now local buses make the 120 km journey in somewhat over four hours – too long for a day trip. Jacqui made all the arrangements for a group of nine of us to visit the city in comparative luxury. Later that evening she called us on radio and reminded us to bring our bathing suits as we were to visit a lake. It seemed just too good to be true – surrounded as we were by desert sands and rocky mountains, and I began to dream of a pine-clad hillside with cool inviting *fresh* water beneath!

We were underway by 7.30, travelling west along the single-lane paved road which passes through the barren coastal plains dotted with the striped tents of nomadic sheep-herders. Huge road-gangs were rebuilding sections of roadway that had been destroyed in the war. Many of the men wore army fatigues, and some carried rifles and automatics – we felt quite ill at ease lest some skirmish might occur. Our guide was a boy of about twelve who had quite good English. His father had been killed in the rebellion, and he was now working for our driver, his uncle, and sending money back to his mother in Ethiopia. He seemed extremely street-wise for his age, and won our hearts. Soon we were rising into the mountain chain on a series of switch-back roads, and everything suddenly became green and lush – something that really surprised me as I felt it would be even more barren here. Abundant rain causes the rich volcanic soil to produce frequent crops, and several large towns looked really prosperous. Below us snaked the defunct rail line, burrowing through mountain folds and emerging into wide valleys.

Asmara itself was a complete culture shock! Italianate and thriving, it had been spared the ravages of war, and seemed totally cosmopolitan and unrelated to Massawa. The covered market took up about two acres in the city centre. Fresh produce remained the domain of women traders, who were very amused at Frank buying vegetables – this was surely women's work! The general section had a vast array of empty tin cans, plastic bottles, pieces of rope, baskets, harness, terracotta jars and pots, and the ubiquitous novelties section with drums, fly swats, colourful crafts and hair ornaments. In the same area were streets devoted to single trades – bazaar style – with tailors near cloth-sellers, upholsters near furniture-makers, and bicycle-repairers near tyre merchants on the perimeter. Donkeys and carts carried the heavier loads, and bicycles were abundant. In contrast, the main street boasted western-style bookshops, clothes shops, shoe shops and printers, and several banks and government departments housed in magnificent colonial buildings, guarded by smartly dressed military personnel. Churches were in prominent positions, and we met an Irish nun who had been teaching in Ethiopia for 30 years, but never lost her midlands accent. It was difficult to imagine that this city had so recently seen two countries torn apart by wars and famines – and as I write, sad history is repeating itself.

We had wondered at what stage of the day our lake-swim would be introduced, and after lunch put the question to our young guide. There seemed to be some difficulty between him and his uncle, and the bus went whizzing off around the city – strange to find a lake here, we thought. Finally we ended up at the tiny, none-too-clean indoor municipal pool, but none of us felt like swimming. The translation of *pool* as *lake* had to make us laugh! At least we had extra shopping time!

Next day we fuelled up – by borrowed jerrycan as usual, and were soon away. We were now quite close to disputed border regions between northern Eritrea and southern Sudan, and were very careful to stay well offshore so as not to offend anyone. We decided to go as far north as we could into Sudanese waters before seeking shelter, and headed off into a strongish northerly wind. In the middle of the night our friends on *Alb* were approached by a gun boat manned by armed, un-uniformed men who demanded their passports. They were naturally reluctant to comply, but had little option in the circumstances. Luckily the incident passed off without trouble and Carol wisely kept in radio communication with us and other boats during the boarding. One really never knows what might happen in this region, and who might be taken for spies. We were all nervous, but knew we *must* keep together, stay well offshore and radio for help at the sign of any possible trouble on board. After three days we reached a sheltered anchorage well north of the border, and set off the following morning to navigate the tricky reef-strewn channel leading to southern Sudan's major port. It was a hard beat into the wind, and we tucked into yet another anchorage at 19.00 in darkness, gratefully using *September Ripple's* lights and radio-relayed instructions as guide.

Next evening, following in the wake of the *Ripple* and *Violetta* we were heading for our last anchorage before Port Sudan, a reef-fringed islet called Long Island. It had good shelter from the northerlies which were making our going difficult, and we reached the surrounding reef shortly after noon, doing quite well under sail. We decided to motor the last half mile so as to avoid the scattered coral heads more easily, and as Frank handled the sails I started the engine. There was a strange sound as we neared the five-metre wide pass, and suddenly we were assailed by a horrible burning smell. Frank leapt to open the engine hatches – and black smoke came billowing out. Straight away he turned off the engine, but the starter key was stuck. He immediately dropped the anchor to prevent us drifting onto the reef, and we were able to assess the situation. It seemed clear that we had burnt out the starter motor, and would have to go through the reef under sail. It took an hour of tacking back and forth before we were safely anchored.

Once there all hands came aboard and we were given all sorts of advice, but the picture didn't look good as a burnt-out motor needs at least a machine shop for help. Fred offered to come and crew for us on the 30-mile beat into Suakin, the nearest port, which was through some very difficult waters. That night other boats joined us, among them *Island Wind* whose skipper Connie was a contributor to the *SiOui* net. He put out an emergency call next morning to see if any boat in the vicinity had a spare starter motor – a long shot! – but he was answered almost immediately by a Swiss boat *Jonathan Seagull* whose skipper Peter had quite a reputation for engine repair, and who was only a few hours away. Peter spent almost all that day working on the motor, but pronounced it beyond his repair capabilities without machinery. However, he did offer to tow us with his sturdy Fisher 36, and we set off next day at 7.00. After about 17 miles the going became too tough for him, as the wind had risen on the nose, and we set sails and severed our tie. There followed a long, tiresome haul, and we would never have managed without Fred's cheerful help and hard work. We soon realised that we wouldn't make Suakin harbour in daylight, but we had no option but head onwards. We were in constant radio contact with both *Jonathan Seagull* and *Island Wind*. Peter, safely in port, mentioned that there were big guns at the entry to the harbour mouth, but that no one seemed to man them, and that Harbour Control generally didn't answer radio calls, so we should just come in whenever we could, and friends would help us negotiate the trickier shallows within the anchorage.

By now it was pitch dark, and our radar and GPS were working overtime to alert us to the presence of reefs. We were tired and dispirited, convinced that we would have a lot of difficulties effecting repairs in Suakin and might be stuck there for a few weeks, with the northerlies building stronger as the weeks went by. Eventually we began to make out the faint lights of the town, and the last few miles seemed like an eternity as we struggled back and forth between the shore and the reef. We needed to round a long spit of coral before gaining a clear run to the inner harbour, and were almost thrown upon it through misjudging the leading lights, but thankfully I heard the sound of breaking waves just in time. A hurried final tack and we were in line for the entry, with the wind now helping us up the quarter mile channel.

I had tried calling the port authorities several times, but no one responded. All seemed deathly quiet and inky black in the outer channel as the port lights were quite a way upstream. Suddenly the tense silence was shattered by shrill whistle-blowing and shouts, and then the horrific sound of machine-gun fire. We felt extremely threatened, but were totally at the mercy of wind and sail, and could do nothing but continue onwards. Frank flashed a torchlight over the sails, while Fred and I ducked for cover, far less brave. In my heart of hearts I knew that we would not be killed – but it was an extremely scary time, and our friends ashore, hearing the shooting, were even more terrified than us. Finally Connie radioed to say he had explained the position to the port authorities, who were asking the military to halt their fire. We would be escorted to our berth by the port launch, and Connie himself would be on hand to help us in. Having experienced such a reception we were naturally a little suspicious of local help, and refused to take a line from the chubby boat filled with turbaned Sudanese, for fear they would charge us towing fees, but they insisted on leading us to the inner harbour. Connie in his little dinghy provided engine power, nudging us gently forward with his 3 HP outboard motor, and helped us anchor. As far as we were concerned he had saved our lives, and we owe him a great debt.

It was very very late before the adrenaline had returned to normal, and the whiskey bottle was almost dry. We were all so relieved that neither we nor the boat had suffered damage. The warning went out to others not to attempt a night arrival, but we didn't want to elaborate further as the harbour people had seemed very embarrassed by the incident and didn't need further loss of face. Suakin is trying desperately to keep its port alive, and to attract the yachting fraternity, and such an incident reported widely would have done their image a lot of damage.

Everything looked utterly different in the morning light. We found ourselves in a sheltered bay with about ten other yachts, on the nearest shore a bombed-out, crumbling ghost-town peopled only by sea eagles, whose ruins suggested fine Islamic architecture. A line of Yemeni fishing boats were anchored stern to the shore, high prows and hardwood dog-houses teeming with cheerful fishermen and boys in colourful garb. Rows of drying shark fin hung from the masts, their strong smell pervading the area. Opposite them stretched the 'modern' town, scattered cubes of adobe buildings rising from the sand. Groups of raggle taggle children cheered and waved from the shore, and occasionally a well-dressed man with briefcase would appear on the water's edge – this was Ahmid, the shipping agent, in search of customers. As he had neither VHF nor dinghy, he hoped that recently arrived boats would spot him and collect him, to conduct the business of entry and exit on board. We pumped up the dinghy and returned Fred to *Violetta* (John was anxious not to delay their departure any longer), and picked up Ahmid, to whom we explained our predicament. We made arrangements with him to bring the defective starter motor to Port Sudan next morning by bus. He felt we would be well looked after there, and though we didn't have the same confidence we trusted his competent manner, and dropping him off on another boat, we set out to explore our immediate surroundings.

The old ruined town on the near shore had been declared a heritage site, protected from further ravishment by UNESCO, but we had little desire to climb its mounds of rubble, and headed instead for the 'new' town where the daily market was in full swing. Sandy streets led past primitive wooden stalls where strange concoctions were being fried or boiled to order. Magnificent weathered men in white or palest lilac robes and brightly-coloured headcloths hunkered on the ground, or sat on crude benches, eating or drinking coffee. Tiny shanty shops kept only a shelf or two of provisions, and in one area two millers worked side by side with diesel-driven crushers, grinding corn and wheat and grains to customers' requirements. With delight I purchased wheat from women seated on the ground with huge baskets, and brought it to the miller. There was no need for any language as my requirements were self evident, and I soon had three kilos of freshly-ground weevil-free wholemeal flour, the first obtainable since Australia! In the fruit and vegetable market we chose lush tomatoes and sweet oranges to replenish our supplies. There were good mangoes and yams, and eggs, and trays of sweet bread rolls, carefully covered against the flies. Nearby in the general market camels were waiting patiently while men sifted through piles of de-stranded rope, ancient harnesses, old tin cans, UN-issue blue plastic sheeting (a ubiquitous item in third world markets), empty sacks, even an old army tent which would prove invaluable as additional accommodation to these nomadic traders. A little apart the only female sellers, sturdy tribeswomen with veiled faces, silver nose rings and heavy fuchsia-coloured robes, were presiding over cotton tents of second-hand western clothing, and vibrant hand-woven cloth in brilliant shades of red and orange, together with silver combs, nose-rings and other artifacts. When we showed interest the prices trebled! They would not allow photographs to be taken, whereas the young men and boys were begging to have their pictures made, and posed elaborately for me! They carried swords pushed into belts around their waists, and many offered to sell these family heirlooms, but we were not interested. Our needs were all food-related, and had been met for the present.

Water was carried in an ingenious 'tanker' made from two twenty-gallon drums welded together, with a tap at one end. This was placed on an old car axle, and towed by a willing donkey. Luckily we had our 130 gallon tank aboard, with a good supply which would take us as far as Cyprus. We had by now acquired a personal guide, a little boy of about six, who, together with his deaf-mute friend, became our shadows for the next few days. We

180

communicated with hand signs and smiles, but wished that the boys would go to school rather than waiting to escort us each day.

At 6.00 next morning we headed for Port Sudan, with Ahmid. The aged bus was packed with white-robed, weather-lined men and colourful, heavily clad women, and the narrow aisle was filled with sacks of grain, spancelled hens and even a young, quiet goat. The unsurfaced pot-holed road ran parallel to the coast through fields of straggling crops: irrigation was a major problem, and little grew in the arid ground. Herds of thin goats gleaned a meagre diet, watched over by nomadic families in dun-coloured tents, whose thorn-scrub boundaries kept young animals safely within and scavengers without. Inland rose majestic mountains – the same chain we had crossed over to visit Asmara, with this slim finger of coastal plain prey to almost constant drought. Frank cradled the heavy starter motor in a cotton carrier bag, and we transferred to a taxi when we reached the scruffy, industrialised outskirts of Port Sudan. In a tiny, non-descript workshop near the railway line a wrinkled mechanic in his late fifties greeted us in excellent English. He put the Bosch starter on his workbench, examined it and heard our story. Then, bending down to a dusty pile of engine parts on the floor beneath the bench, he pulled out as if by magic an almost identical motor. He rubbed the dust off the serial number, and we were amazed to see that it was the same as ours, though the armature or body was slightly longer. Frank could not believe our luck – it would only take this man a few hours to reconstruct a good-as-new motor, and the cost would be far less than a new replacement (which would take weeks to have delivered here). We were overjoyed at this good turn of fortune, and were convinced of the value of all those prayers that friends and family at home had promised. Happily we taxied back to the city centre, in search of a bank which would accept our credit-cards, but none were geared for such transactions. We would just have to wait until Egypt and hope for the best! Paying for the repair would almost finish our reserves of dollars, but we had plenty of tinned food, potatoes and onions aboard and we would not go hungry. An hour later we collected a shining motor and after lengthy interchange between Ahmid and our saviour, we handed over $190 in a thick wad of $10 bills. Unused to haggling, we probably gave twice the going rate, but we presumed that some of this would later be returned to the agent as commission, and were glad that what in the circumstances was reasonable to us was probably a great amount to them.

All afternoon Frank worked patiently down in the cramped engine, getting Richard to come and check his progress from time to time, as there was an elaborate amount of wiring involved and he was terrified of causing a short. Finally the installation was complete, and the moment of reckoning at hand – would the motor respond when the key was turned. I was pale with apprehension as Frank depressed and turned the fatal key – and the engine burst into life with a steady throb! We had quite a celebration on board that night, though our alcohol supplies were dry!

September Ripple and *Violetta* left next morning, and we visited the town once more, to complete our exit procedures. I gave our faithful little follower a pair of lurid, wrap-around sunglasses, and he thought he was in heaven! We also gave him a big food parcel for his family, having seen the limited supplies that were available. Other boats made similar gestures, and while we worried at the children foregoing school in the hope of better immediate gain, the yachting season is short and hopefully we do more overall good than bad in places like this. Being exposed to so much poverty made us often feel ill at ease, and ashamed of our own abundant wealth: it certainly hardened us against the selfishness and greed of the 'developed' world.

It was St Patrick's Day and *Grey Dawn*, an Australian boat from Mooloolaba YC, gave us a case of beer, hearing of our drought, and held a party which we really enjoyed. Next morning we were off once more, feeling rather sad at leaving this seductive, almost-biblical place, though we shuddered as we passed the big anti aircraft gun in daylight: was it only three nights ago we almost met our end here?

After three days of *marsa*-hopping (sheltered anchorages surrounded with coral that dot the coastline) we were near the disputed Sudanese/Egyptian border, and when the wind turned south we decided to go on as far north as we could in the good conditions. Two days later we were safely into Marsa Halaib, in an area still contested between Sudan and Egypt, but with an Egyptian patrol boat in situ we felt more secure. Frank had to bring passports and boat papers to the captain, who subsequently visited *Atlantic Islander* and asked for books and cigarettes, or any other 'gifts' – alcohol, though not really allowed, would be acceptable! We were impressed at the skilful entry of a tiny catamaran, 5.8

metres long, skippered by a lone Englishman who had neither radio, engine, nor GPS – and had come all the way round the world. *Cooking Fat* was a spoonerism for *F**king Cat!*

Three days later we reached Mina Safaga, Egypt's southern-most official entry port: from this date our month-long Egyptian visa would come into operation. Almost two-thirds of the Red Sea now lay behind us, and we were much relieved. This merited some quality time ashore, and once we had completed the lengthy im-migration procedures at the busy commercial port, we headed to a free anchorage off the resort area of Ras Abu Soma, where the *enormous* Safaga Paradise Hotel reminded us all how fortunate we were to be among tens rather than thousands of fellow 'tourists'. To the pink-skinned sun-seeker arriving here, it must have been a total culture shock to wander from the resort area into the make-shift town where standards were light years below those enjoyed at the hotel. Once again we tried local banks in search of cash, but none could help us. We were assured that Port Suez would accept our credit cards, and fervently prayed that this would be so as we were now down to about $50.

Reunited with the *Ripple* and with Fred and John, we foolish-ly decided to blow our remaining cash and once more take a trip inland together – this was probably our best opportunity to visit Luxor, and a local bus ran each morning, with an evening return. We could thus organise an overnight stay, see all the major sights, and be back by the following night, well within budget. En route in the comfortable if uncared-for bus, we watched an official cor-don of tourist coaches with their attendant army patrol streak on ahead of us. We felt far more secure among locals on a low-key regular service – at one hundredth the price! In Luxor friendly Hussein (whose nephew had met us en route) packed all six of us into a taxi with himself and driver. The Central Garden hotel was indeed central – about 10 minutes walk from the Temple of Luxor – but there was little trace of any garden. However, the rooms were quite passable (at $8.00 per night!), with en suite facilities, and we dumped our small packs and set out to discover this much-visited city.

Almost immediately we realised how lucky we were to be based in Safaga, where the tentacles of major tourism have not yet really reached. Despite our downbeat appearance and lack of ob-vious wealth, we were besieged by touts, who cajoled, begged and almost bludgeoned us to use their services/shop/tour/skill: no amount of 'No, Thank You!' would do, and I finally found that the only thing that deterred them was to suddenly drop into an imbecilic stance and pretend to be totally deranged. This they didn't like, and immediately turned tail. But after several hours I was worn out, Frank was sick from laughing, and we escaped into the sanctuary of the temple where one's entry ticket eliminated all but official guides, who graciously accepted a 'no' if their services were not required. Later we returned to experience the evening's *son et lumière* as the magnificent second century temple's history was played out in poetic recordings and dramatic light displays.

Early next morning we crossed the fast-flowing Nile and visited the City of the Dead – the lavishly painted tombs of the kings, queens and nobles of ancient Egypt. For this we had the services of an excellent guide – a teacher in Cairo University. With a magical lift of his finger he was able to keep the unwanted touts at bay. By 8.00 the heat was already intense, and the lack of air within the tombs took much of the joy away, as I felt like fainting each time we went below ground. It was really disheartening to see the extent to which sheer tourist numbers have effected the deterioration of these incomparable frescoes. It looks like Egypt is hell-bent on killing the golden goose by allowing the natural heritage to be destroyed and hassling visitors past the point of 'no return'. This was the first country that we seriously did not want to revisit. However, nothing can take away from the beauty of the tomb paintings, or the sheer magnificence of the temples.

We completed our day with a felucca cruise on the legendary Nile, though due to the lack of breeze and the heaviness of a much repaired and battered sail, we had to be content with a downstream glide and an upstream row, as our intrepid young 'captain' hauled us back to the Right Bank with the crudest oars we have ever seen – they seemed like door posts. Unexpectedly the evening bus – a full-blown coach with air-conditioning – was booked solid. There was nothing for it but to bring our bags back to the hotel, and stay another night! That worked out cheaper than taking the coach, and we were off early next morning after a bonus night on the town. It was good to travel by daylight and enjoy the sights – the lush green of the river belt, where vegetables grew in abundance, and cattle and sheep were fat and well watered, then the semi-rich alluvial plain, and beyond it the coastal range where not a blade of grass nor any tree or shrub was seen. Back 'home' we completed our provisioning with some excellent local cheese very like Parmesan, ferried endless cans of diesel from a nearby garage by taxi, and were off the following morning.

A final push through heavy winds, sheltering at nights, and we were through the narrow Straits of Gubal which divide mainland Egypt from the Sinai peninsula. *Enarkay* had managed to collect our Aden mail, and at an anchorage beyond the straits passed over the precious packet containing our GPS batteries. Port Suez was only a few days away, and we went as fast as we could sailing through the night on the eastern edge of the shipping lane, arriving in darkness. We were jubilant to have survived the dreaded Red Sea, and though we were tired and dust-covered, it looked like we would make our Cyprus rendez-vous without too much trouble. But first we *had* to find a bank which accepted credit-cards!! We presented ourselves to the Bank of Egypt, which *did* have such a service. But ... the phone links were down, and there was nothing they could do for us! Our transit of the canal was scheduled for 9.00 am next morning, and we were penniless and desperate. To have come so far, and be unable to pay for the Suez transit ... what could we do? Frank, inspired, offered the agent our hand-held VHF radio – he didn't seem to have one – in exchange for our fees (about $250), and the Prince of the Red Sea (for such was his name!) was very interested. However, the bank *had* advised us to return after 17.00, and our prayers were rewarded with repaired phonelines and a fistful of dollars! We had a meal out in celebration, and vowed that we would never again travel the Red Sea without plenty of cash.

The canal transit takes two days and was unremarkable and annoying. Empty desert stretches to the horizon on both sides, enlivened by the odd signal station, which monitors canal traffic. Our pilot did not want to take the wheel, but sat and communicated occasionally with other pilots by VHF. As the first forty-four miles drew to a close near the Bitter Lakes, where there is a compulsory overnight stop, he mentioned the subject of his 'present'. We gave the compulsory packages of cigarettes, together with a small gift for his daughter, and some perfume for his wife. He wanted more. I lost my cool and demanded all be returned, mentioning a few home truths about the greedy character of the average Egyptian, and what it would eventually do to the tourist industry in gener-

185

al. He was sorry – genuinely so – and I felt how stupid we all were to be falling into this ridiculous *backsheesh* trap. If every boat refused point blank to give 'gifts' no such blackmail could thrive – but tales of ramming boats and other forms of sabotage have been so well circulated now that everyone is afraid to act according to their heads.

Next morning a new pilot bore fresh loaves of bread, but was dour and taciturn, and we were as well pleased. The second segment of the transit is much shorter, and technically one should be out into the Med by mid afternoon. We had completed all paperwork in Suez, and were cleared to leave Egypt. All that remained was to drop our pilot off in Port Said, and dole out packets of cigarettes to various officials who were involved in the offload. Meanwhile the wind was rising from the north-west and it looked like we would be very foolish to head out on the long journey to Cyprus. So we decided to take shelter in the small dirty yacht club basin a few hundred yards from the harbour mouth. No sooner were we in than we were being asked for ridiculously high fees – this caused a lot of dissent among the assembled boats. We hoped to leave next morning, but the winds did not abate until two days later. Meanwhile we were forced to remain on board as we had technically exited the country: to step ashore would cost us lots more dollars. It was a trying few days and time was running out for our rendezvous in Cyprus with David on his first stint as crew, together with old-timer Rachel. We were so looking forward to the Mediterranean ahead – but wondered if it would be kind to us weary world-worn wanderers? The signs did not seem good.

19

MEDITERRANEAN

Early on Saturday morning, 11 April, we finally escaped from storm-bound Port Said, together with a large group of relieved 'independent' and Trade Winds Rally boats. The anchorage at Port Faoud Yacht Centre had been filthy, the reception bitter, and a bad taste of Egypt still remained in our mouths. Our boats and rigging all bore the telltale ochre sand of the desert-rimmed sea, and we were eager to hasten to ports where we could wash away the grime with plentiful fresh water. Some boats were heading for recently opened marinas in Israel, others for Malta, and many for Larnaca in Cyprus, where Rachel and Dave would arrive the following day. We were under pressure to make the 300-odd mile journey as fast as possible – but the winds were still against us.

We had had no funds in Port Suez to refuel before the canal transit, and now realised that we were seriously short of diesel. That evening in response to a radio appeal, Graham and Mary completed a tricky manoeuvre to share their spare fuel with us. They brought *Hilda* alongside, threw us a long line which we looped around a stanchion and then passed back to them. By knotting the ends together around the handle of their jerrycan, we could haul the can to our stern and lift it aboard. This we did twice, and were thus better off by 50 litres of precious fuel, which we would repay in kind on reaching Cyprus. We gratefully bade our benefactors *bon voyage* as they were making better headway than we were, and concentrated on combining sail and engine to best advantage to make our journey as fuel-efficient as possible. But the wind turned even more against us, and unable to make a north-easterly direction, we finally arrived some 40 miles west of Larnaca at Episcopy Bay, where *Hilda* and *Alb* had already tucked into shelter. Another Trade Winds boat, *Ocean Gypsy*, was also at anchor, celebrating the completion of their circumnavigation which had commenced from Cyprus in 1995. Early next morning we shared in their excitement when the RAF's Red Arrows put on a brilliant aerobatics display for the skipper who had previously been a member of the team. On Tuesday Rachel and David joined us at Limassol marina and sailed with us to Larnaca. On the short journey in

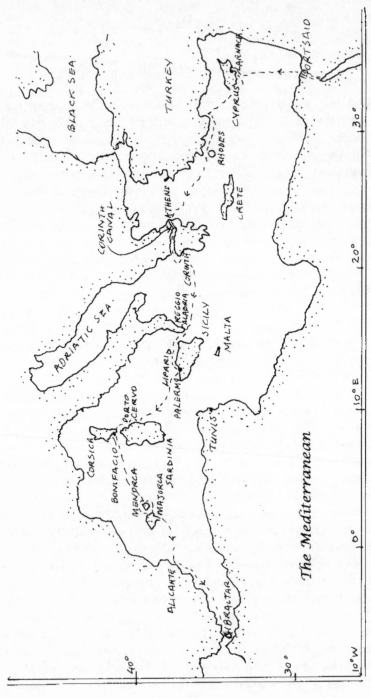

The Mediterranean

calm conditions we had the most spectacular view of dolphins – so clear in the aquamarine water that it was almost impossible to tell whether they were above or below the surface.

We were glad of the two extra crew to tuck ourselves into a tricky berth in tightly packed Larnaca Marina, one of the most helpful in the world. We hired a car for next to nothing, and spent what was left of their week's holiday driving, shopping and dining out. We had one full-day excursion, and visited war-torn Nicosia with its UN-patrolled Demilitarised Zone – on one side flies the red and white Turkish crescent, on the other the Greek Cypriot flag bears a map of the whole island, clearly laying its claim to all the island.

Since the collapse of the Berlin wall, this is now the only capital city in Europe divided by war. Dave introduced us to email and the Internet in our first-ever cybercafe. Why hadn't I known about these before? An hour later we were throwing snowballs in the high Troodos Mountains, and driving through Alpine-like villages with ancient, steeply roofed houses and tiny churches. In the afternoon we walked the sunny promenade in sophisticated Limassol, before heading back for some delicious Irish steaks in a 'Tudor' Pub in Larnaca. Rachel and David had a nice apartment nearby which we swapped one night for *Atlantic Islander* – to give us the luxury of real beds, a balcony, and plentiful water for showers and hairwashing! I'm not sure what they gained in exchange! Before they left we threw a party for twenty Red Sea Veterans, to introduce them to old and new-found friends.

The following week was one of more reunions, excuses for parties, and joint shopping sprees in excellent supermarkets where locally produced wines and spirits were *exceedingly* cheap (£3 for a bottle of brandy!) A week later we were joined by two very close friends from home – the only non-family members who had managed to co-ordinate plans in order to sail with us. After a day to settle in, we brought them on a rough two-night passage to Turkey, where we anchored in beautiful, mountain-girt Kekova Roads. They were glad to have big seas behind them, as they had suffered quite a bit of seasickness with great patience and endurance, not shirking night watch even once.

Dark clouds and a threat of rain did not deter us, as we inflated the dinghy and set out to explore the marvellous ruins of Kale Köy – a mediaeval castle sitting on a rocky knoll, with an ancient village of tiny stone houses tumbling down the slope beneath to the smooth waters of the roads – Kekova Island protects a long stretch of mainland from the easterly winds. Local schoolgirls watched our dinghy come ashore and their nimble figures clad in baggy trousers threaded the narrow paths like mountain goats. Smiling they proffered baskets of hand-edged headscarves and fine embroidery work, huge brown eyes shining from under their own embroidered headgear. They were delightfully innocent in many ways, well educated and courteous, but total business women when it came to selling their goods. Local *gulets* – elegant wooden sailing boats now built mainly for the tourist trade – visit these coasts, laden with souvenir-hungry holiday-makers, and the village communities which were until recently cut off from tourist incursions have spotted an easy target.

We dined that evening at the tiny village of Uçajiz, right at the water's edge, tying our dinghy to the rickety jetty provided for sea-borne diners. Our wizened host proposed grilled fish and salad, and though the generator broke down after ten minutes, leaving us in pitch darkness, this did not deter anyone. Candles were lit, the cooking was completed over an open fire, and a good local wine washed down our delicious feast. When lights and radio eventually blared into action we were rather regretful – but the owner got us up to dance, and we entered into the spirit with gusto.

Heavy rain next morning brought out the wet-weather gear, and Frank and John kindly did most of the outdoor work while Monika and I attended to cabin duties. Within a few hours we were in Greece – and a sign on Kastellórizo island welcomed us to the easternmost outpost of the EU! A mere three miles off the Turkish mainland, this is a cautious enclave in the simmering fear and hatred between these neighbours. Like most of the Dodecanese, this island was originally Turkish, became part of an independent Greece in 1830 and was taken over by the Italians in 1912. Thanks to its marvellous natural harbour this was once an important centre in the trade between Europe and the Levant. In the 1800s there was a population of 20,000 – today it stands at around 200, but the recent filming of the Italian movie, *Mediterraneo*, has awakened the possibilities of tourism, and slowly but surely homes burned out as British troops evacuated the island at the end of WWII are being carefully restored. All the stone houses are of uniform shape and design – two storeys with high ceilings, tall windows, upper balconies, flat roofs and an almost Georgian feel.

A twice-weekly ferry links the island to Rhodes, its nearest Greek neighbour, 70 miles to the NW. But the main presence here is the Greek army, billeted in all sorts of nooks and crannies, eyes ever northwards towards the potential Turkish invasion. A recently built airport would enable rapid deployment of military support if necessary. At present yachts provide most of the tourist visitors, some coming on day trips from Turkey, and waterside cafes and restaurants capitalise on their spending power, providing poor food at EU rates, as we were to discover. It was pleasant to moor stern-to at the empty, crescent-shaped quay, which was really the village's main street. We were helped ashore in pouring rain by a tall English woman – who turned out to be the writer of a well-known and respected book on sail repair, the owner of a 'bring and buy or sell' second-hand chandlery in her tiny home nearby. Lisa Carr moved here some seven years ago and lives with a local man – both involved in servicing yachts and boats. Her tiny hall and stairwall are covered in boat names and 'murals' – many done cleverly by Lisa. Fellow sailors Clare and Ken Dixon, who had left Crosshaven some years before us, were the only names we recognised apart from *Alb!*

We had been warned that the anchorage in Rhodes fills up quickly, so next evening, after a delightful walk into the mountains, and an early dinner on board, we cast off and nudged out into the channel as the setting sun threw purple shadows on the nearby Turkish mountains. By now our new crew had good sea legs and we had an excellent night's sail under a sky dense with stars. The watches worked perfectly, and we reached Rhodes in the early hours of Sunday morning. There was just enough space for us to tuck in to – right in the heart of the new town and just across the street from the GPO – how much more central can one get?

Next day we took the local bus and visited beautiful Lindos. We were almost sorry that we hadn't decided to anchor there as it must be one of the most picturesque harbours anywhere. However, the shelter is not as good as Rhodes, and as I had decided to make a flying visit to Cambodia where Cathy was suffering the pangs of early pregnancy compounded with a bout of dysentery, Rhodes would be a better place for Frank to stay in my absence, with excellent chandlers and stores near to hand.

My week in Phnom Penh was enriched by a three-night visit

to Siam Reap, near the legendary ruins of Ankor Wat. Cathy, cheered by my visit, was feeling well enough to act as an excellent guide, and we spent hours enthralled at many of the surrounding temples in this sacred place – a symphony of carved stone and architectural extravagance slowly being reclaimed by encroaching jungle despite the best efforts of conservationists and UNESCO.

Frank meanwhile was busy looking after sails, hull, and woodwork and *Atlantic Islander* looked bright and clean on my return. He had ingeniously found a sturdy pram chassis in some city-centre junk shop, and used this as his 'four-wheel-drive' to ferry cans of diesel from a garage some distance away – as well as transporting heavier pieces of equipment to and from the boat. We gave ourselves a few extra days after my return to restock the larder, and to socialise with friends, before setting off through the Dodecanese and Eastern Cyclades towards Piraeus and Athens. Everyone we met had their favourite anchorages and islands, and we well knew that we would have time to barely scratch the surface of these eastern-Mediterranean islands which have attracted sailors for hundreds of years. Armed with another excellent pilot guide, we traced a path from beautifully uncommercialised Symi to Kos and then on through Kalimnos, a big charter centre where we spotted an Irish ensign but did not get to meet the crew, to Amorgos – surprisingly green and lush compared to most of its barren, rocky neighbours – where the cult film *Le Grand Bleu* was made.

Serifos is an excellent watering stop for yachts, blessed with abundant rainfall. A wealth of flowers, shrubs and trees flourish in the richly cultivated soil, and these are home to countless birds. Reeds, rushes and running streams had an incredibly cooling, soothing effect, and reminded us of home. How much we longed to be there now, yet we savoured the beauties of these eastern islands. We climbed up into the old mountaintop town in the late afternoon. During siesta even the dogs were quiet. As we rose we began to see signs of life: an old man tending a tiny garden, a glorious tenor singing in a shady alleyway, a gaggle of black-clad women in the small general store, murmured conversations behind closed doors and shutters. We saw an old loom in the corner of a tiny, white-washed room, and a settle bed strewn with subtly-coloured yarns. Further down the same street a cobbler's tools and hand-made shoes lay in a doorway. Up and up we trudged, glad that it was now nearly 17.30 and at this altitude the sun had lost some of its fierceness. On the very top stand three churches, with St Helen's in the pride of place – we peeped in the tiny window to see a simple interior spotlessly kept – flag floor, sugán chairs, tapers, lectern, and simple icons.

Piraeus – the port of Athens – was packed tight with huge, ostentatious motor launches, and we had to be content with a very rocky berth against the harbour wall: each time one of the frequent hydrofoils passed we were dashed alarmingly onto the concrete, and needed all fenders out to protect ourselves. But we knew it would be worth a bit of discomfort to see the Acropolis, and the following morning we were on a 7.30 train to the capital – a mere 20 minute's ride away. Once we were out of the station we could immediately see our goal – the Parthenon is visible from all over Athens, and we had seen it from miles off the coast the previous day. We walked through the ancient Agora at the foot of the hill, and reached the entrance before opening time, so were among the early ones to arrive in the old city without the crush of tour-bused hoards. The age and craftsmanship is stunning – all this in 450 BC – the simplicity and perfection of form, and later in the museum, complexity of sculpting, the beauty of the friezes, the lifelike quality of clothing, hair, muscles, feet – living marble of lavish beauty that takes one's breath away.

The next leg of our journey led us through the Corinth Canal: our third and shortest – and most expensive. (Suez was next and Panama the cheapest!) Built a little over a hundred years ago, it looks like it has had no maintenance since then and is slowly but surely crumbling away. Nero tried to dig a canal in 67 AD with some 7,000 Jewish slaves, many of who perished. The Egyptians discovered that the Ionian and Sporades seas were at different heights, and that to progress would lead to flooding, so plans were abandoned until last century. Instead a paved road – the Dioklos – was built to haul the laden ships from east to west.

We tied up against the harbour wall at modern Corinth, a clean, prosperous town, and explored the Corinth of St Paul. While very little remains standing, the sheer size of the place, and the complexity and sophistication of the baths and drainage systems, the extent of the huge basilicas, shopping arcades and open spaces are quite staggering. We had the whole site to ourselves, and with a helpful local guidebook which showed a reconstructed model we were able to marvel at the beauty combined with functionality displayed by the city planners of 2,200 years ago.

Fortified with ancient culture, we set off next morning for a three-day passage to Reggio Calabria in southernmost Italy. However, the wind was on our nose all through the narrow Gulf of Corinth, and we decided to slip into the sheltered anchorage of Nisos Trizonia, some 45 miles west. Next day we set off again, wind still against us, and motored for many hours. Later it was glorious to watch the sun set over the end of Kefallonia, the last Greek island we would see – a swirl of salmon cloud tinting the sea, and spreading outward. Gradually the sky darkened to merge with the black lofty silhouette of 1,632-metre Mount Énos, and a hundred twinkling lights from shore-side towns shone brighter than the millions of stars above. The milky way streaked an arc of star-spawn over boat and island, and ahead a slim crescent moon cast a thousand glittering splinters in her path. These shimmered and split in the shifting black of the sea. I had managed to set the sails, sick of a day of motoring, and was able to revel in near- silence at the glory of the night. Just before coming off watch a falling star streaked towards the west. I thanked the good Lord for all the wonders we have and so enjoy – good health, a sturdy boat, a family of strong, intelligent individuals, and each other. But more than anything, a capacity to be moved by nature.

Three days later we were safely tied up in the busy commercial harbour in Reggio Calabria. Our second eldest son Gary would be joining us here and we were really looking forward to having his company. Together we travelled through the famous Straits of Messina between Sicily and the toe of Italy, and could understand the fears of Odysseus as he met the terrible whirlpools of Charybdis. The sea floor drops dramatically in this narrow patch – we are in sight of the highest volcano in Europe, Mount Etna – and this causes huge currents and eddies which tug at the boat even in full revs. The cross-straits traffic is intense, with some ferries carrying entire trains across to Sicily! We needed full concentration, and were really glad of the extra crew. Safely through the straits we headed for the Aeolian island of Lipari, passing Vulcano, which last erupted in 1890, with its constant plume of smoke. There is something fatally attractive about volcanoes, and next morning we took a long climb to see as much as we could of the neighbouring spectacle. Lipari is a beautiful island which attracted the Greeks back in 580 BC, has a magnificently-sited town on the main harbour, and is thronged with holiday-makers in the summer months. A neighbouring naval boat had been exceedingly noisy all night long, and we left that afternoon, when an onshore wind began to pick up! Later we heard that a few months before several boats had been sunk here in similar winds, moored as we were to the harbour wall!

We reached Palermo, capital of Sicily, next afternoon, and initial impressions were not good. The harbour area stank so badly it was stomach turning, and getting fresh water was an almost impossible procedure. But we made friends with Paul and Cathy who arrived on a lovely Moody shortly after us, and stayed on because the winds were really too high and in the wrong direction for Sardinia. We used the time to explore some of the grimy suburbs of the city which had a strange appeal, and to visit the lively street market where we once again stocked up on fresh vegetables and meat. Here the Mafia hold sway, and we were quite on edge particularly at night, although the marina was well guarded by the navy. A local man, on holidays from 'Noo Yoik' insisted on showing us the sights, and would not take no for an answer! When he told us that he claimed a lot of respect, we felt obliged to go with him! He proudly brought us to the amazing grotto of Santa Rosalia, high on Monte Pellegrino, where Palermo's patron saint lies buried: throngs of the faithful come to intercede here for the sick and dying, and hang silver tokens of the affected parts – legs, hearts, liver, kidneys, breasts, heads, arms, around the shrine. A miraculous spring gushes healing waters, and we witnessed great faith here. Sergio insisted on buying us souvenirs as he firmly believed in the efficacy of the patron. We then drove to the peak of Pilgrimage Mountain and looked down on all of Palermo, as well as the delightful crescent bay at nearby Mondello.

We hoped to get away on the third day, but a gale warning held us until the following morning. And then we discovered that our anchor was wedged solidly to the bottom – snarled in sunken mooring lines. Despite it being the filthiest place we had ever been – bar Port Said – Frank once again donned wetsuit and went over the side, with help from Paul in his dinghy. After a quarter-hour of hauling himself up and down the anchor chain, trying to free the snag, while Gary winched by hand, we were released at last – but Paul and Cathy then discovered they too were held fast, and once again Frank did the diving! He instantly became Cathy's hero! It took a lot of shampoo and water to get rid of Palermo's putrid smell.

Two days later we were in the clean air of Sardinia's east coast, in the sheltered (we thought!) harbour of Cala Gonone. Frank had been heading for nearby La Caleta but my guide book didn't give it many stars and so I had my way. *'Beautifully sited at the base of 900-metre-high mountains, this once tiny settlement was until recently accessible only by boat'*

There was only one tiny space for us to manoeuvre into, and kindly German neighbours were most welcoming, despite their concerns with the rising wind. At midnight Frank and Gary were up securing extra lines to the dockside, and at 01.00 I woke to a terrible grating sound: our bow anchor had slipped, and we were being dashed against the davits on a heavy wooden boat which lay alongside the quay. All hands on deck as Frank started the engine, Gary cast off the sternlines, and I pushed with all my might to keep our aerials from getting damaged. By now the winds were over 45 miles per hour, and our German neighbours had their deck lights on and were frantically trying to haul on their anchor to get further from the quay wall. It was a terrifying time, with the wind seething down the mountains relentlessly, and sheets and rigging raging against the masts. We managed to reposition ourselves alongside the strong local boat, and put out every fender we possessed, including all the deck cushions, to prevent damage to it. We had to maintain full anchor watch, and I found it the scariest night of the whole journey, as potential catastrophe seemed very real. At sea there is room to manoeuvre, and to run before the wind, but here we had no further place to go, and should any other boat come undone it would spell disaster for all. And so we had our first experience of the legendary meltemi which can last for anything from a few hours to *nine* days – we just continued to pray that it would soon abate. I resolved to let Frank pick the safer havens in future! Next day our prayers were answered, and we headed for the safety of dull, comfortable La Caleta.

We had one other stop – at anchor – before reaching the legendary Porto Cervo on the Costa Smeralda. 'Discovered' in the late 1950s by the Aga Khan as a excellent area for cruising, he managed to buy up about 10 kilometres of coastline and develop it in an extremely exclusive manner with strict planning regulations. All the houses are discreetly set into the pink granite and maquis surroundings, and Porto Cervo itself is more like an architectural model of Mediterranean chic than a living community. To berth here at the huge marina would cost us £46 per night (off season), and £60 in July and August. That really ensures that one does not have to mix with the riff raff! However, just outside the marina is a relatively sheltered bay, surrounded by manicured grounds and tasteful homes, and this is where the boat people throw anchor! We dinghied ashore to explore this exclusive place, and found it rather soulless. In a few weeks the famous Sardinia Cup would draw top racing boats in Europe and beyond, with all the attendant razz matazz: for the moment it remained quiet and unassuming.

With strong winds forecast for next day – yet again! – we were awake before dawn and under way by 6.00 to make the 25 miles to Bonifacio in Corsica by early afternoon. The Straits of Bonifacio have a bad reputation, but we were blessed with a millpond. This white city is perched on the edge of eroded chalky cliffs – 304 m above sea level, and is one of the most dramatic places we visited. Inside the totally sheltered harbour is a lovely marina, surrounded by *la belle France* – where *patisseries, boulangeries, boucheries* and *tabacs* abound, and the tourists are nearly all French. I set off eagerly to explore the citadel, climbing 152 steps in the searing heat to gain entry by one of the two gates with drawbridges – complete with delicately balanced iron wheel mechanism which drew up the wooden bridge with ease. Inside were narrow alleyways between six-storey houses – arches holding both sides apart at quite a height. Like Rhodes, tourist shops abound, but there is absolutely no hard or even soft-sell, so it is all very pleasant, and quality seems excellent – even in the postcards. Houses on the sheer seaward face must have occupants with no fear of heights! At £20 per night the marina was not cheap, but we had noticed some 'free parking' a little out of town, and went there the following evening, having enjoyed a full day on shore power, using the nearby laundrette (what luxury after weeks of hand washing), cleaning the boat and exploring.

Two days later we were away by 6.00 after a very early swim. Contrasting forecasts came from French and Italian stations, and it was difficult to get a true weather picture, but we decided to make a go for it. As we sped westwards the winds increased from ideal to frightening, with many sail changes, thunder and lightning, blocked loos, seasickness, and finally flat calm, before we entered the sheltered arms of Mahon, capital of Menorca, two days later. It was our fastest passage of the voyage, but just a little too near the edges of safety, and we were so glad to have Gary with us! We briefly visited the lovely old town, before setting off for Cala Ratjada in Majorca, to meet Frank's brother Liam who was finally joining us for a fortnight. Then back to Menorca to complete a circuit of the island, with delightful anchorages particularly at Ciutadella, the handsome former capital. I flew home for a week to be with my brother John who was visiting Sue for a short break, leaving the three 'boys' to enjoy some all-male sailing. On my return Liam had flown home and Gary was soon to follow suit, so we sailed to Alicante and dropped him for a train to Paris. This is one of the most successful city-centre marinas we have been in, an extension of the lively promenade where the residents and visitors can stroll in the cool of the evening, and wine and dine in the huge variety of reasonably priced establishments that overlook the harbour.

A three-night passage brought us through the ancient Pillars of Hercules and out of the Mediterranean. Gibraltar was an astonishing mix of the familiar and the improbable: an English enclave on foreign soil – most of it on land reclaimed from the sea, with colonial gardens gasping for water. The marina was friendly, cheap (£7 per night), and had a bird's eye view of the imposing rock, but was just a little too near the military runway, where huge air-force transport planes roared their way back and forth on practice runs, deafening us all in the process. We downed glasses of best bitter, and watched the fireworks as *Britannia* left the harbour, on her last visit as the Royal Yacht. She was en route from Hong Kong and the handover ceremonies of another former colony, and we wondered how long Gibraltar would remain part of the United Kingdom.

We went to see the cheeky Barbary Apes, and walked the treacherous Mediterranean Steps to bid that windy sea farewell. The roughest of paths led across the wild eastern slopes: but we had received ample warning that they were not easy, and travelled with care and not a few thrills, with breath-taking views back over the Middle Sea. We stayed in Gib for only three nights, but seemed to get a lot done in that time, including a big shop in

Sainsbury's, and buying gifts for friends back home. Diesel at £1 per gallon was not as good as Margarita or Malé but better value than back home! There were gales in the straits and we were anxious for good weather to get through, as this is another notorious area for strong currents and difficult conditions. But home was now just over the horizon, so to speak, and we were anxious to be away.

20

HOME STRAITS

On 31 July we paid our reasonable dues and headed into the Straits of Gibraltar, with winds strong and from astern: *Atlantic Islander* was reaching record speeds of 9.4 knots – too good to waste. We headed for Cádiz, and steamed in there after midnight. The RCC pilot book mentioned a possible anchorage in the Old Fishing Harbour inside the main commercial port, where we tied alongside a dredger for the night. We were hardly into the celebratory whiskeys when a security man and a Guardia Civil arrived alongside and ordered us to leave. The 'bit of lingo' came in handy and we invited the pair to join us. Only the Guardia Civil would agree – but would take nothing alcoholic, just a small coffee – he had stones in the kidneys, and I commiserated with him from first-hand knowledge. He was impressed with our progress around the world, and was quite delightful. He assured us we could stay until morning, though this was not generally allowed. We finally fell into bed after 1.30.

By 8.30 we were on our way to the municipal marina which we hadn't know existed – beside the RCNC (Real Club Nautico de Cádiz) – just inside the harbour mouth. It is a bit out of town, but not as far away as the recommended Puerto Sherry. There was hardly a tourist in sight, not a postcard to be bought, and the town was totally animated by residents, who shopped and sipped coffee and ate tapas in glorious shady squares or in narrow alleys between tall, balconied eighteenth century palacios, now subdivided into apartments. We visited the Museo de Cádiz which is across the square from the tourist office – its pride some moving Zurberan's of saintly-looking monks from the Cartuja de Jerez.

We found a good supermarket that would deliver free to the marina, where beer was 22p a can! We chose some good riojas to bring home, and visited the nearby lively food market. That evening there was a big fiesta – the *Feria de los Angelitos*, or Little Angels – where all the little girls and boys dressed in their best flamenco gear, flouncy dresses, hair-combs and shawls for the *niñas*, box jackets and smart hats on the boys: a mini version of the marvellous Feria in Seville. A throbbing, pulsating mobile fairground offered dodgems, ferris wheels and flying saucers, complete with screaming occupants. Professional photographers had set up 'traditional' interiors – sugán chairs, guitars, and even a stuffed *caballo* that little Rosito or Paco could sit up on and be immortalised in all their style – *à la Sevillana!* To my great dismay there wasn't a single note of traditional music to be heard – but then we *were* there at midnight and things still seemed a bit early! Instead there was deafening rock that made all talk impossible.

Mazagón was our next port of call, on the edge of the Coto Doñana, which was formerly the vast hunting estate of the kings of Spain, and now a famous nature reserve which we had visited many years before. Sadly development is encroaching the perimeter, and the huge tourism complex at Matalascañas is already having a detrimental effect on the wildlife. Columbus left from this area and prayed near here before leaving. The Franciscan Abbot of La Rábida monastery was instrumental in getting Los Reyes Católicos to support his scheme. Its fitting that this was to be our last port in Spain until we got to Bayona, as the *Pinta* did!

Back in Portugal our first port was Lagos with quite a tricky entry, particularly in winds of 20/25 knots. One has to request the pedestrian bridge to be raised, and then negotiate a narrow, busy marina which is not easy in near gale force. However, the town was lively and delightful, and we were visited by a knowledgeable contributor to the admiralty pilot book who gave us lots of really useful tips for our passage north.

Sagres is a busy fishing harbour with a few yachts anchored. Another early start for Sines before the strong afternoon northerlies set in. We passed the famous Cabo San Vincente, the southwesternmost part of Portugal, at 6.00 and had my Benedictine uncle Vincent to thank for perfect weather. Patron of this region, we had prayed at St Vincent's shrine in Lagos.

On 9 August we completed our world circumnavigation, when we motored into the Tagus estuary. It had been one year, nine months and nineteen days since we left Lisbon behind us, and we celebrated the achievement a day later when eldest son Andy and his girlfriend Ruth came to join us for the second-last week of the voyage. This was a double cause for celebration and the very last bottle of Australian 'champagne' was opened! But the following day I learnt with great sadness of the death of a good friend back home, after a brave struggle with cancer. It reminded me just how lucky we had been to survive such a long and hazardous journey with only minor accidents.

With two extra crew we day-hopped up the Portuguese coast, visiting entrancing resorts where most of the holidaymakers were natives. Peniche had changed beyond recognition – the fact that we could see it without fog made a huge difference, and they had put in a rather basic marina (no loos or showers or office!), situated right near the heart of the walled town, and we were able to come alongside an outside berth, to be immediately interrogated by the *policia*, ever vigilant on the Portuguese coast.

Next morning there were 30 knots of wind – from the north! As we were expected home by the end of the month, we were obliged to leave harbour and struggle against the wind, but limited ourselves to a 35 mile push to Nazaré, where a small marina shares shelter with a busy fishing fleet. Ruth was really brave and fought off seasickness by staying up on deck. Once safely tied up, we decided we deserved a meal out despite the mile-long hike to town, and were disturbed to see many local buses filled with Portuguese who were clearly sleeping rough – in tiny tents on the beach, or in sleeping bags on the carpark tarmac. The beach was a rolling stretch of fine sand, very windswept with huge rollers thundering in, and the 'posh' sheltered part was totally covered with tiny square tents, pink or blue striped or white cotton, rather like a jousting scene in mediaeval times. In the sharp slanted evening light it looked really magical: a total contrast to the rougher side of town. Gutted fish were stretched out to dry on wooden racks – the smell overpowering in the evening heat. Older women still wear traditional black garb and bright headscarves tied against the constant wind, and carry burdens on their heads, though despite all their hard work many are fat and ill-figured.

Next morning was windless, but a huge northerly swell remained. We didn't even try to sail as we wanted to make time, but with full revs we were doing 4 knots at best and didn't arrive into Figueira da Foz until 20.30 – using the radar to great effect as the shore was practically invisible for most of the day. Miles and miles of beach here give a totally flat outline on the screen, with the harbour moles standing out clearly enabling us to make a good heading for the tricky entry, which thankfully a returning fishing boat confirmed for us. Apparently the bar is quite shallow, and in big seas they actually close the entrance if the swell is over two metres.

It was good to be totally in the shelter – and with four mackerel caught by Ruth we had an excellent and very welcome dinner.

Here the marina was in the centre of town, and we enjoyed a lazy day on 15 August – the second anniversary of our departure from Crosshaven! Ruth and I shopped while Andy put his electronics know-how to work and helped Frank re-programme the SSB radio. We were sorry we hadn't had his knowledge for the thousands of miles behind us, but were pleased that we could make the last few hundred miles with improved radio contact. That evening we shared a final meal on board, and reminisced on a memorable week. We would greatly miss the young people's enthusiasm and company.

Next morning Andy and Ruth pushed us off the marina, wistfully waved us goodbye and headed for their train, while we made a go for Bayona, 78 miles north. It was a lumpy, bumpy ride with wind again on the nose, a huge swell, and slow speeds even motoring. We were quite emotional at the prospects of the voyage so soon coming to an end, unsure of our futures, knowing we would be initially like displaced persons without job, home or car, somewhat shell-shocked. We had been under pressure to arrive back in Crosshaven by 23 August which was now simply unfeasible: during the day we had the first call on our newly acquired mobile phone – a gift from Rachel – telling us that we would not be expected until 29 August, and we breathed a sigh of relief. Now we could relax a bit in Bayona, and prepare ourselves for one of the most difficult parts of the entire journey: the last few hundred miles through Biscay – one of the North Atlantic's most storm-tossed regions.

A full moon lit our way into the sheltering arms of Bayona, and we dropped anchor at 1.30 to sleep gratefully til morning. Just across the bay from us lay the replica of the *Pinta*, the first boat to return from the just discovered New World.

Late next afternoon, after laundry and general maintenance, we explored Bayona, discovering the magnificent thirteenth century cathedral – solid, almost windowless, and wonderfully unadorned apart from the fine Baroque retablos over the main and side altars. The statues, as in so many old churches, were really evocative, and we were particularly drawn to a sweet-faced virgin and child to whom shipwrecked souls were raising their hands from the encroaching waves. I lit two candles here – or

203

rather dropped in suitable coins which automatically lit two electric candles – no at all as satisfactory as the old method, but possibly safer? The 'proprietor' as Frank called the middle-aged *padre*, was pacing up and down the side aisle, and his heavy footsteps echoed through the vaulted building. He intimated the church's age with a shrug, '*Muy, muy vieja* '. Its lack of adornment, and the weathering of the hard granite pointed to well before Columbus' time.

On 19 August we set off with far more butterflies than normal. We were heading into 700 miles of uncertain weather, though the long range forecast seemed good. We were leaving behind a lifestyle that had a lot of attraction, and were returning to an unknown future. For the first few nights Frank had trouble sleeping – feeling too much anxiety about the passage and the forthcoming changes in our lives. We read a lot, spoke very little, argued quite a bit, and did a lot of soul-searching. How would we accommodate to the sometimes humdrum reality of life ashore? Would we be able to pick up the pieces of our old lives? The only certainty we had was the joy we would experience being reunited with family and friends.

Day 5 had very little of interest: drizzle and wind on the nose, with some attempt at sailing for a few hours, which drove us too far east – we were heading nicely for the Scillies, which, given unlimited time, would be lovely – but we must speed northwards to waiting friends. We were by now picking up local radio very well, and the meliflulous tones of Micheál Ó Muireheartaig brought unexpected joy. Home news seemed depressing as always – killings, gangster element at large, a price on the state pathologist's head, Cobh fishermen stop tunnel work with a high-court injunction: it will ruin their livelihood. There were the old chestnuts, pollution of the rivers – are the farmers or the county councils to blame? I vowed to stay tuned to FM only and save my rage if possible. Though the content depressed us, it *was* exciting to hear again the 'lilting tones of the Gael' and to anticipate the welcome that Frank especially would get from so many he hadn't seen for almost over two years – family, friends, and business associates.

We each summed up the benefits and negative aspects of this two year sabbatical – it seemed that good far outweighed the bad, but it had put a strain, physical, mental and emotional on both of us, and also on those back home when we were out of contact.

How would we cope with life on land, with the realities of everyday working life, earning an income, selling the boat, building a house? So many uncertainties lay ahead. We were to become grandparents, and take on that new role, as well as reclaiming our old role as parents. How would we cope? How would old relationships re-establish themselves? There were a thousand unknowns, but sighting the dim gleam of Fastnet Light, over the horizon, brought us back to the practical reality that Home was almost in sight, and by 2.00 on Monday 25 August, we picked up a mooring in quiet, sheltered Oysterhaven Bay, and before contacting anyone, collapsed *exhaustedly* into bed, surrounded with green.

Twelve hours later we were tied up to a marina in Kinsale, with the help of Liam who had made the whole dream possible. Sue was next to arrive, jubilant and intensely relieved to drop the mantle of responsibility that she had worn, and to cease worrying about our welfare. Liam's wife Brid hugged us in tears, and soon we were joined by the rest of the immediate family whom Frank hadn't seen for over two years. Our official arrival wasn't planned for another three days, and we were so glad of this opportunity to be emotional with some privacy!

Thursday dawned with winds forecast to Force 9, and my heart sank. How would we possibly get ourselves out of a tricky marina in these conditions? It would be unthinkable to arrive at the RCYC without *Atlantic Islander*, and it was equally unthinkable to postpone the event which had been greatly publicised and at which a large crowd was expected. So with help and perseverance from Liam, marina personnel, and neighbouring boats we made an undignified but thankfully unpublicised exit from Castle Park Marina. With a handkerchief of sail we tried to slow down our arrival at Roche's Point, but its difficult to go slowly when a Force 8 is following! We sailed to and fro off Ringabella, in sight of the plot of land we had purchased before going away, and then proceeded with as much decorum as we could muster towards the rendez-vous. *Who* would be crazy enough to come out and meet us in these conditions, we thought: but then we saw them – a dozen boats from the Club, led by Frank Lane's *Oisín*, neighbour Paul's *Tuanella* and Noel Smyth's *Laragh* with close friends and family aboard. We started shouting and cheering and jumping in the air. It was real – we *really* were home! Tears, smiles, waves, handshakes, hugs, kisses, shouts, horns, bunting, cannon, champagne – a sea of warmth surrounded us and led us to a place of honour at the club bar, where we presented the Admiral Conor O'Donovan with our worn and patched club ensign, which we had been proud to fly in 33 countries and 166 ports of call. In turn we were presented with a beautifully inscribed illuminated globe. *Atlantic Islander* was the first Royal Cork boat to go around the world!

For weeks we lived in a daze. Treated as minor celebrities we had TV and radio interviews, gave talks, answered a hundred questions, and relived the past two years several times over. We had friends for dinner on *Atlantic Islander* and continued to live aboard – this after all was our only *home*. We tried to decide what to do with our futures, envying all the while the young Coveney family who were about to set out on a similar adventure – but for marvellous philanthropic ends. We kept in touch with sailing friends to prolong the good feelings, and I was slow to come ashore, in mind and in body.

But the birth of our first grandchild brought me back to reality, and Ciara was a focus for all our lives. The weather turned wet and cold, and I gave in to Frank's pleas. We moved to welcome accommodation on land: when we sold *Solimar*, we had agreed with Sue that we could go and live with her until our new home in Fountainstown was complete. She had lived with us some five years before while building her lovely house overlooking all of Crosshaven and half of Cork Harbour. Little then did we know what a cruel twist of fate lay ahead for her. Oblivious to the future we settled down to a regular working day back at the office, and bought a car.

'How is it to be back?' people would ask.

'Wonderful,' we would say, sometimes without full enthusiasm.

'Would you do it again?'

'Yes! or something similar,' *emphatically*.

Life ashore was indeed very strange. To use Naomi James' phrase, we felt literally 'at sea on land', and clung tenaciously to our memories. Very few understood fully what we were going through at this time of re-adjustment. Though we were basically the same couple who had left two years before, we were perceived in a different way, and people distanced themselves from us because of our experience. Perhaps we were to blame for this ourselves, in having become so self-sufficient and self-reliant, but it was difficult to go back to where we started.

We blossomed when talking about our experiences, reliving every good and bad moment of the trip, and listeners in the main seemed really interested in our tales of adventure. But one cannot live in the past, and gradually we became more drawn into the here and now, as we re-built our business and re-established our working lives.

Things that had bothered me only slightly before going away became really annoying, like the huge amount of waste that was taken for granted, or the supermarkets' reckless use of non-bio-degradable plastic bags. Wholesale complaining of how badly off we were as a country just didn't ring true, and the national tendency to depend on others irked. Soon the faraway hills looked green once more, and far off seas attractive. But all this would seem very insignificant before very long, as we faced what was to become the most difficult and painful period of our lives.

*

EPILOGUE

From the time we moved in with her, six weeks after our return, Sue complained of severe stomach cramps. Initially the doctor felt she was suffering from food allergies, but six weeks later she was found to have a large cyst in one ovary and in the course of investigative surgery underwent a radical hysterectomy for cervical cancer, followed by massive doses of chemotherapy. Within 15 months she was dead. She died in her own home, in our care, and it seemed fitting that I should devote myself to her final months after two years of withdrawing from family responsibilities. What a price it was to pay for our adventure. I became tortured with guilt and doubts. Had her anxieties about us contributed in some way to her illness? We seldom appreciated the amount of worry that those back home went through on our behalf – every time there was a storm forecast in this section of the world she had fretted that we might be threatened with similar winds. The family at home had had to endure long weeks without any contact, not sure whether we were alive or dead, while we were so busy getting on with the day-to-day business of sailing that we worried less on their behalf. We were constantly gratified by their concern, but never gave it any in-depth thought: they were there for us when we needed them, that was all that really mattered to us. Why did she have to die after only 45 years while we were still fit and well into our mid-fifties? Were we in some way responsible for her death through lack of knowledge about her true condition on our return? Why did we not see the signs? We left these things to the medical profession, falsely lulled into a sense of diminished responsibility.

The voyage had taught me a lot about self-reliance, made me physically and mentally fit, and this helped me to care for Sue calmly and with an apparent measure of contentment. I strangely found these hopeless times often fulfilling and rewarding. For her part, a finely-tuned stoicism led her to accept her deteriorating situation without a cry of protest. Everyone remarked how marvellous it was that we were home to help her when she needed us: deep down we knew how little our help could achieve, and that caused us to grieve deeply. Each evening near the end she would look up with a glowing smile as I bade her good night, and say 'Thanks for everything' All I could ever reply, with a breaking heart, was 'Thank *you!*' Thank you for never crying, never protesting, never saying 'Why? Why me? Why not *you*?' It was a time of deep, unspoken, unspeakable suffering.

Through her we came to realise the importance of saying 'I love you' and 'Thank you for being wonderful' – and not taking close ones for granted. Up until now we were not a demonstrative family, but these words became important. If this were the only benefit we were to reap, it was indeed an essential one. All the grief we would share together so soon after the joys of reunion, bonded us closer together as we tried to help each other through the hardest time of our lives.

Now, washed with the sadness of death, the beauty we have seen around the world seems somewhat muted and removed. On the voyage we were cheered by the constant, incomparable glory of nature, at peace in the sunsets, angry in storms, lush in the tropics, arid in the deserts, magnificent in the coral reefs, frightening in the *meltemi*, unsurpassed in nights of stars. There was the constant camaraderie of sailing friends, the unstinting sharing of expertise and experience, the unspoken assurance that all would come to the aid of the one in trouble. Having left behind so much in the way of friendship, family, and certainty, ocean-going yachtsmen and women need to rely heavily on each other, and firm friendships are struck in moments.

All those we met were unanimous in one thing: none of us could enjoy the ultimate freedom to wander the face of the globe without the dedication of some friend or family member back home, who took on the task of holding bank managers at bay, re-addressing mail, keeping people in touch, and administering all the daily minutiae essential to modern life. Sue had held so many strings for us we could have never have made the trip without her. Neither could we have conceived what a huge price she and we would so soon have to pay.

She died as the first daffodils pushed their way through the hard wet soil of winter, a sign of hope and of renewal. She showed us in her life and in her death that true courage does not lie in sailing a small boat in dangerous waters, but in navigating with calm through the rough seas of life.

GLOSSARY

aft: behind, back end of boat

aft cabin: cabin at back of boat

angle of keel: degree to which boat tilts in wind

auto-pilot: electrical steering device which is connected to the tiller

battens: narrow strips of timber or plastic used to stiffen sail

berth: place at a marina or bunk in a boat

bilges: part under the flooring

boom: metal or wooden part under the mainsail which keeps it in shape and taut

bottom: part of the hull which is underwater

bow: front of boat

burgee: small flag, triangular, flown from top of mast

coach roof: cover, usually solid, over forward part of the cockpit, which protects crew from elements

cockpit: outdoor control centre where crew usually sit when on watch

companionway: steps leading into main saloon

depth sounder: electronic device which gauges depth of water

dinghy: in our case we used an inflatable rubber dinghy which we deflated for long passages at sea and tied down securely on deck.

*dodgers:*protective strips of sailcloth which shelter the cockpit from wind

ensign: flag flown as the symbol of nationality: in our case with the RCYC emblem on blue ground, flown at stern of boat

fairlead: hole through toerail which guides mooring ropes and prevents chafing

fenders: air-filled buffers hung over side to protect hull from damage at marinas

forward/fore; front of boat, in front

forepeak: cabin area under the bow of a boat

furling: system of rolling sail into itself or into the mast

foresail: sail in front of mast

forestay: steel wire support for mast, running from foredeck to a point near top of mast

galley: kitchen

gimbals: system of keeping compass or cooker level at any angle of keel

genoa/genny: forward sail, usually bigger than mainsail

GPS: Global Positioning System

guardrail: plastic-covered wire led through stanchions around the deck edge to prevent crew falling overboard

halyard: rope through the mast that pulls sail into position (from *haul yard*)

heads: marine toilet

hull: lower part of boat

jib: small foresail used in heavy weather

knot: measurement of speed of boat or wind (one nautical mile per hour)

lay-day: day ashore during sailing events

lee cloth: strip of cloth or canvas attached to bunk which clips onto hooks overhead to secure the sleeper in rough weather

mainsail: sail on main mast

mast: large pole which carries mainsail and boom

mile/nm: nautical mile, one-sixtieth of a degree of latitude, slightly shorter than standard mile

mizen mast: small mast usually behind mainmast on ketch

mooring: method of securing boat when not sailing – by anchor or attached to fixed mooring buoy.

mole: breakwater

motu: small island on coral reef

pilot/pilot book: navigational information

rigging: all the wires that secure masts to the deck

roads: anchorage

sheets: ropes used to control sails

shrouds: lateral support for the mast

spinnaker: lightweight semi-cylindrical sail used when wind is from behind

spinnaker pole: metal pole which holds out spinnaker foot on windward side to keep it secure and manageable. Also used with genoa in downwind sailing

stanchion: post which holds guardrail in position

spreaders: lightweight horizontal poles on the mast which keep rigging in place

spring lines: warps which are strung in an X-shape to prevent the boat surging forward or backwards while at a berth

SSB: Single Sideband Radio, long range transmitter / receiver

stays: wire ropes tied to deck which keep mast stable

stern: back end of boat

toerail: small rim with drainage holes which runs around top of deck, under the guard-rail, to prevent slipping overboard

topsides: part of hull usually above water

twin headsails: two foresails attached to forestay, poled out out on either side to catch wind from astern. More stable than spinnaker.

VHF: radio telephone with average range of up to thirty miles

warps: ropes used to secure boat to anchor or berth

Weatherfax: fax machine programmed to radio fax weather transmissions

winch: rotating drum which tightens halyards or sheets, operated with *winch handle*

wind-vane: system of self steering with its own rudder which uses no electricity and is attached to the stern of the boat

INDEX

214